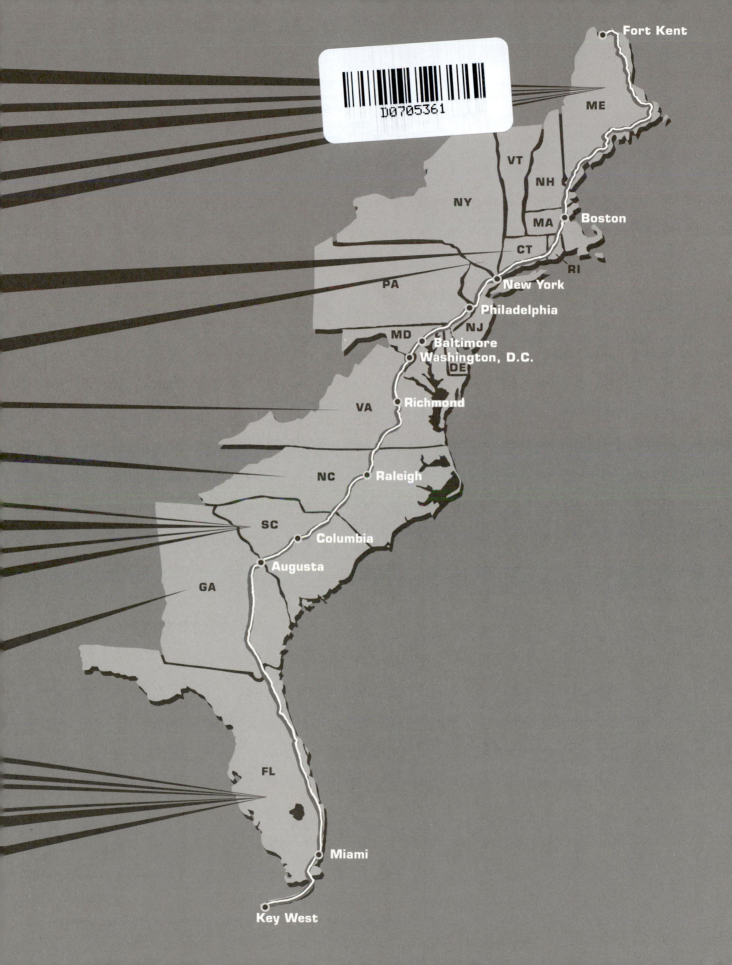

Fort Kent

ME

VT

NH

NY

MA — Boston

CT

RI

PA

New York

Philadelphia

MD

NJ

Baltimore

Washington, D.C.

DE

VA — Richmond

NC — Raleigh

SC — Columbia

Augusta

GA

FL

Miami

Key West

THE GREAT AMERICAN ROAD TRIP

THE GREAT AMERICAN ROAD TRIP

U.S. 1, MAINE TO FLORIDA

PETER GENOVESE

RUTGERS UNIVERSITY PRESS

New Brunswick, New Jersey

"Old Lem," from *The Collected Poems of Sterling A. Brown,* edited by Michael S. Harper. © 1980 by Sterling A. Brown. Reprinted by permission of HarperCollins Publishers Inc. New York.

"Flipper," by Henry Vars and By Dunham. © 1963 Metro-Goldwyn-Mayer Inc. and Ivan Tors Film, Inc. © renewed EMI Feist Catalog Inc. All rights reserved. Used by permission. Warner Bros. Publications U.S. Inc., Miami, Fla. 33014.

Library of Congress Cataloging-in-Publication Data

Genovese, Peter, 1952–
    The great American road trip : U.S. 1, Maine to Florida / Peter Genovese.
       p.   cm.
     ISBN 0–8135–2741–4 (alk. paper)
     1. East (U.S.)—Description and travel. 2. East (U.S.)—History, Local.
3. East (U.S.)—Social life and customs. 4. United States Highway 1.
5. Genovese, Peter, 1952–   —Journeys—East (U.S.).   I. Title
E169.04.G465 1999
917.404'43—dc21   99–27381
                                                     CIP

British Cataloging-in-Publication data for this book
is available from the British Library

Manufactured in the United States of America

To wanderers everywhere—
roam, if you want to

CONTENTS

THE GREAT AMERICAN ROAD TRIP

INTRODUCTION

In a spacious but modestly furnished building on Main Street in Fort Kent, Maine, Charles Pelletier and Vaughan Martin watch the border. Outside the window of Pelletier's office is the bridge over the Saint John River, and, at the other end of it, Canada.

It is a damp, chilly day, the kind that has you thinking of a hot bowl of soup—maybe from Rock's Motel Diner, across the street. Pelletier is port director for the U.S. Customs Service's Border Patrol. Martin, a former schoolteacher, is one of his seven inspectors. The two men talk about the items people are forever trying to sneak past them: drugs, alcohol, fruit, plants, animals, Cuban cigars, and lottery tickets.

"One time a guy had nothing to declare, but he had a half dozen burlap bags in the back seat of his car," Martin recalls.

"When I picked up the bag, it let out a squeal."

"A pig?"

"I almost had a heart attack," he says, smiling.

On the same road 2,400 miles south, on one of those warm, languorous days that have you thinking of tall drinks with little umbrellas, Laura Catlow sits in her office, watching Buck, Alita, and other students in one of the more unusual "schools" in the country.

Alita and classmates are dolphins, those playful, ever-smiling creatures who, unlike the rest of us, never seem to have a bad day. Of course, if you lived at the Dolphin Research Center in Grassy Key, Florida, 59 miles from Key West, you wouldn't have many bad days, either. You'd get twenty to twenty-five pounds of fish every day, free run of the pens perched in the Gulf of Mexico, and a chance to yuk it up with busloads of enthralled schoolchildren.

The most famous dolphin of all, Flipper, lived here. Several dolphins acted the part of Flipper in the 1963 movie and subsequent TV show. But the original Flipper—her real name was Mitzi—lived here, in Milton Santini's Porpoise School.

"One researcher from England has asked to study humor in dolphins," Catlow says. "Is there such a thing?"

There's plenty of humor, and drama, and life, along U.S. 1. It is literally and figuratively America's main drag. The Main Streets of dozens of towns and cities along the East Coast are on U.S. 1. For much of its length, the highway follows the route of the old Boston Post Road, the most important road linking the original thirteen colonies. Even today, sections of the highway through New York and Connecticut retain the name.

> "The most important road, everything considered, in the United States."
>
> Federal Bureau of Roads, 1927

The misconceptions about the highway are legion: that it is America's "first" road; that there's not much on it except every fast-food franchise on Earth; that the interstate highway system, particularly I-95, has relegated U.S. 1 to a minor highway—culturally barren, commercially insignificant, and boring.

It's safe to say U.S. 1 is this country's most misunderstood and maligned highway. Route 66 had its own TV show, plus books, videos, magazines, museums, fan clubs, T-shirts, and coffee mugs. There was one previous book on U.S. 1 ten years ago. A documentary on the highway aired on NBC—in 1962. The U.S. 1 Highway Association is long since defunct. There are no fan clubs, no museums, and definitely no T-shirts.

This book hopes to correct all that. I spent more than two years, in all, on U.S. 1, traveling tens of thousands of miles, braving several snowstorms in Maine and New Hampshire and more sunny days in Florida than I care to remember (you know how tough it is to work on those kinds of days?).

I met hundreds of people who lived and worked on the highway, from the chainsaw-wielding Wild Mountain Man in Maine to Ellen Dierenfeld, who oversees the menus of the animals at the Bronx

Zoo; from the waitresses at the Little Tavern in Laurel, Maryland, to James Fulmer, who sells fireworks and tomatoes along U.S. 1 in Clearwater, South Carolina; from Lamar Deal, resident wit of Okefenokee Swamp, to Metro Dade Officer Javier Giovane, who took me on patrol along the Dixie Highway in Miami one night.

This book is their story, and the story of a woefully underappreciated highway. U.S. 1 is not the most scenic highway in America (not with all those fast-food joints, convenience stores, rundown motels, gun shops, and go-go bars, it isn't) nor the quickest-moving one.

As far as I'm concerned, though, it's the best damn highway in America. I've driven nearly a million miles around the country in the past twenty-five years. No other road matches U.S. 1's combination of history, culture, scenery, roadside attractions, variety, and vitality.

> "The ugliest road in America."
>
> *Life* magazine, in the 1930s

The one previous book about U.S. 1, and countless newspaper and magazine stories over the years, often skirted the highway, ending up on "more interesting" side roads and in nearby towns that have no connection to U.S. 1. For example, it seems like every piece ever written about U.S. 1 from Maine to Florida makes mention of Mallory Square in Key West. It's a colorful spot, but it's not on U.S. 1, so it's not in this book.

Every sight, sign, attraction, business, person, and town mentioned or profiled in this book (with the exception of the Federal Highway Administration historian, the Tragedy in U.S. Museum, and the

Astronaut Hall of Fame, just off the highway) is on U.S. 1. Not near it, *on* it.

U.S. 1 runs through Boston, New York City, Baltimore, Washington, D.C., Richmond, and Miami, among other cities. It takes in the George Washington Bridge and the Pulaski Skyway, the Bronx Zoo and Okefenokee Swamp, the National Museum of Natural History, the National Museum of American Art, and the Mushroom Museum, the Federal Bureau of Investigation and countless local police departments, Dow Jones and Company and the *National Enquirer*. The Star-Spangled Banner is on U.S. 1. Madonna lived on U.S. 1, until she sold her house in Miami to Rosie O'Donnell.

> "Not a single annoying and expensive toll bridge or ferry is encountered along the entire route. This gratifying condition should result in material conservation of time and tempers, energy and expense. . . . Dense fogs are unknown on 'The Sunshine Route,' and the absence of these dangerous, inconvenient, and time-devouring irritants also should appeal to travelers contemplating a southward pilgrimage. It is a happy circumstance that U.S. No. 1 is free of these schedule-gremlins and deceptive and baffling foes of visibility, composure, and safety."
>
> *Official U.S. No. 1 Guide Book,* U.S. No. 1 Highway Association, circa 1940

It zig-zags along the wild and beautiful Maine coast and soars over the Atlantic Ocean as the Overseas Highway through the Florida Keys, one of the most spectacular stretches of road anywhere. U.S. 1, the most visually diverse major highway in the country, makes all other long-distance highways seem lonely and lifeless by comparison. (U.S. 1 is not to be confused with Route 1—the much shorter Pacific Coast Highway—in California.)

U.S. 1 is Main Street and Miracle Mile, two-lane blacktop and six-lane expressway, straight as an arrow in some places and twistier than a Philadelphia soft pretzel in others. There are 2,244 traffic lights on U.S. 1 from Fort Kent to Key West. How do I know? I counted every one.

U.S. 1 is often compared to I-95; the two run parallel down much of the East Coast. I-95 starts in Houlton, Maine (U.S. 1 runs another 100 miles north to Fort Kent) and ends, quite unceremoniously, in Miami, as nothing more than an off-ramp onto U.S. 1, which runs another 150 miles before ending at the corner of Fleming and Whitehead streets in Key West. What's the most interesting thing along I-95, anyway? South of the Border?

Route 66 (what's left of it; the highway was officially decommissioned in 1985) has surface charm and flash; U.S. 1 has depth and substance. Route 66 is in the past, nostalgic and romantic; U.S. 1 is here-and-now, in-your-face, and a little on the wild side.

———

It's time we see it. We'll start at the Border Patrol office, where U.S. 1 begins, and end, 2,450 miles later, in fun-loving Key West. The top is up on the Jeep, but don't worry, it'll be down long before we hit Miami.

Ready? The highway, to echo Bruce Springsteen, is alive tonight.

MAINE

U.S 1 in Maine runs close to the coast from one end of the state to the other. . . . There are two coasts of Maine. The coast known to most visitors has spruce-tipped hills and hard beaches dappled with the red, orange, green, blue, and white raiment of visitors, blue green waters broken by tilting sails and the wakes of speeding motorboats, and a brilliant blue sky . . . the second coast of Maine is for four or five months muffled in snow; travel is at times difficult. . . . The glory of this Maine is its sky, unreal saffron after the gray light that comes before the dawn, blue as Persian tiles for a brief time at midday, and an unearthly pale green streaked with rose in the late afternoon, turning the snow pale heliotrope with purple shadows.

—*U.S. One, Maine to Florida*, American Guide Series, 1938

The sign marking the beginning—or end, if you will—of U.S. 1 can be found in the parking lot of a tax- and duty-free shop in Fort Kent, Maine, which is somehow appropriate, because this is an everyday, workingman's (and woman's) kind of highway, a supremely democratic road that includes everything from old-fashioned hardware stores to brand-new Home Depots, from village groceries to state-of-the-art supermarkets, from tiny post offices to golden-domed state capitols, from six-stool greasy spoons to multimillion-dollar restaurants.

U.S. 1, one realizes soon enough, is the fast-food-franchise, discount store-chain, hubcap-dealer, gun-shop, video arcade, go-go-bar capital of the world. To paraphrase Arlo Guthrie, you can get anything you want on U.S. 1.

As it will be in scores of cities and towns along the way, U.S. 1 is Main Street in Fort Kent. The town was settled by French refugees from Acadia (U.S. 1 around Orland, Maine, is still marked Acadia Highway) and named after Edward Kent, a former governor of Maine.

Across the street from the tax- and duty-free shop and the Fort Kent Masonic Lodge is Rock's Motel and Diner, a favorite haunt of U.S. and Canadian truckers, who are conversant in English and

A sign marks the beginning of U.S. 1 in Fort Kent. The mileage, however, is off by about 200 miles.

French (Fort Kent is 40 miles north of Quebec). The Customs/Immigration border crossing, where U.S. 1 officially begins, is next door to the duty-free shop. There are two port directors—Charles Pelletier, for Customs, and Michael Dahlgren, for Immigration.

"Eighty percent of the traffic we see is local," Pelletier explains. "Half of the time you converse in French. It's not a requirement of the job, but it's a big help."

Apart from the occasional pig and exotic bird, most of the stuff people try to sneak past Border Patrol officer Vaughan Martin and the other inspectors are everyday items.

"This morning we confiscated a couple perennial plants—bleeding hearts," Pelletier says with a smile.

Drugs that are available by prescription only in the United States but can be bought over the counter in Canada—Claritin, for example—are often smuggled across. The inspectors are more on the lookout for illegal drugs—marijuana, hashish, and cocaine in particular. For small amounts, the fine is five hundred dollars; if you don't have cash or a check, your car is confiscated.

"We pull drug paraphernalia from hoods, engine compartments, and other places," Martin says. "Narcotics in people's underwear."

"And underage kids try to hide beer," Martin adds.

"Kids from this side go over to New Brunswick, where the legal age is eighteen," Pelletier explains.

You don't need a passport to cross between the two countries; a driver's license will do. How often do inspectors stop someone, or how do they spot the shady types?

"Every twentieth car or so, or someone who exhibits nervousness," Martin notes. "It's a judgment call for the most part. We do not need permission to ask someone to open their trunk."

"Or a lady's purse," Pelletier adds. "For us, it's the same as a bag or box."

The border, like a good convenience store, never closes—it's open twenty-four hours, seven days a week.

The 200-mile Can-Am Sled Dog Race starts on U.S. 1 in Fort Kent. It's held in February, just about when the Maine winters turn Arctic.

Border Patrol officer Vaughan Martin at the Fort Kent Customs/Immigration border checkpoint.

"We got 120–130 inches of snow last winter," Pelletier says. "It's not always that bad. Some winters you don't have to shovel the snow off your roof."

Main Street (U.S. 1) in Fort Kent runs past Route 1 Fashions, Nadeau's House of Furniture, a small Sears store, and Fort Kent Pharmacy, "home of the 99-cent greeting cards." "Welcome to Fort Kent, Friendly Town, Sporting Paradise," reads the first of countless town welcome signs along U.S. 1 (see endpapers). On the way out of town, the road passes Saint Louis Cemetery, with its commanding view over the Saint John River, and heads, in the first of many surprises in the next 2,400-plus miles, *north*,

Do those giant lobsters drink milk? Presque Isle.

Information booth in Van Buren for Village Acadien, the "largest historical site in Maine."

toward Frenchville ("A Small Town with a Big Heart," according to its welcome sign) and Madawaska. The town, which translates, in the Micmac Indian dialect, variously as "where one river runs into the other," and "where there is much hay," is the scene, every October, of "the world's largest garage sale," at Madawaska High School.

———

It is pretty much all downhill from here on U.S. 1, all the way to Key West. The highway runs from Madawaska (elevation, 595 feet) to Grand Isle (elevation, 510 feet), to Van Buren (495 feet), where bags of fresh potatoes are sold at the Tulsa gas station and U.S. 1 makes a hard right, heading inland to Caribou ("The Community of Choice").

The road passes Quaggy Joe Mountain and Garey's Custom Slaughtering in Mars Hill, which features old-fashioned angled parking and the law firm of Hussey and Hussey. Along both sides of the highway are roadside potato stands where, if no one's around, you put your money in tin cans on slanted wooden counters. Lining the road are tractor deal-

Road sign, U.S. 1, Maine.
From *North & South:
Berenice Abbott's U.S. Route 1.*
Courtesy of the Syracuse University
Art Collection.

ers, farms, and mobile homes with firewood stacked outside, snowmobiles on the front lawn, and satellite dishes on the roofs.

> "A comrade in the horticultural trenches likes to tell people that his supreme goal in gardening is to make his yard look like Route 1.
> And he doesn't mean that painfully quaint strip of outlet stores in Freeport or the manicured lawns of Wiscasset. He's talking about the unkempt stretches in between the two-lane RV-bahn, bounded by overgrown verges and gullies, woods' edges and old barnyards that together form a long, untidy, but authentically Down East sort of botanical garden, free and open to all."
>
> Richard Grant, *Down East*, September 1995

In Littleton, just before Houlton, hubcaps are strewn on the ground or strung on the fence. That's Hubcap Heaven. One cold winter night, in Littleton, I had a flat tire, the only car problem I would encounter in my two years on U.S. 1. A guy who worked at C & W Citgo on U.S. 1 in Littleton helped me fix it; I practically had to force him to take twenty dollars.

After 100 miles of small towns and wilderness, Houlton, full of truckstops and motels, seems like a major metropolis.

Houlton to Calais, the next major town, is 86 miles of wild, desolate beauty. In 1954, famed photographer Berenice Abbott covered U.S. 1 from Fort Kent to Key West with a young man named Damon Gadd, who offered to drive her in exchange for photography lessons. Abbott took some twenty-five hundred photos of the trip with her Century Universal and Rolleiflex cameras. She returned to settle in Maine in 1960. "I was never sorry I settled here," she once told *Yankee* magazine. "Never. Maine is hard to define. The minute you get over the bridge at Kittery you want to say hallelujah!"

The hamlets roll by: North Amity, Orient, and Weston, where the Million Dollar View Restaurant is on U.S. 1.

Two common sights here are the redemption centers (one in Calais is called Tin Can Alley), where you

> "I knew U.S. 1, stretching from the Canadian border to Key West, was capable of putting a man in an institution of one kind or another—at least it once was—but I hoped things had changed. . . . They hadn't. The highway was still a nightmare vision of the twentieth century, a four-lane representing (as Mencken has it) 'the American lust for the hideous, the delight in ugliness for its own sake.'"

William Least Heat Moon, *Blue Highways: A Journey into America*, Little Brown, 1982

can turn in recyclables, and Grange halls. Danforth is the first town in Washington County, called the "Sunrise County" because the sun rises first in the United States there. "Scenic highway next eight miles," says a sign on 1 north of Danforth. The road is breathtakingly scenic, and bumpy. Off to the right, Mount Katahdin, Maine's highest peak, rises majestically above the early morning mist.

Near Princeton, there's Pocomoonshine Lake and aptly named Big Lake. Princeton is on the Indian Township reservation, run by the Passamaquoddy Indians. In 1794, the Commonwealth of Massachusetts (which then included what would become Maine) took by treaty hundreds of thousands of acres of Passamaquoddy land, except for the 23,000 acres that now make up Indian Township. The Passamaquoddies gained 140,000 acres of land in Maine as part of the Maine Indian Claims Settlement Act of 1980.

Passamaquoddy Big-Money Bingo is on U.S. 1. The Passamaquoddies want to build casinos on their regained land, much like the Mashantucket Pequots did with the Foxwoods Casino in Connecticut. But the Passamaquoddies have run into resistance from state officials. They also want to be governed by their own law, not the state's.

"It would give me a sense of identity," tribe member William Altvater told the *Portland Press Herald*. "It says to me that I am different. It says to me that I can say neither the state of Maine nor the federal government can put me under their thumb."

Calais (pronounced "callous"), with the state's highest unemployment rate, sits in the middle of what Mainers call the Appalachia of the Atlantic. The town, according to one account, "is tired of teetering at the edge of America," and, envious of the prosperity enjoyed by St. Stephen (across the river, and border, in New Brunswick) is pinning its future on a superhighway that would connect one part of Canada with another by cutting across northern Maine, starting with Calais. Right now, though, the highway is no more than a four-lane fantasy.

Katy's Fudge, in a can't-miss bright yellow house, is on 1 in Robbinston. Several miles south is Perry, named after War of 1812 naval hero Oliver H. Perry,

Lobster is the kitsch of choice along U.S. 1 in Maine. Perry.

Drive-through lobster:
N & N Seafood bus,
Jonesboro.

and home of one of the more intriguing roadside markers on the entire length of U.S. 1.

"Welcome to Perry," reads a sign almost hidden in the bushes. "Halfway between the North Pole and the Equator."

Which comes as little consolation if you're up here in the winter, when it seems the North Pole is just around the next bend and the Equator on another planet.

Tired? You can stop at the 45th Parallel Rest Area, on 1. Five miles south of Perry is Pembroke; Fulton's Cabins, a set of ten multicolored cabins in a neat row, stand on the highway's southbound side. A garbage truck rumbles by; painted on its side are the words "Moose Island Solid Waste Disposal." Dennysville, several miles south, is named not after the fast-food chain but after an Indian chief whose hunting grounds were in the vicinity. As you head north on 1 from here, each bridge, each river crossing seems to take you deeper into the Maine wilderness.

Archibald's One Stop is in East Machias. Machias is Indian for "bad little falls." The barren fields of win-

ter are transformed, in summer, into blueberry fields. The University of Maine's Blueberry Hill experiment station is on 1 in Machias. The N & N Seafood bus is parked on 1 southbound in Jonesboro.

North of Cherryfield ("Blueberry Capital of the World") is the Down East Museum of Natural History, which is part museum and part antiques shop, with its colorful collection of road signs, farming implements, fishing tackle, motorcycles, and hubcaps on the front lawn.

Penobscot Bay, and the Atlantic Ocean, start to make frequent appearances on the left as the road heads south. "Welcome to Ellsworth," says a welcome sign, "Crossroads of Downeast Maine."

The Maine glimpsed from U.S. 1 from Fort Kent to Ellsworth is wild, desolate, and beautiful, a whole lot of almost-nothing. South of Ellsworth is the more developed, populated, touristy end of Maine, a string of small towns that try to outdo each other for the distinction of being Maine's prettiest or most scenic town.

"Welcome to Belfast, a Waterfront Community," reads the welcome sign, as if Belfast were the only

The Down East Museum in Cherryfield is a rich trove of roadside memorabilia.

town on the waterfront. Bath is heralded as "One of the 100 Best Small Cities in America," Wiscasset "the Prettiest Village in Maine." Some towns advertise their biggest, or most noteworthy, attraction. Waldoboro is "Home of the 5-Masted Schooner."

The long, slow, scenic stretch of 1 from Ellsworth to the state line at Kittery (in summer, the traffic is just as bad as your favorite bottleneck back home) is filled with motels, fast-food chains, gift and souvenir shops. There is abundant display of the sort of

roadside art (giant lobstermen, crab traps, and lighthouses) Maine does better than any other state along U.S. 1 with the exception of Florida.

But there are many empty, rural stretches where the most distinctive feature is the rocky Maine coast, a white clapboard country church, or a handmade sign by the side of the road that says something like "Home of the Wild Mountain Man."

If a sign like that doesn't make you pull over, nothing will.

——

On a cold, wintry Maine night, with a bitter wind blowing off nearby Penobscot Bay, Ray Murphy, artist, is outside, hard at work. His studio, on U.S. 1 south several miles north of Ellsworth, is an open-air log cabin rigged with a portable generator. A lantern is hooked to one wall, and music sputters from a scratchy radio. Murphy says he's not cold; the chainsaw provides heat.

The saw, which sounds, at such close quarters, like a jet engine, is the Wild Mountain Man's paintbrush. Wood chips fly everywhere; some are

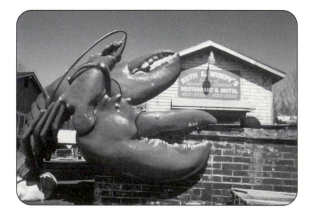

More giant lobsters! Ruth and Wimpy's, Ellsworth.

Ray Murphy works year-round
in his open-air studio on U.S. 1.

lodged in Murphy's thick beard. You take one look at his cheery, roly-poly face and his chainsaw, and you're not sure whether he'd be a better Santa Claus or Leatherface, from *The Texas Chainsaw Massacre*.

"I met him once," Murphy says of Gunnar Hansen, who played the chainsaw-wielding killer in the 1974 cult movie. Murphy looks across the highway, toward the bay. "He lives over there, on an island."

Murphy invites me into his cozy log cabin. He's finishing a splendid eagle, one of tens of thousands of pieces—birds, bears, moose, beavers, horses, squirrels, and other animals—he has chainsaw-sculpted in the past forty years.

"I'm sitting at 43,429 pieces," he says above the blast of the chainsaw. He smiles. "By the end of the day maybe it'll be 43,430."

His grandfather, Jim Baker, was "a famous mountain man." His great-grandfather was an Indian chief. As a kid, Murphy lived on a reservation in Wyoming. He remembers carrying firewood home as a four-year-old. When Murphy was ten, his father—"he had the reputation of being the toughest son of a gun in the state"—bought a chainsaw to cut ice. Murphy used the saw without his father's permission, and got a good spanking. By the time he was fifteen, Murphy had his own business—making furniture on the reservation.

By the time he was twenty, he was on his own, wandering around Idaho, Washington, and Oregon, working for logging companies, sculpting on the side.

He moved to South Dakota, and started to make a name for himself as an artist. He made it into *Ripley's Believe It or Not.* "Ray Murphy of Rapid City, S.D., carved the entire alphabet on a lead pencil with a chainsaw," according to the entry.

In the early eighties, Murphy left Rapid City and headed east.

"My artwork wasn't doing well," he recalled. "The economy was going downhill. I had to get the heck out of there."

He lived and worked in New York State and New Hampshire. One year, he and his wife drove to Myrtle Beach in the GM bus that has been everywhere from Alaska to Central America. Their roundabout route included a stop in Bar Harbor. They liked what they saw of the area. The Wild Mountain Man wanted to set up shop along Bar Harbor Road, but ran into local opposition. He found several acres on U.S. 1 in Ellsworth, 20 miles away, and it was there he built his home and log cabin studio.

Ray Murphy's bears stand along U.S. 1
as if waiting for a bus. Ellsworth.

"Chainsaw art—buy it now before prices really go sky-high and before too many wannabee chainsaw artists flood the market," said the 1995 *Old Farmer's Almanac*. "Creations range from a full-size moose sculpture sold for $4,000 at the Spinning Wheel gift shop in Waterbury Center, Vt., to the stunts of such experts as Ray Murphy of Ellsworth, Me. Ray carves names on wooden belt buckles while the owners wear them."

"There are hundreds of these wannabees who use hammers and chisels along with chainsaws," the Wild Mountain Man says. "That ain't chainsaw art; that's wood carving. There are maybe thirty of us worldwide who are true chainsaw artists."

A hand-lettered sign on his spacious lot, where his carved eagles clutch fish in their talons and bears stand along the road as if waiting for a bus, describes his accomplishments:

Originated the art of sculpturing with chainsaw.
Featured worldwide: TV, radio, magazines.
Over 8,000 newspaper articles.
Wrote alphabet on pencil 1979.
Only person to sculpt with two chainsaws at same time.
Eagle in White House, 1982–88.
Dubbed by peers "World's foremost trick artist with chainsaw."
Work in 45 museums.

The eagle in the White House? Murphy says he carved an eagle with a black jellybean in its beak and sent it to Ronald Reagan, who had it on display.

The piece he's most proud of, though, is a pair of eagles fighting over a fish. Who owns the piece?

"Let's say this," he replies cagily. "The woman who owns it doesn't want her name disclosed. She's rather famous and lives in Tennessee."

He uses white pine for his larger figures, cedar for the small ones. Every year, he goes through 3,000–4,000 feet of pine—and several chainsaws. Chainsaw sculpting is not for the unsteady of hand or weak of nerve.

"I've had twenty-nine major injuries," the Wild Mountain Man says matter-of-factly.

The worst one?

"Went and cut my throat one time; the saw got away from me," he replies. He points to a scar above his eye, and then runs his finger from his ear down to his throat, revealing a long, jagged scar not immediately noticeable because of the beard.

He was cutting a tree when the saw got caught and then flew into his face.

"I thought I cut my ear off," he recalls. "If I didn't have my hard hat on, it would have gone right through here," he adds, running a finger down the middle of his face.

Another time, he got some toxic resin under the skin. "One knee swelled up like a basketball, the other like a football," he recalls. "I ended up in a wheelchair."

There's another side to the Wild Mountain Man. The last few summers, he has participated in Camp Postcard (Police Officers Striving to Create and Reinforce Dreams), a local program for at-risk youth. He knows how lives can go wrong in an instant. Murphy stopped drinking twenty years ago, on New Year's Eve. Asked why, he replies, "Almost killed someone in a barroom brawl," and says nothing more.

Today, the Wild Mountain Man is healthy and happy. His trusty GM bus, with more than a million miles on the odometer, is parked next to the log cabin, and serves as storage space/gallery. There's plenty of wood nearby, and the artist has a good spot on what he is convinced is an up-and-coming highway.

How long will he keep being the Wild Mountain Man?

"Haven't thought about that," he says. "I'll probably die with a saw in my hands."

———

About 10 miles south of Ellsworth is the state's largest antiquarian book dealer and antiques shop, located in just about the last place you'd expect: a chicken barn.

The Big Chicken Barn, to be exact.

"It was built in the fifties, and it was a chicken barn until 1976," says Annegret Cukierski, owner of the Big Chicken Barn.

The Big Chicken Barn's staff: John Curtis, Dick Bond, Annegret Cukierski, Mike Cukierski.

She bought the building from a previous book/antiques dealer who sold books upstairs and leased space to dealers downstairs.

"My husband stopped by one day, looked at the place and said 'Wow!'" Cukierski recalled. "I had a few kids and was looking for a little business." She laughed. "It's just sort of grown."

The Big Chicken Barn, open nine-to-five, seven days a week, is longer than a football field, home to more than a hundred thousand books, ten thousand magazines, and countless antiques, spread over nooks and crannies, shelves and display cases on two floors. Fifty dealers have space. What can you find at the Big Chicken Barn? Everything from 1930s clothing and 1940s appliances to 1960s albums and 1980s toys. Weird stuff? How about a dentist's chair from the 1920s? Not weird enough? How about a life-size Mr. Spock, a body bag (body not included), or a couch that had been burned during the making of *Pet Sematary*, by Maine's own Stephen King?

"You really don't know what you're going to find in here," Cukierski says.

"We're a prime supplier of Dale Evans memorabilia," says salesman John Curtis.

Five years ago, a couple stopped in hoping to find a 1940s issue of *Life* magazine in which, they said, they had been on the cover. No problem.

The first floor is crammed with enough knick-knacks and paddywacks to stock several dozen antiques stores. Old board games, like Cracker in My Bed, and jack-in-the-boxes. Kodak Tourist cameras and a 1940s Electric Lunch Box, which you'd plug in to heat your little tins of food. Beer steins from the 1991 Munich Oktoberfest. Mounted deer heads and raccoon coats. More snowshoes than you're likely to encounter anywhere else. Rockers and toy horses, Ouija boards and cowbells, dollhouses and dressers. A genuine Allagash portage boat, "for easy portage on the Allagash River," according to a sign. What, you can't use it on any other river?

An Armour Pure Lard Bucket, chicken-shaped butter dishes, and what might be the world's largest coffee cup. Kiss albums and carved Indian heads. Fedoras and flapper outfits, a sanitary scale for your butcher shop, and a pair of block and tackles "off an old ship."

Where else are you going to find a Jones Quality Codfish box, or a tin of George Washington Greatest American Cut tobacco?

"There is a very strict order to this madness," explains Cukierski, referring to the coded dealer tags on every antique.

Upstairs are all the books and magazines. The first book to catch my eye is John Gould's 1963 work *Monstrous Depravity: A Jeremiad and a Lamentation about Things to Eat*, which begins: "If the fine art of cookery is to survive, we men must step in, for the trend is toward oblivion otherwise."

You can find *The Adventures of Poor Mrs. Quack*, and a 1900 pamphlet titled *The Great Round World and What's in It*, published by The Great Round World Company on Fifth Avenue in New York City. In bins

down the center aisle are vintage magazine food ads, including a Karo Table Syrup ad featuring the Dionne quintuplets ("Of course we eat Karo . . . rich in dextrose, the food energy sugar").

A directory on the wall lists the Big Chicken Barn's magazine collection; there are fifty-nine titles

> "The road inland from Bar Harbor to Bangor, which winds through magnificent forests, past lakes and rolling mountains and little old New England farmhouses, is decorated with increasing reminders to ask for Magooslum's Maine-Made Mayonnaise, Smoke Oakum Cigars, and vote for Muddle for Sheriff, to say nothing of B.O. Tobacco, visiting Fuss' Overnight Camps, buying a nice pair of four-dollar shoes from Buzzard's, picking up a Boston bag at Roorback-Skillet Company's Bangor store and attending a Lions meeting while in the city."
>
> John Jakle, *The Tourist: Travel in Twentieth-Century North America*, University of Nebraska Press, 1985

beginning with "A," from *American Boy* and *American Needlewoman* to *The Auk*. You can pick up copies of *Your Big Backyard*, *Sexual Medicine Today*, *Muzzle Blasts*, and *Uncle Ray's Magazine*. *Life* magazines from 1937 are here, plus copies of *Sports Illustrated* back to 1954, when it was called *Weekly Sports Illustrated* and cost a quarter a copy. This is the place you can fill out that *National Geographic* collection. And yes, the moose head on the landing is for sale—four hundred dollars.

It was getting near closing time, and I couldn't leave the Big Chicken Barn without buying something. I almost bought an old library card catalog (fond memories of the Dewey Decimal System), and settled on a car speaker from a long-gone Maine drive-in movie theater.

"I bought a bunch of them," Mike Cukierski said. "I traded one for a piano."

About 8 miles south of the Big Chicken Barn, on the northbound side of U.S. 1, a big sign announces, "Handcrafts at H.O.M.E. Village." What is it? Store? Co-op? Gallery? Artists' colony?

H.O.M.E. (Homeworkers Organized for More Employment) turned out to be all of the above and more, sanctuary for the down and out, a haven for the artistically minded, and home for those not embarrassed to admit they want to change the world, or at least this small corner of it.

It started with Lucy Poulin, an ex-Carmelite nun who in 1970 saw that many older women in Maine were subsisting on their old-age pensions, which brought them a mere $100–$250 a month. Many of the women were crafters; Poulin and several others opened a little store on U.S. 1 in 1971 for crafts, particularly quilts. "New ideas," recalls one H.O.M.E. employee, "fell into place." Project Woodstove, to provide free wood for low-income families to heat their homes, was started after Poulin found an elderly woman trying to heat her house with charcoal briquettes. More nuns and lay people got involved. Using their hands, donated materials, and grants, they slowly transformed 150 acres of land along U.S. 1 into a self-sufficient community designed to give the less fortunate a chance to start over, or pick themselves up.

"My first day was the 28th of December, 1971," recalls Lorraine, a longtime employee (many of the women who have come here for help prefer to use their first names only). "Lucy was building a storage barn and she put me on a board as counterweight while she was sawing. In her eyes I could see her thinking, 'Mmm, poor little nun.'"

Lorraine, a former nun, had lived in a monastery for twelve years. This was her first job "outside."

"It started as a crafts co-op, but it became quickly evident people needed much more," Lucy Poulin says in her office. She wears a blue denim work shirt with a cross stitched on front. "Basic education. Learning how to read. Day care. Employment. Eventually, housing."

"It started with the piecework, then the craft store, and now there is so much more," Lorraine explains. "You have the sawmill, learning center, pottery, weaving shop, museum. And that's typically Lucy. She is very diverse. She listens to everybody, but she likes also to try new things."

"There was tremendous prejudice from townspeople at first," says Poulin. Asked to elaborate, she shakes her head. "It's much less today."

H.O.M.E. is one of three Emmaus communities in the United States, and three hundred worldwide. The humanitarian organization was founded by Abbé Pierre, a French priest, who helped homeless people build rough-and-ready housing in Paris after World War II. Other Emmaus communities in the United States are Emmaus Harlem and St. Francis Community, founded here by Sister Lucy in 1976.

H.O.M.E. includes a soup kitchen and free health clinic; the Goodness Sake Food Co-Op, which sells organic foods, dried herbs, spices, teas, coffees, beans, and rices; an auto repair garage that takes in outside work; a cobbler shop; a shingle mill and sawmill; a farm where chickens and ducks are raised; food banks here and in Ellsworth; five area shelters; and a transitional home in Ellsworth.

Firewood, lumber, shingles, and cedar posts are available from the sawmill. The museum, next to the chapel, is like walking through grandmother's attic, with its haphazard collection of Underwood typewriters, steamer trunks, spinning wheels, bottles, farm tools, lanterns, cast-iron muffin pans, and just inside the screen door, a venerable upright piano.

"Perhaps the most impressive thing about the whole operation," columnist Molly Ivins wrote after a visit, "is that it is not terribly impressive. There is no posh administration building, no fancy anything anywhere."

H.O.M.E.'s continued existence depends on residents, staff, and many volunteers and benefactors, like Paul Robotham of Unionville and Tom Starr of Durham, Connecticut, who every Thanksgiving load up a U-Haul truck with donated furniture and drive to H.O.M.E.

Hunched over a bench in the village woodshop is someone who's found a home here.

"A lot of the people here have some social problems, drinking problems, stuff like that," Richard Turner says. "They're trying to clear themselves of that, trying to make it on their own."

Turner is from California. He worked for a crop duster, Weather Aviation, in Lincoln, California, and other airplane outfits. Steve Ames, a buddy he knew from California, ended up at H.O.M.E. as construction manager. Out of work, Turner called Ames. "He said, 'Come on out.'"

Turner's day in the shop begins at 7:30 a.m. He makes cabinets and chairs, tabletops and "little doodads that go in the craft store." The shop made fifty pine display racks for a pet supply store owner in Massachusetts, who wants fifty more.

"There's talk of a thousand after that," Turner says.

He's not a skilled woodworker, having learned on the job instead. He also does some maintenance work around the complex.

"I generally learn things fast, and I'm not stupid," he says, grinning.

Turner, like the others who end up at the cooperative community along U.S. 1, is trying to start over again.

"I'm looking around for some property, but I don't have a credit history," he explains. "Fifty years old, I never bought anything on credit."

At his feet is a sign that will be installed in H.O.M.E.'s chapel next door. The white-ceilinged chapel is spare but beautiful, with five pews on either side, plus three more against each wall. A notice in the vestibule says: "We hope the quiet of this wayside chapel will refresh you in this busy world."

Back in her office, Poulin talks about the future. In just three years and three months, a six-member H.O.M.E. construction crew built twelve homes in Sedgewick, about 15 miles way. On the drawing board are twelve farmhouses, to be built on H.O.M.E.'s 150 acres. Lucy hopes to open a store in Bar Harbor. With eighty people on the payroll, H.O.M.E. is the third largest employer in Hancock County. But the cooperative is desperate for supplies. A "wish list" pyramid in H.O.M.E.'s *This Time* newsletter ranked Money at the top, a variety of items (food, garden tools, wheelbarrows, chairs, pots, and pans) in the middle, and Money Money Money Money Money at the bottom.

"From an economic perspective, our needs here are enormous," Poulin says. "You drive along Route 1, you see the beautiful old homes. But there is a tremendous need among the underclass—from the homeless to teenagers to the elderly. All the problems we have in the city we have out here."

——

From H.O.M.E., U.S. 1 winds through Bucksport, across the green wrought-iron bridge over the Penobscot River (for a great view, stop at the Sail Inn, at the other end of the bridge), and on to Searsport (the Penobscot Marine Museum and Hard to Beat Hardware), Belfast (the bridge at the end of town became

You don't even have to get out of your car to check the merchandise at Tuttles Shoes in Rockland.

one of my favorite running routes), and Northport, home to a U.S. 1 gift shop known as Pussy's Port o' Call. Snow Hill Lodge—"the view with a motel"—is on the highway just south of Lincolnville center. Camden is one of the most popular of all Maine coast towns, and would give Wiscasset a good run for the money as "Maine's Prettiest Village." Want to stay in a castle? You can, at Norumbega, a turreted Victorian stone castle on 1, that, according to its owners, is "the most photographed structure on the coast of Maine."

It's 2 miles to Rockport, and 6 more to Rockland. *Down East* magazine/catalog showroom is on the highway just north of Rockland center. In town are E. L. Spear Hardware, established 1900, and Wassee's Hot Dogs, "absolutely the best hot dogs anywhere."

But it's at a Rockland lighthouse, that preeminent Maine landmark, that we're going to stop. This is not just any lighthouse; it's a fifteen-foot-high coffee-serving lighthouse.

———

"We're from Seattle; we've been drinking this stuff for twenty-five years," Kathy Searle says from inside the cozy confines of the drive-through Lighthouse Espresso.

You may question the sanity of someone who exchanged the latte winters of Seattle for the iced mocha winters of Maine, but Kathy and her husband, Kurt, picked a good spot for their business. The lighthouse overlooks Rockland Harbor, filled with everything from schooners and sailboats to lobster boats.

The couple moved here in 1996 from Seattle. "It's getting too big," Kathy says of Seattle. "We were part of the exodus." Why Maine, and Rockland? "The view," she adds, looking around her. "Maybe the Mainers take it for granted, but we don't."

They did their coffee research in Seattle before heading out here, and drew up plans for the lighthouse. When it first opened, some people mistook it for an information center or vending machine.

Where else to put a drive-through Maine coffee stand than in a lighthouse? Lighthouse Espresso, Rockland.

The first winter—make that *every* winter—was rough.

"Sixty-, seventy-mile-an-hour winds blowing off the water, zero wind chill," Kathy recalls.

"We stayed open," her husband notes proudly. "It rocked a little bit. The foundation froze to the ground. I re-anchored it."

The lighthouse is heated and air-conditioned, but it's tight quarters inside. Good thing the two are married.

"This was supposed to be my bucolic lifestyle," Kathy says, laughing. "I don't even have a garden yet. But he's great," she added, looking at her husband. "He's my honeydew."

"Yeah, it's honey do this, honey do that," Kurt jokes.

Business was slow at first, but it's picking up.

"It wasn't quite as good as we hoped at first, but Mainers are slow to accept new things," Kathy says. "Eventually they'll be drinking coffee like we do." She smiles. "They'll see the light."

———

Four miles south of Rockland is Thomaston. Dragon Cement, New England's only cement manufacturing plant, is on 1 in Thomaston. So is Maine State Prison. Next door is the Maine State Prison Showroom, one of the more unusual outlet stores in outlet-happy Maine. The shop sells items made by state prison inmates—desks, chairs, tables, bookcases, boats, lamps, toys, plaques, and other items, with crafts-manship—and prices—that are hard to match.

I've bought an oak bookcase, an oak chest, various toy logging trucks and school buses, and a three-foot-long red and black caboose I haven't figured out what to do with yet. The Thomaston store is run by the state; its independently owned sister store in York will be profiled later in this chapter.

Got a flat on Route 1?
Get it fixed at Route 1 Tire, Warren.

U.S. 1—signs along this stretch read Atlantic Highway, a reminder of an old Maine-to-Florida road—runs 12 miles to Waldoboro. There, a neon beacon on U.S. 1—not a lighthouse—beckons hungry, weary travelers. We've arrived at Moody's Diner/Motel.

Percy Moody started the motel on the hill, on what was then Old U.S. 1, in 1927.

"There were three cabins, and an outhouse," Debbie Bellows, one of Percy's daughters, says from behind the diner counter. "My father gave each guest a bottle of water. He charged them a dollar a person a night." She remembers when her brother Harvey would carry her around in his wheelbarrow as he delivered firewood to the cabins.

In 1929, Percy opened a food stand. The state built a new road—it would become part of a realigned U.S. 1—and Percy added his own little road, connecting his motel with the highway. He was a tree farmer, a fish peddler, "a lot of different things," Debbie says. "He told me there had to be a better way to make a living than picking beans."

That better way became the diner, which evolved from the humble roadside stand.

"When it first started, it was just a little stand

MOODY'S DINER LUNCH AND FILLING STATION, WALDOBORO, MAINE

Moody's Diner Lunch and Filling Station, Waldoboro.

with an open serving window," Alvah Moody says. "Dad moved it down to the new Route 1. The floor of the original stand is under here, somewhere."

The diner has been expanded no less than fourteen times, most recently in 1994. New vinyl seat covers, made by inmates at Maine State Prison in Thomaston, were added one year. The diner now seats 105.

"Dad always said, 'Give people good food at a fair price,'" Debbie says. "We have people who get most of their meals here. It's not uncommon for people to drive 70 miles to eat here."

This day's special is smothered beef—tender chunks of beef with onions. The diner is also known for baked goods.

"A woman from New Jersey called the other day, asking for the recipe for our doughnuts," Debbie says.

What's Cooking at Moody's Diner, by Nancy Moody Guenther, one of Percy and Bertha Moody's nine children, contains recipes for everything from Bubbling Squeak (tomato soup, ground beef and onions, plus peas, potatoes and carrots, brought to a boil and then simmered in frying pan) to Million-

aire's Pie and Aunt Bertha's By Cracky Bars. The book is available at the diner.

One day, the food editor for a major women's magazine from "away"—the Mainer's term for out of state—called the diner and asked if it could fly a crew up the following week to shoot the making of a New England Boiled Dinner.

Nancy said they were welcome to come, but the diner served boiled dinner only on Thursdays. The food editor said, don't worry, we're bringing our own meat and recipe; we'd just like to use your kitchen. Alvah got on the phone and laid down the rules: You're welcome to show up Thursday— without the groceries.

Moody's Diner is closed one day a year— Christmas. The motel's eighteen units are open May 15–October 15. "Just far enough from Route 1 for quiet and privacy," according to the brochure. The motel does business the old-fashioned way: cash only.

"I've been coming here for sixty years," says Woodrow Verge. "Every morning we're in here. The clam chowder's good. Everything's good in here."

Verge, from Waldoboro, drives a bus. Verge is eighty-one years old.

"Have to take the basketball team today," he says.

He remembers the little lunch wagon up on the hill, Percy Moody selling his hot dogs at baseball games in town, and Bertha Moody taking leftover egg whites and making angel food cake.

Percy Moody, then eighty-nine, was asked if he was surprised by the diner's success.

"Of course not," he replied. "It's run by Moodys."

———

The highway is alive day and night, alive with promise and possibility, with the everyday stories that never get page-one headlines but that make up the road's, and this country's, history as surely as the most dramatic events.

> "U.S. Route 1, the coast road, a brutally congested strip mall of sham and scams . . ."
>
> Christopher Corbett, *Washington Post*, December 24, 1989

Here is one story. It happened in a nursing home on U.S. 1 in Camden two years ago. A man named Clyde Sukeforth, from Waldoboro, is sitting in his room. He is ninety-five, and wears a Toronto Blue Jays cap backwards on his head.

"I can remember it like yesterday," the old man tells his visitor, a reporter for the *Boston Globe*. He had broken his hip several weeks before, but his mind is as sharp as ever.

In 1945, Sukeforth was a scout for the Brooklyn Dodgers. Branch Rickey, the Dodgers owner, called Sukeforth into his office one day and asked him to take the overnight train to Chicago and catch a Negro League game between the Kansas City Monarchs and Lincoln Giants in Comiskey Park.

Rickey was interested in a shortstop named Jackie Robinson. Robinson would not actually play in that game because he had hurt his arm. Sukeforth invited him back to his hotel, where the two talked for hours.

"The longer it lasted, the greater became my opinion of Robinson," Sukeforth recalled.

The next day, Robinson and Sukeforth took the train back to New York, and headed to the Dodgers offices on Montague Street in Brooklyn. Sukeforth introduced Robinson to Rickey.

"Jack, all my life I've been looking for a great colored player," Rickey told Robinson. The club owner had one question—would Robinson be able to accept the worst abuse that could be heaped on one man—and not retaliate?

"If you want to take this gamble, I promise you there'll be no incidents," Robinson said.

It was what Rickey wanted to hear. Robinson signed a $3,500 contract to play for the Dodgers' AAA team in Montreal. In 1947, Robinson became the first black player in the major leagues.

Several days before the start of the 1947 season, Dodger manager Leo Durocher was banned from baseball for a year "for conduct detrimental to the game." Rickey needed an interim manager, and chose Sukeforth, who managed the first three games in Jackie Robinson's first season in the big leagues.

As the sky darkened outside, threatening snow, Sukeforth sat in his nursing home room and talked about the ballplayer who had changed baseball forever. Some Dodgers, according to Sukeforth, did not welcome Robinson as a teammate.

"Some guys would come up to you and want to argue the situation, and I'd tell them what I thought," he said.

Which was?

"That Jackie Robinson was a very good ballplayer, and a very good man."

———

U.S. 1 makes a graceful sweep toward Wiscasset, 15 miles from Waldoboro. A red phone booth stands outside Ma's Antiques. Several Maine Coast Railroad trains are parked along the road south of the Damariscotta turnoff. "Fresh jerky ahead," reads a small sign.

Wiscasset, the self-proclaimed "Prettiest Village in Maine," is next. Red's Eats, a tiny red-awninged roadside stand known for its lobster rolls, is on Main Street (U.S. 1), just over the bridge. Nearby is a siding for the Maine Coast Railroad trains that run over the tidal rivers and marshes between Wiscasset and Bath in the summer and fall.

Five miles south of town is the Center of Native American Art. Five more miles is another bridge, this one over the Kennebec River, into Bath, the city of ships. In 1608 the first ship built in the New World was launched 12 miles downriver; ever since, ships of all classes have been built here. In World War II, Bath Iron Works delivered two destroyers a month. "Welcome to Bath," a tourist brochure says, "17th best small city in America."

Words to live by. North Edgecomb.

Just north of Brunswick, U.S. 1 widens into a four-lane freeway through thick stands of pine. All roads in Maine, or so it seems, lead to Freeport, with nearly two hundred outlets, stores, B & B's, and restaurants, and world-renowned L. L. Bean, on U.S. 1, where you can pick up a fly rod or package of freeze-dried food at three in the morning. We're going to spend the night not in one of Freeport's thirty inns, hotels, and B & B's, but in a cozy little place almost hidden in the trees 2 1/2 miles, and another world, north of town. Welcome to the Maine Idyll Motor Court.

———

It's four in the afternoon. My Jeep is parked in the gravel in front of Cabin 10. There's an old rocker on the porch, along with a pile of wood and some newspaper. The room inside is rich with the smell of pine, wood smoke, and summertime memories.

The twenty cottages are spread in a grove of pine, hemlock, oak, and spruce. The only sound is a faint whoosh of cars behind me; I-95 is just a short walk through the woods. The units have individually controlled thermostats, but you're missing out on the true Maine Idyll experience if you don't gather a few logs from the porch and start a fire. It can be cool at night, even in the summer.

"Well," says owner Louis Marsteller, "my folks started this in 1932. My dad was in the lumber business. He had lumber to sell, but there were no buyers. It was the Depression."

The first thing you notice about Marsteller is his hands: big and callused, from a lifetime of working outside. His father, Ernest, was from Texas. He dropped out of school in the eighth grade to help support the family. Ernest bought the property, eyeing the trees for timber. But the business failed, so he decided to build cabins for the tourist trade.

Louis Marsteller, owner of the
Maine Idyll Motor Court, Freeport.

"People said he was crazy, putting in a motel," Louis said, smiling.

There were eight cabins at first, including my number 10. Ernest Marsteller chose the name Idyll "because it was an Old English word for natural setting," according to his son.

The motel then included the main house, the office, and a public dining room where you could get a steak dinner, with apple pie for dessert, for a dollar. Showers and toilets were behind the building; Ernest Marsteller would bring a bucket of hot water to guests in the morning if they requested it.

"In the thirties, there were a lot of people walking the roads, hoboes," Louis says. "My parents would give them dinner. Eventually, they quit doing that and just gave them a sandwich in a bag."

Seven cabins were added between 1934 and 1940, three more in the early fifties, the final two in 1990.

Cabin 18 is special. It looks like a treehouse built on the ground, with rough-hewn doors. The cabin was built entirely from one Maine pine.

"We get some city folks," says Louis, his face breaking into a smile, "who think it's pretty rough

A favorite among
Maine Idyll visitors is Cabin 18,
made from one Maine pine.

and don't want to stay there. But the beds, and the bathrooms, are the same as the others."

Cars race by on the interstate; nowhere else are U.S. 1 and 95 closer, except where they join or intersect.

"Used to be quiet around here," Louis says ruefully.

It sure sounds quiet to me.

"Half our customers are repeat," Louis says. "A few we pick up off the road."

All the cabins have refrigerators and televisions (mine offered eight channels, including the Canadian Broadcast Network). Many of the units have fireplaces and kitchenettes. The Maine Idyll does not take credit cards.

"We've stayed away from that, and managed," Louis says.

A lot of people, he adds, "don't know how to build a fire anymore." He shows them a trick. Toss in some sticks, light them, add a log, then hold a newspaper up against the fireplace, "to get a good draft going." The fire will burst forth as if by magic. Works every time.

"Some people worry about wild animals," says Louis, who seems perpetually amused by the ways of city folk. "Someone asked me if porcupines could come down the chimney [they can't; the chimneys are screened]. We see a moose every once in a while."

Ernest Marsteller and his wife, Lelia, were active in the Quaker meeting. Lelia wrote poetry; she composed "The Ideals of the Planner and Builder of the Maine Idyll Motor Court," which can be found on the wall in every cabin.

"You who stop here should forget your troubles and grief, your feuds and hate," the note says. "Think of the trees, the fields, the sky."

Copies of Lelia's poems can also be found in the cabins. Here is her "December Weather Report":

The sky is a gray blanket
spread across the naked treetops
that someone did not tuck in.
On the cold side
and the icy wind
is blowing underneath
making the dead leaves
and bits of paper
run around in circles
and huddle in corners.
If it snows
that will blow in, too.

———

What's on the 66-mile stretch from Freeport to Kittery? Oh, just fifty-five traffic lights, eight towns, four cities, eight McDonald's, five miniature golf courses, two water parks, one minor league baseball stadium, one potato chip factory, and scores of roadside motels, including the Sleepy Hollow Motel, the

> U.S. 1 between Portland and Kittery is lined "with doggeries and crab-meateries and doughnuteries and clammeries and booths that dispense home cooking on oil cloth and inch-thick china in an aura of kerosene stoves, frying onions, and stale grease."
>
> Kenneth Roberts, quoted in John Jakle, *The Tourist: Travel in Twentieth-Century North America*, University of Nebraska Press, 1985

Sleepy Time Motel, the Sleepy Haven Motel, and the Sleepy Town Motel. No town in this busy stretch is sleepy, at least in the summer.

Just south of Freeport, in Casco Bay, a three-story-high Indian with a red and white headdress towers over the highway in front of the American Skiing Company. Nearby, Even Keel Road intersects 1.

There are hundreds of outlets along U.S. 1, but DeLorme manages to be different. DeLorme, whose state-by-state Atlas & Gazetteer series is the country's

Portland Sea Dogs players and two kids stand during the playing of the National Anthem before a game.

A magnificent roadside Indian in Casco Bay greets Freeport-bound motorists.

best-selling series of recreational maps, is head-quartered on 1 in Yarmouth. Maps, software, and travel guides are available at the gift shop. A forty-one-foot-diameter rotating globe, the world's largest, is in the lobby.

In Portland, the highway piggy-backs, briefly, onto I-295, then makes a scenic loop around the lake-like Back Cove, popular with joggers and bicyclists. U.S. 1 runs through Portland, making a left turn in front of a brick edifice that echoes, in the summer, with the sound of wooden bat meeting ball. This is Hadlock Field, home of the Portland Sea Dogs.

It is Maine's only professional baseball team. The previous professional team in Portland were the Portland Pilots, who won the New England League championship in 1949, only to see the league cease operations after that season.

"If the people don't want to come out to the park, nobody's going to stop them," the inimitable Yogi Berra once said.

Mainers were not going to be stopped one way or the other. The Sea Dogs have been among the league's attendance leaders, averaging 400,000 fans a year. The Sea Dogs rewarded their fans' support, winning three Eastern League Northern Division titles in their first four years.

Minor league ball is baseball as it's meant to be played: in the cozy confines of a small park where you can hear the umpire call balls and strikes and where the top ticket price, at Hadlock Field, is six dollars—for a box seat. In 1998, minor league baseball attendance nationwide topped 35 million people—more than the National Football League and National Hockey League combined.

The atmosphere is friendly, the food and drink cheap, and there are plenty of giveaways, from free meals at the local burger joint to cars and vacations. Dizzy-bat races are a crowd favorite; two contestants run around a bat a half dozen or so times, then race, always crookedly, toward the finish line.

If a Sea Dog player hits the giant inflatable glove in right field—"the biggest glove in Maine"—he and a favorite charity split the pot, which increases one hundred dollars every game.

On this night, the Sea Dogs are playing the Reading Phillies, Double-A affiliate of my favorite baseball team, the Philadelphia Phillies. Josh Booty is playing third base for the Sea Dogs. You can have a cap embroidered with your name for only three dollars. I ask the woman behind the counter to put "Route 1 Guy" on mine.

———

Humpty-Dumpty Potato Chips, with its grinning, red-hatted Humpty-Dumpty on the façade, is on 1 in Scarborough. I'm not a big potato chip eater, but their pretzels are great. The State o' Maine Bowling Center is on the northbound side. The Saco Drive-In, with its rusty but splendid circular neon sign, is open for another night of schlock and shock. The

The Saco Drive-In is one of three operating drive-ins on U.S. 1.

"Sleepy" is a popular name for motels along the southern Maine coast. Scarborough.

drive-in, which celebrated its sixtieth anniversary in 1998, is one of only three operating drive-ins on 1 (we'll visit another, the Raleigh Road, in Henderson, North Carolina, later in the book).

The double-bill tonight is *Can't Hardly Wait* and *Armageddon*, the first one silly, the second one silly but at least intermittently fun.

Car speakers have gone the way of kiddie rides and playgrounds at most drive-ins; at the Saco, you tune in the sound on your FM radio. What makes a night at the Saco memorable is the series of classic drive-in trailers played before the movies begin.

"If you want to see girls who'll do anything for kicks, see *The Dirt Gang*," announces the trailer for the 1972 Roger Corman–produced biker movie.

"*Tentacles*—eight tons of bone-crushing terror! . . . You realize there is nothing to do but wait and SQUIRM!"

"*Schizoid*," a clinical-sounding voice says, "is not recommended for people with schizophrenic tendencies."

In 1958, there were more than four thousand drive-ins around the country; today there are less than one thousand, most of them in the South and Southwest. New Jersey, birthplace of the drive-in, has none left. There are five in all of Maine.

U.S. 1 from Saco to Kittery is a mostly commercial strip, but an enjoyable one, free of the usual clutter and billboard overkill. The sign outside Casket Supreme, on 1 in Biddeford, says: "Buy

A roly-poly figure in front of a motel/ miniature golf course in Biddeford.

A smiling mouse welcomes customers to a wine and cheese store in Wells.

direct. Bypass the middleman." You want a souvenir lighthouse? The Lighthouse Depot, on 1 in Wells, is the world's largest lighthouse gift and collectible store. The store's founders, Tim and Kathy, are co-editors of the monthly *Lighthouse Digest*.

The Maine Diner, on northbound 1 in Wells, is a must-stop. It doesn't have quite the history of Moody's—the Maine Diner opened in the early fifties—but is a landmark nevertheless. Socrates "Louie" Toton started the diner; brothers Myles and Dick Henry took it over in 1983. Their first day of business, they made forty-two dollars. Since then, more than a million customers have walked through the doors.

"When the diner came up for sale, I was a general manager for Red Lobster, and Dick was a school-

Don't ask. Biddeford.

teacher," says Myles Henry, sitting at the front counter. "When we opened up, I don't think we had more than fifteen hundred dollars in the bank. Now we spend that much every day on seafood.

"Our first ten years, I wouldn't want to repeat," he adds, laughing. "The first six months you ate the specials. I don't think I have the energy or the balls to do it again. It was a once-in-a-lifetime thing."

He, Dick, another brother, Bruce, "and any family member we could scrounge up" spent thirty days cleaning and renovating the diner.

The new Maine Diner's first customer in 1983, Myles likes to say, came here quite by accident. "He drove his car into a pole near our parking lot," he

An abandoned seafood takeout stand, Kittery.

recalls. "Seems he mistook us for a bar, and zigged when he should have zagged."

The guy stayed, and had a meal with his coffee.

"On the first day one customer ordered poached eggs and oatmeal," Myles says. "We didn't have either."

Under Louie Toton, the diner was open from the day after Labor Day to the day before Memorial Day.

"He wanted no part of the tourist trade," Myles says. "He just wanted to schmooze with the locals. He'd use the summers to grow his vegetables out back."

The garden still provides fresh produce for the diner. The Maine Diner served 250,000 people last year; its first eight years, it had 75,000 customers combined. The diner does 65 percent of its business from May to October, when more than 250,000 people drive through the Wells-Ogunquit area. The Maine is open year-round but not around the clock.

"It's a good time to be an independent business," Myles explains. "We're always going to be a little friendlier than the next guy. With these chains,

you don't know if you're in Tulsa, Oklahoma, or Springfield, Missouri. It gets to the point where there's no regional taste to the food."

The diner is proud of its lobster pie (featured on NBC's *Today* show), its seafood chowder (best chowder at Ogunquit Chowderfest five years in a row), and Grandmother Woodman's Center Cut Ham, among other dishes. Like clams? Try the Clam-O-Rama—a cup of clam chowder, fried whole clams, clam strips, and a clam cake. Desserts include red raspberry pie and Grape Nuts custard pudding.

> "The single, principal highway entering the State of Maine from the south over the new bridge joining Kittery, Maine, to Portsmouth, New Hampshire, has been badly congested every summer for a number of years."
>
> *Concrete Highways and Public Improvements Magazine*, November 1927

If there's a line at the door—and there often is—you can walk next door, to the diner's excellent gift shop. You won't miss your turn; they'll give you a beeper.

"I'm a pretty good marketer," Myles, forty-two, says of his Maine Diner T-shirts, sweatshirts, pot holders, and other items. "No one's going to toot your horn; you have to do it yourself. You almost have to create your own aura."

There's even a Maine Diner newsletter; 7,000 people are on the mailing list.

Famous customers? Sen. Edmund Muskie was a regular here. But Maine's most famous summer resident hasn't eaten in the Maine Diner.

"Mr. [George] Bush [who lives in nearby Kennebunkport] hasn't made it in yet, I don't know why," Myles says. "His Secret Service guys have, though."

For a while, he says, the Maine Turnpike (I-95 here, I-495 north of Portland) put U.S. 1 "on the back burner." But 1 has experienced a resurgence. "Route 1 has become a busier road. It's gotten stronger in the last five or ten years, for sure."

——

The highway makes one last dash, through Ogunquit ("Beautiful Place by the Sea"), home of ocean-view motels, Ogunquit Theatre ("America's Foremost Summer Theatre"), and Yum Mee Chinese restaurant, and York, where Flo's Hot Dogs, housed in a low-slung red shack, is a roadside landmark. There are no tables, six wooden stools, and only one item on the menu. Flo lives out back; her daughter-in-law, Gail Stacy, runs the place.

Two miles south of Flo's, on the northbound side of 1, is an institution where the inmates really have taken over, and J. D. Maloney couldn't be happier.

In Maine, there are factory outlets for everything from jeans, underwear, and shoes to vitamins, bread, and coffee, so why not a prison goods outlet, where the public can buy items made by inmates? The Maine State Prison Showroom in Thomaston

Roadside giant, Kittery.

and the Woods to Goods store in York may look alike, but the resemblance ends there.

The first is state-owned and operated; the second is independently owned. The prices are cheaper at the state store, but the selection at the York store is better. The shelves are stocked with bath towels, jewelry boxes, cribbage boards, chess sets, salad bowls, humidors, CD towers, lamps, rocking horses, tables made from lobster pots, wooden piggy banks, and hundreds of other items, made by inmates in Maine, New Hampshire, Arizona, Oklahoma, and New York.

"We are the only store like this that I'm aware of," owner J. D. Maloney says in his small office.

Woods to Goods was started by Dave Machum in 1993. By then, Maloney had been laid off from the Portsmouth Naval Shipyard, where he had worked seventeen years.

"I have a relative who's an inmate at Maine State Prison," Maloney explains. "During a visit we started tossing around ideas."

Machum wanted to retire; after "two or three hours of gabbing," Maloney bought the store.

In Maine, inmates can make up to five different items for the two stores. Their designs, however, must be approved by an in-prison juried committee. Inmates choose prices for their items; the state marks the prices up to pay for supplies. Inmates get paid about eight dollars an hour; the state takes 80 percent of their salary for room and board and a victims' restitution fund.

"The victims make out OK, the state makes out OK, and the inmate makes out OK," Maloney says. "When inmates [make items], it's got to reduce recidivism. It's only common sense."

Inmates at the "supermax" prison facility 10 miles from Thomaston do not make items for his store. "We like to emphasize to the public that nothing comes from the incorrigible inmates, but from inmates who can be rehabilitated, those who can leave with a marketable skill under their belt," Maloney explains.

The artists' names do not appear on their items, but tags indicate what prison system they're from: pink for Maine, gray for New Hampshire, blue for Oregon, yellow for the few civilian craftsmen the store uses. The Prison Blues line of clothing on display here, made by Oregon inmates, is a success nationwide. "Made on the inside to be worn on the outside," is the Prison Blues slogan.

Maloney does much of his shopping at the Thomaston store—"I'm their biggest customer"—while also making regular "runs" to prisons in New Hampshire and New York State.

The store is open ten–six every day except Thanksgiving, Christmas, and "the occasional blizzard," Maloney says. His best-selling items: model ships. Other items include duck-shaped boxes, banana and grape hangers, and signs for your favorite fishermen: "A fisherman . . . A jerk at one end of the line waiting for a jerk at the other."

"We've been asked, when are you going to put in another store, when are you going to franchise," says Maloney, whose wife, Jane, also works in the store. "It's food for thought. We're growing at a comfortable rate here."

Kittery is outlet city, U.S.A., with more than 120 outlets along U.S. 1, more than Freeport. There's a drive-through grocery store at the Kittery circle. You cross the bridge over the Piscataqua River, and just like that, you're in New Hampshire.

N E W
H A M P S H I R E

> US 1 spans the restless Piscataqua River; the current of this turbulent stream is so swift that the water never freezes even when the temperature is far below zero. From the earliest days the road between Portsmouth, N.H., and Newburyport, Mass., often followed or closely paralleled by the line of the modern highway, served to bind the sparse settlement together. Over this country road a lone horseman carried the mail between Portsmouth and Boston until the coming of the stagecoach. He forded rivers, crossed treacherous salt marshes, and, when necessary, fought off Indians and wolves in the discharge of his duties.
>
> —*U.S. One, Maine to Florida*, American Guide Series, 1938

U.S. 1 slices through downtown Portsmouth as State Street, passing a series of colorful shops, including Divine Dungeon. A sign in front of a house advertises Extremely Motivated Home Improvements. South of the Portsmouth traffic circle is Yoken's Restaurant, with its great neon whale sign ("Thar She Blows!"). Henry and Clarice Yoken opened the restaurant in 1947 in the former Parkway Restaurant and Lodge. The current Whaler Room was the entire restaurant then, with nine booths and two counters. Attached to the restaurant is Yoken's Gift Shop, the largest gift shop in New England.

Portsmouth is one of several dozen U.S. 1 towns involved in an ambitious program to plant elm trees along the highway from Maine to Florida. The New Hampshire–based Elm Research Institute chose the highway because it represented America.

"Route 1 is Main Street America," institute executive director John Hansel told the *Boston Globe*. "It tied all the colonies together and is a history lesson in itself. You can spot an elm tree a mile away, because of its vase shape. It gets ornamental very quickly, and I would say Route 1 deserves some ornaments."

Hansel is hopeful that many, if not all, of the 1,350 towns along U.S. 1 will join the program.

———

About 5 miles south of Portsmouth, in North Hampton, is the largest collection of *stuff* along the entire

You really can get anything on U.S. 1. Portsmouth.

length of U.S. 1. The sign says "Mel's Truck Sales," but the yard is jammed with old cars, pickup trucks, panel trucks, locomotives, cabooses, railroad equipment, license plates, and signs. Inside the office is a cantankerous, stubborn, but otherwise lovable guy named Mel Clark, one-time owner of the World's Largest Tire and the Moxie House.

"This is my last day in business," Mel announces on my first visit to his yard.

Two months later, Mel was there, and three months after that, he was still there. He wasn't there on my third visit, but only because he was in Montana. Mel is still at Mel's, and he's as ornery as ever, and it's hard to imagine him being happy anywhere else.

"Everything's for sale," says Mel, sitting in an old-time barber's chair in his office. "Just bring a truckload of money and you can have all this shit. I'm being forced out of business."

"I thought New Hampshire was a great place to do business."

"Fuck no. The only thing we don't have is a sales tax. The property tax is so high; everything is so high."

He listed the property himself, then finally gave it "to a goddamn real estate man."

A guy walks in, asks about a Corvette he heard was for sale.

"Donna can handle that," Mel says. "She's talking right now," he says, raising his voice. "As soon as she shuts up, she can help you."

Donna Jones, Mel's girlfriend, walks in from the other room. She heard what Mel said, as he intended.

Mel's Truck Sales, North Hampton.

A vintage gasoline sign, Mel's Truck Sales.

The facade of Mel's office is ablaze with signs, plaques, even a car.

Knothead even knows how to kick the tires. Mel's Truck Sales.

Mel Clark in his barber chair.

"If there weren't people around," she says, "I would say something. But I'm one of those nice Maine women—with all her teeth. I have all my teeth and I don't own a skidder [chainsaw]."

Mel's sixty, Donna's forty-six. The two were definitely made for each other.

"Found her up in Maine," Mel explains.

"Where's she from?"

"Brownville."

"Where's that near?"

"Nothing."

"He came up to Brownville to buy my property," Donna says of the first time she met Mel. "I

told him it wasn't for sale. He said I stomped my foot. I don't think I did."

They had something in common—both had fought cancer.

"I'm queen of the junkyard," Donna says. "There are worse things to be. I used to be queen of the water and sewer department, for twenty years."

"When I go to Maine, everybody asks, 'How's Donna?'" Mel says. "When I go to the post office here, it's 'How's Knothead?' Nobody gives a shit about me."

Knothead is Mel's faithful guard dog. If he's not eating, he's sleeping. Mel has him trained to kick car tires, in case people want to check a car or truck in the yard and don't want to kick the tires themselves.

"I got him fourteen years ago," says Mel, who has a flat-top haircut and a voice that sounds like a truck grinding its gears. "I bought this semi from Boston. Inside was this dead puppy. I said, 'We better bury him.' Somebody said, 'I think he's moving.'"

Mel was born in his parents' house, next door to the yard. His dad, an electrical lineman, was killed on the job when Mel was eight.

Mel was a born salesman. "I sold bicycles when I was twelve," he recalls. "In fact, this all started when I went from selling bicycles to selling cars. I was sixteen."

"You sold cars when you were sixteen?"

"Oh yeah. I was selling cars before I was sixteen. I didn't do much kid stuff. This teacher wanted to take me back to school. I told her, 'I made seven hundred bucks this week.'"

A friend pops his head in the office and says, "You have a locomotive out there blocking things."

Haunting reminder of an old amusement park.
Mel's Truck Sales.

"A locomotive?" Mel says, surprised, as if the locomotive showed up in his yard in the middle of the night.

He's a wheeler-dealer in antique trucks and cars, trains, boats, gas pumps, roadside memorabilia, and whatever else catches his eye. He bought the Moxie House, a house shaped like a bottle of the vintage soda pop, which had been at a Manchester, New Hampshire, amusement park. Then he turned around and sold it. Back in 1972, he bought what was then the world's largest tire. He sold that, too.

> "Route 1 is almost suffocated with access. Many folks back out of their driveways onto it. Where it struggles through huge and indifferent cities, it's just another street. In the country, it divides a landscape of sagging toolsheds, guest cottages, old billboards, and rusting gas pumps overgrown with wisteria. Have you ever driven through a museum? That's Route 1, an open-air exhibition whose displays change with the season. . . . This grand attic of a highway . . ."
>
> Bruce Dale, "A Journey down Old U.S. 1," *National Geographic*, December 1984

He bought a Central Maine Express passenger car that is now home to a radio station in Dover, Maine. Another railroad car is up in Brownville Junction; it serves as Mel's "world headquarters." He just bought eighteen cabooses from Canaan, Connecticut, to add to the fifty-six he already has. What will he do with them?

"Sell them," Mel replies. "But I have nothing to do with them. Donna's the caboose lady."

"He's got twenty trailers out back with antiques he hasn't looked at in twenty years," Donna says.

Mel read one day that "industrial vacuums" were being sold at an auction. He figured he had to have at least one, so he sent a representative to the auction. The guy called a few hours later, and said,

Can't wait to order. Seabrook.

"Mel, we have a problem; these vacuums are thirty feet long and fifteen feet high." Mel smiles as he tells the story. "They used these vacuums to clean airport runways. We bought all of them. We had to get a special trailer."

He bought a Simon the Pieman figure from a Howard Johnson's off the Maine Turnpike. But his most prized possession over the years? An Ahrens-Fox fire engine—cream-colored, with blue fenders. "The Duesenberg of fire trucks," Mel says. Arthur Fiedler rode on it one year to a Boston Pops concert. Mel eventually sold it, of course.

Mel asks Donna several times about an upcoming wedding they've been invited to. She tells him several times she doesn't have the invitation in front of her; she'll check later.

"I'm just trying to get my social calendar straightened out," he says.

"He bought a brand-new suit, and now he wants to go everywhere," Donna says.

"I've done million-dollar deals, and I never had a suit," Mel says sheepishly.

He'd like to move some of his cars, trucks, and

trains from the U.S. 1 yard to Brownville Junction, and build a village of false-front buildings—a saloon, general store, bank, and so on. It sounds like a great roadside attraction—MelWorld?—but it wouldn't be open to the public.

"In Maine, taxes are seven dollars a thousand," Mel says. "Nobody fucks with you. No zoning. You can do what you want."

A friend stops in, asks how long Mel is going to stay in business.

"I'm going to lock the gate, and go to Maine," he replies. "I'll be here next Tuesday, then through the weekend, and then I'll be gone forever."

U.S. 1 lasts just 16 miles in New Hampshire, the shortest distance of the fourteen states it traverses. The highway passes the Road Kill Cafe in Seabrook and slips over the border into Massachusetts. In Salisbury, it runs past the Sunshine Cabins and Ann's Diner, crosses the Merrimack River into Newburyport, and heads, now more country road than anything else, toward Boston. There's a familiar sound in the air, the sound of a thousand summer nights across America. The fair's in town. This one is the oldest fair of all, and it's right on U.S. 1.

MASSACHUSETTS

U.S. 1 is the most direct route, though not the most scenic, between Portsmouth, N.H., and Pawtucket, R.I. Even in the days of stagecoaches the section of highway between Newburyport and Boston was known as the "airline route" because of its unwavering course. In its 35 miles it deviates only 83 feet from a straight line; it runs through pleasant farm lands north of Newburyport, then over the glacial hills of Topsfield and Danvers. There are no unnecessary hindrances to traffic in Boston on the through route, which follows a wooded parkway with overpasses and a staggered system of traffic lights.

—*U.S. One, Maine to Florida*, American Guide Series, 1938

In 1818, several Essex County, Massachusetts, farmers put ads in local newspapers inviting all those interested in forming an agricultural society to meet in Cyrus Cummings's tavern in Topsfield. Twenty men showed up. They formed the Essex Agricultural Society, and decided to hold a livestock show that year, and in subsequent years.

The Civil War didn't stop the farm show, which had become a showplace for the latest agricultural inventions, including Raymond's Hay Elevator, True's Potato Planter, and Willis' Seed-Sow.

In the 1890s, the shows were moved to Peabody, but in 1910, after a series of poorly attended events, they returned to Topsfield. In 1929, the midway was filled with rides and games of chance; the headline act of the 1934 fair was Zacchini, the Human Cannon Ball. In 1935, Bud Hamilton performed his famous "Dive of Death," seventy feet into a tank of water. He missed the tank on his first try and hit the ground, but only broke his arm.

Ever wonder how good a speller you'd be if you had a dictionary? Salisbury.

Buckle up. The Topsfield Fair, 1940s.

The Vinson Twins, a synchronized swimming team that performed at the Topsfield Fair in the 1950s.

The Topsfield Fair, America's oldest country fair, is held on U.S. 1 in Topsfield every October, drawing a half million–plus people over ten days. There are livestock shows, beekeeping exhibits (including appearances by the American Honey Queen and the American Honey Princess), milking demonstrations, chick hatching exhibits, antique tractor displays, New England's premier fall flower show, and the annual All–New England Giant Pumpkin Weigh-Off.

Last year's winner was a 920-pound behemoth grown by Warren and Barbara Cole of Warwick, Rhode Island. The secret to their success? Five gallons of fish emulsion and Stress-X, a seaweed concentrate.

"We've found the main reason people come to the fair is for the agricultural exhibits," says Alvin Craig, fair manager since 1985.

Craig, walkie-talkie in hand, is walking through the fairgrounds. He looks as if he hasn't slept in days, which is understandable. The hard part comes in organizing the thousands of exhibits, shows, displays, rides, entertainment, and food vendors. It requires the help of a 30-member paid staff and 350 volunteers.

"On any given day, there are one hundred school buses here," says Craig, who puts in fifteen-hour days during the fair.

Until the early 1970s, the fair began the Labor Day weekend. When the fair was moved to October,

A happy fairgoer. The Topsfield Fair.

Alvin Craig, manager of the Topsfield Fair.

The Topsfield Fair.

The Topsfield Fair.

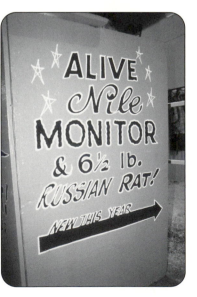

Boy, I'm scared. The Topsfield Fair.

many people thought it would die. Some death. The year 1975 saw the largest number of agricultural exhibits in the fair's history. In 1983, the fair topped the 500,000-attendance figure for the first time. In 1996, attendance was 512,450; in 1998, 525,000.

At night, the Ferris wheel is brilliantly lit in red and orange neon. Kids on the Tilt-a-Whirl shriek with delight. A little girl bobs up and down on the carousel. A boy asks his dad if he can go on a ride just one more time.

"Hey, sir," one wheel operator shouts, "a winner in every race, a prize every game."

"Come on over here," another operator whispers as he walks past, "and get ripped off for only a dollar."

"Killer snakes from around the world!" screams the sign on a freak-and-oddity show. "Giant Pythons! Stinging Scorpions! Big Hairy Spiders!"

One trailer promises a "Pygmy Mud Man" and an "alien in a spacecraft." The mud man is made of mud, all right, and not very well. The alien turns out to be a beady-eyed figure resting in a capsule covered with what looks like Reynolds Wrap. Illumination

The Topsfield Fair.

inside the capsule is provided by a GE kitchen and bath dome light.

The 180 food vendors range from Big Al's Spicy Italian Village and The Original Kielbasa Shop to Anne's Fried Dough and Aunt Hatty's Old-Time Fudge.

But there is only one "Sausage King." Nick Sabpag has been at the fair the past fifteen years. "Good food is not cheap, cheap food is not good," reads a sign in the Sausage King's tent. Both his rent ($1,875

for ten days) and the number of competing vendors have increased over the years, so Nick, wrapped in several jackets against the chill, wonders how he's going to make money. If the quality of his sausage sandwich (huge, only four dollars) is any indication, he'll do just fine.

"We're off to a great start," Craig says the next day. "Weather is everything now."

He looks haggard, but he doesn't seem to mind.

"The day goes by so fast," he says. "You just bounce from one thing to another."

———

Five miles south of Topsfield begins one of the more amazing stretches of U.S. 1. This section, from I-95 to the Tobin Bridge in Boston, is not for the faint-hearted, lead-footed, or aesthetically sensitive. If you cringe at the sight of a sixty-seven-foot-high cactus, a Chinese restaurant that resembles the Forbidden City, a giant ship moored in a sea of black-top, a slightly leaning tower of pizza, and roadside motels that should pay you to stay there, jump immediately on I-95.

You will not only save time but increase your chances of living another day, since this 10-mile-long

Nick Sabpag, the Sausage King. The Topsfield Fair.

A hard-to-spot sign with a powerful message. West Revere turnoff.

ride—part Indy 500, part Demolition Derby, and best taken, if you're a passenger, with eyes closed—is the most chaotic and hair-raising stretch along U.S 1's entire length.

I'm on the road at night, which is the only way to see this stretch of 1 in all its wonderfully garish neon glory. I'm in safe hands. Well, I think so, anyway. Arthur Krim is behind the wheel, and he knows this road as well as anyone. It's not his driving I'm worried about, but the fact that he has to drive and talk at the same time. Krim, a Cambridge-based geographer and roadside aficionado, is my tour guide through the very gates of traffic hell.

U.S. 1 doesn't get much respect, and this stretch of 1 may get the least respect of all—"an enduring monument to wretched excess," according to the *Boston Globe*. In Robert Parker's 1974 novel, *God Save the Child*, his gumshoe, Spenser, calls the highway overpasses tying together the suburban towns "culverts over a sewer of commerce."

"The 10-mile stretch of Route 1 that snakes its way through Boston's northern suburbs from the Tobin Bridge to Interstate 95 is an enduring monument to wretched excess. It's an unmoveable (and to some, preferably removable) feast of tackiness, tawdriness, weirdness, and exuberant tastelessness: a swatch of real estate that was actually improved four years ago by the addition of a million-square-foot mall, and one that remains without peer locally for sheer commercial variety and visual clutter—even as its loopiest features are being Starbuck'ed and Staple'ed onto the endangered species list."

Joseph P. Kahn, *Boston Globe*, June 1998

In other words, Krim's—and my—sort of highway. He concedes the road's excesses—every chain and franchise known to humanity seems to be located here—but admires what's left of the 1940s and 1950s roadside architecture.

Weylu's, probably the biggest Chinese restaurant in the country. Saugus.

Our tour runs takes in the Saugus portion of 1, from the Hilltop Steak House, home of the sixty-seven-foot-high plastic cactus, south to Route 1 Miniature Golf, then back north to The Ship, and is punctuated by Krim's observations, a mixture of academe and boheme, with one hand on the wheel at all times.

"Heroic monumental," he says, describing Weylu's, the huge, pagoda-shaped Chinese restaurant that stands atop a rocky ridge overlooking U.S. 1 northbound.

Weylu's, probably the country's largest Chinese restaurant, was the grandest of a six-restaurant chain of restaurants owned by Rick and Wilma Chang, two immigrants who started with big dreams—the Weylu's in Saugus alone cost 13 million dollars—but ended up in court, plagued with delinquent mortgages and tax liens. The restaurant has since been sold, but its extravagance still astounds. Flanking dragon statues and brass doors greet customers. Inside are twenty-four-karat-gold–plated columns and rooms stocked with marble, teak, and carvings. Seating capacity: 1,500.

Next stop is the Kowloon Restaurant, with its amazing Polynesian tiki facade and pagoda-roofed sign that includes two pink neon cocktail glasses.

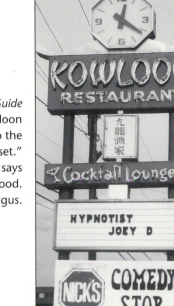

The *Zagat Guide* says the Kowloon "caters to the puffy hair set." Arthur Krim says the food's good. Saugus.

The *Zagat Guide* to Boston restaurants describes the Kowloon as "a plumber's conception of Kublai Khan's pleasure palace," one that caters to "the puffy hair set." Actually, Krim says, the food's pretty good.

The highway—paved in 1922, designated U.S. 1 in 1926, and widened in 1953—"offered the true sense of interstate travel" in its less cluttered, pre-interstate heyday, according to Krim. "This became really a tourist route," he explains. "It wasn't just a local route."

The interstate robbed 1 of that role, and now 1 is a high-speed local expressway along Boston's North Shore suburbs. More than one hundred thousand vehicles charge through here every day. There are no jughandles; U-turns are accomplished with the greatest of unease, by taking local turnoffs, swinging around, and jumping back on the highway, with its nonexistent or limited shoulders. All this requires nerves of steel and extremely quick pickup in one's car.

Krim veers into Fern's Motel parking lot, where we admire the motel's splendid neon fifties sign—"Fern's" in green, "Air Conditioned" in orange, "Motel" in pink, "Vacancy" in red. But my tour guide does not want to linger.

"It's *Psycho* material," he says, glancing nervously at the motel, as if expecting Norman Bates to open the office door.

We reach Lynnfield and turn around, heading south on 1, and reach The Ship, a restaurant (now known as the Weathervane) whose bowsprit is barnacled to the adjacent building, a replica New England fishing village. The building houses the Christmas Tree Shops, which, as befits the unreal atmosphere of this portion of U.S. 1, sells mostly non-Christmas items. Krim loves The Ship. He thinks it's more authentic than the U.S.S. *Constitution*, which, ironically, can be glimpsed from the Tobin Bridge (U.S. 1 in Boston).

"There's more wood on [The Ship] than the U.S.S. *Constitution*," he says. "The *Constitution* has been rebuilt so many times it's not even real anymore."

He drives past the leaning tower of pizza at Prince's Restaurant, built in 1958. The International House of Pancakes on the other side of the highway nearby was the scene of mayhem in 1989. Reputed mob enforcer "Cadillac Frank" Salemme was in the IHOP parking lot when four gunmen dressed in camo fatigues opened fire. Salemme staggered into a nearby pizzeria, taking a bullet in the leg on the way. He survived, and became the alleged boss of the New England mob.

Maybe the most famous accident in the highway's history occurred in 1918, when Francis Stanley, inventor of the Stanley Steamer motorcar, was killed driving his invention on what was then called the Newburyport Turnpike.

Krim stops in his favorite U.S. 1 shop, Russo's Candy House, a beautiful, well-preserved 1954 house, which looks both elegant and lost amid the highway's neon-lit excesses. One is nearly overcome with the aphrodisiacal smell of chocolate inside the shop.

We stop in the Border Cafe, a Mexican restaurant on 1 with a big neon "Eat" sign out front. Krim, instrumental in saving the famous Citgo sign in Kenmore Square, Boston, is writing a book about Route 66.

"I can't seem to get off the damn highway," he complains good-naturedly.

It is time for us to get off our own damn highway. The gigantic neon cactus at the Hilltop Steak House, maybe the most wondrous of all U.S. 1's sights, looms ahead. The Hilltop, one of the top-volume restaurants in the country, was started by Frank Giuffrida, who loved John Wayne so much he plastered portraits of the Duke along the main stairway. Giuffrida has since sold the restaurant to a Denver-based company. But the spectacular neon cactus remains.

"It's a remarkable highway," Krim says in the Hilltop parking lot.

———

There are scores of miniature golf courses along U.S. 1, but only one Route 1 Miniature Golf. It's on the southbound side of the highway in Saugus. Just look for the big orange dinosaur with the not-so-fearsome set of pearly-white teeth. His name's Nick, after Nick Melchionna, the course's original owner.

Bob Paino, Nick's brother-in-law, and Diana Fay, Nick's niece, are the current owners. The golf course, open from March to November 1, attracts 30,000–50,000 people a year. The site includes a Dairy Castle, formerly a Carvel's.

"There was this huge cone there, must have been fifty feet tall," Bob, sixty-three, recalls. "It was beautiful."

Nick, who built the holes himself, opened the course in 1958. The magnificent neon sign came from a New Hampshire miniature golf course. Nick

Route 1 Miniature Golf in Saugus is an oasis of calm amid U.S. 1's most chaotic stretch.

Susan and Mary Paino, c. 1969.
Route 1 Miniature Golf, Saugus.

tried several ways of attracting customers, including an archery range, pony rides, and pet animals. One was called Al the goat.

"He didn't work out too well," Bob recalls. "Nick spent most of his time picking up goat droppings."

This is 1950s-style miniature golf, with classic obstacles like tilting windmills, moving rockets, and protruding bowling balls, with none of the fake rugged scenery of so-called "adventure-style" golf courses.

Myrtle Beach, South Carolina, with more than fifty courses, is the capital of miniature golf, but Pinehurst, North Carolina, is its birthplace. The sport—"the feeblest outdoor activity this side of waiting for a bus," someone once said—can be traced to James Barber of Pinehurst, who in 1916 designed a miniature golf course with all the elements of "real" golf. In the 1920s, miniature golf courses started springing up around the country, often in the unlikeliest of locations. In 1926, Drake Delaney and John Ledbetter built New York City's

first outdoor miniature golf course on a skyscraper rooftop.

The Crash of 1929, according to Nina Garfinkel and Maria Reidelbach in their terrific book *Miniature Golf* (with photographs by the inestimable John Margolies; Abbeville Press, 1987), meant boom, not bust, for miniature golf. The sport offered people an escape into a fantasy world. By 1930, as many as fifty thousand miniature golf courses dotted the American roadside. Department stores designed wardrobes specifically for miniature golf.

About ten thousand miniature golf courses remain in the United States. Florida has the most, followed by Pennsylvania and Michigan. At Route 1

Bob Paino and Nick the dinosaur,
Route 1 Miniature Golf, Saugus.

Miniature Golf, the tradition lives on. Nick the orange fiberglass dinosaur keeps a watchful eye over the highway as little kids of all ages do battle with par.

The course is a favorite stop for children's groups and tour buses. What better way to relieve the white-knuckle-terror of U.S. 1 through Saugus than a round of miniature golf?

> "And signs, glory be, what signs!
> Standing on poles, hung from facades,
> stuck on roofs, they promise everything that
> America could possibly want: Taco Salads,
> Coffee in Rooms, Open Nites, We have Diesel,
> Cocktails from 11:30, Same Day Alterations,
> Free HBO, 30 Lanes, Air Conditioned,
> Floor Sample Clearance, Self-Storage, Tan 'n' Tone,
> Over 70 Billion Served . . ."
>
> Nathan Cobb, *Boston Globe*, July 1989

"We have groups come down from Canada to play here," Bob marvels.

The right turn from Route 1 Miniature Golf onto the highway—you must cross over the exit ramp to Route 99—might be the most death-defying thing you'll ever do in your life. If you survive, continue on 1 toward Boston, through Revere and Chelsea, then over the Tobin Bridge, following the spectacular loop down and around Boston Sand and Gravel. U.S. 1 joins Route 3 and I-93 for a stretch, then I-95 (the ultimate insult), ridding itself of the interstate at the Dedham-Westwood boundary. Foxboro Stadium, home of the New England Patriots, is on 1. The Maine Motel is on U.S. 1—in North Attleboro, Massachusetts. It's time to take out the road maps. The reason: We're in Providence.

RHODE ISLAND

The northern section of this route goes through the industrial and commercial area of the state, through Providence, the capital city, and its thickly populated environs of Pawtucket and Cranston. South of the latter city the route passes through a less densely settled section of the state, through the coastal townships of Warwick, East Greenwich, Narragansett, and the Kingstowns, which are rich in historic interest.

—U.S. One, Maine to Florida, American Guide Series, 1938

The highway crosses I-95 and enters Rhode Island in Pawtucket, where U.S. 1 is Broadway. There is a sign for U.S. 1 north but there's no sign for U.S. 1 south. The road suddenly hops onto the expressway—95—and then you hop back off at the first exit because there's a sign for 1 south. You come to a light; the sign for 1 is practically hidden behind a sign for a local hospital. You come to a fork and . . . now what? You give up, get back on 95, take the second U.S. 1 exit (North Main Street), and come to a light. It's not marked. Let's try a right. Nope, wrong direction. A left puts you on North Main, if you know enough that when you end up behind Brooks Pharmacy, you need to make an immediate left, then a right on North Main, which is U.S. 1 and leads right into downtown Providence. U.S. 1, at this point Gaspee Street, passes the state capitol, and then the Amtrak station, and comes to a T, which is of course not marked and you guess left, which leads to Mell's Diner, Downtown Radiator, and G.I. Joe's Lottery Agent, which is all very interesting but it's not U.S. 1. On another occasion, you drive past the Weston Motel and reach another light and another T, and you're clearly not on U.S. 1, and you go back and turn right at the Weston, which is Sabin Street, which becomes Broadway, which somehow puts you on Pocasset Avenue, which is not anywhere near U.S. 1, and you know this because you've just stopped at a Cumberland Farms and bought a Rand McNally map, which you use to get back on U.S. 1, and you come to the conclusion that no highway, especially one this important, SHOULD BE THIS POORLY MARKED!

U.S. 1 runs through Cranston and Greenwich, home of Jigger's Diner, hugging Narragansett Bay before turning oceanward at South Kingstown. Ten miles south is a little meeting hall. There's a light on inside.

This would be enough for me to take up bowling. Cranston Bowl.

——

Before the meeting, someone walks around offering a box of Whitman's Chocolates. The meeting begins with two staff-wielding members who walk from the podium to a dark-blue-velvet-covered table in the center of the room. The organist breaks into "God Bless America" and "Take Me Out to the Ball Game." Members put hands on their breasts and face the flag to recite the Pledge of Allegiance.

"P of H" is stitched on sashes around the room. A meeting of the Patrons of Husbandry—commonly known as the Grange—is underway. This is Quono-chontaug Grange, which holds its meetings on the second and fourth Thursdays of each month in a simple but spacious hall on U.S. 1 in Charlestown.

There are two rows of folding chairs on either side of the hall, but most of them are empty. Only thirteen Grange members are here tonight. It is a sign of what is happening to the Grange nationwide. The organization, headquartered in Washington, D.C., claims 300,000 members; there were more

Another drive-in bites the dust. Hilltop Drive-In, East Greenwich.

than one million before the Depression. Grange halls are closing, and many of the ones open struggle to survive.

"I remember when the average attendance here was seventy-five," says Cassandra Crandall, Quonochontaug Grange master.

"The Grange for years had a purpose," says Monroe Hoxsie, a member since 1926. "Now it doesn't have a purpose as far as I can see. If it has a purpose I would like someone to tell me."

It is a candid admission; Hoxsie is the Grange jokester, but his words still carry weight.

"The Granges, the VFW, American Legion, all of them, are suffering from one invention, the boob tube. Television is killing them all." The eighty-seven-year-old smiles. "I wouldn't live without it."

The Grange was formed in 1867 to help farmers whose livelihoods had been destroyed by the Civil War. The Grange is credited for the introduction, in 1896, of rural free delivery.

"Rural free delivery united the nation," United Postal Service historian Robert West told the *Portland Press Herald*. "After rural free delivery, we were no longer two classes—one in the city, the other on farms. We were one country."

The Grange's long-standing focus on agriculture has given way to a stronger emphasis on community service, with the numbers of family farms—and farmers—shrinking. Washington County Pomona Grange #2, which consists of seven granges, runs the Washington County Fair, Rhode Island's largest fair.

A Grange meeting is filled with rites and rituals that may seem arcane in the 1990s. The gatekeeper greets members as they walk in. The assistant steward and lady assistant steward receive a password. The lecturer acts as a kind of emcee, choosing and moderating the evening programs.

The truth is out there: *X-Files* fans know the Mulder summer home is in Quonochontaug.

The ritual, however, is an integral part of Grange life and a symbol of the organization's enduring nature. The Grange songbook includes "God Bless America," "Go Tell It on the Mountain," "I'm Looking over a Four-Leaf Clover," "Bringing in the Sheaves," and "It's a Good Thing to be a Granger":

It's a good thing to be a Granger.
It's a good thing we know.
It's a good thing to be a Granger
Wherever you may go.

For many years, Quonochontaug Grange had a friendly rivalry with nearby Cowesett Grange to see which would draw more members to meetings. But Cowesett Grange no longer exists. Dave Crandall, Cassandra's husband, a man with a big, booming voice, remembers the square dances at Quonochontaug Grange hall going until two in the morning. They are no more.

"New England states were the hotbed for Granges," Felix Wendelschaefer says. "When this state became industrialized, the Grange went out the window."

A Quonochontaug Grange meeting always includes the "penny social," a raffle. Each member donates an item—vegetables from the garden, toys, clothing, books. "It's a good way to get rid of things you don't want," Wendelschaefer says, grinning. For a dollar, you get twenty-five tickets, which you can distribute any way you like into the cups next to the raffle prizes. If you really want that Danielle Steel novel, put all twenty-five tickets on Danielle Steel. Monroe Hoxsie is the big winner this night, garnering two fat tomatoes, a kaleidoscope, and a wallet.

> "Route 1 is to Route 95 as the pony express is to airmail. . . . You can get a headache trying to look for scenery along the way. It is not much more than a string of undistinguished, tired, monotonous, anonymous, characterless and just plain boring buildings."
>
> John J. Monaghan Jr.,
> *Providence Bulletin*, December 1966

After the meeting, Grange members head downstairs for refreshments. Cassandra Crandall says the Grange is selling its hall and property on U.S. 1 to the local fire department, but will hold the mortgage and, more important, continue to meet here.

"We're going to keep going as long as we can keep going," she says.

———

Any bona fide *X-Files* fan knows the Mulder summer house is in Quonochontaug. The name is an Indian word for "black fish." Tiny Rhode Island—37 miles east to west, 48 miles north to south—is dotted with villages with colorful, tongue-twisting names, the legacies of five Indian tribes who lived here—the Narragansetts, Niantics, Nipmucks, Pequots, and Wampanoags.

Passapaquag Road is in Weekapaug, which is just down the road from Quonochontaug. Usquepaug is famous for its annual Johnny Cake Festival. Johnnycakes are cornmeal cakes fried on the griddle until the crust is crispy.

Pawtucket and Woonsocket are Indian names. And don't forget Chepiwanoxet, Meshanticut, Misquamicut, Pettaquamscutt, Shawomet, and Yawgoo.

CONNECTICUT

The first post rider on the American Continent was dispatched over this route, from New York to Boston, following the old Pequot Path, then only a blazed trail through the wilderness. Over this route in 1773 Paul Revere, spurring his foam-flecked horse, dashed on his way to Philadelphia with news of the Boston Tea Party. When the half-frozen horseman paused at Guilford to bait his horse, the astonished natives gaped wide-eyed at the streaks of war paint on his face. Today, this highway, the Roaring Road, modern and efficiently policed, is the only direct route across southern Connecticut from border to border.

—*U.S. One, Maine to Florida*, American Guide Series, 1938

U.S. 1 runs unerringly from one end of Connecticut to the other, connecting the towns and cities scattered along the coast like some far-flung constellation. The highway is one Main Street after another through the Nutmeg State. The highway enters Connecticut in Pawcatuck, and in 9 miles reaches Mystic. Mystic Pizza is on Main Street—U.S. 1. Six miles south, a submarine-shaped sign by the side of the road welcomes you to Groton, Submarine Capital of the World. "The heck with OPEC," says a sign in front of the Citgo station. Road Kill Cafe and Nowhere Cafe are on 1 in car dealership–crazy New London. Where can you find Weeki Weeki Laundry? In Waterford.

Approaching Lyme, U.S. 1, marked as Ancient Highway here, winds through a scenic countryside of nurseries, roadside stands, farms, and spacious homes. The Rustic Cafe is on 1 in East Lyme; in the summer the Lyme Fire Department, on 1, runs a cow chip raffle. Frankie's, on 1 in Westbrook, advertises "the state's best happy hour." Lupone's Department Store—established in 1902—is a fixture on 1 in Clinton, the self-proclaimed Bluefish Capital of the World. Madison is one of the quintessential U.S. 1 towns in Connecticut, with its shop-filled Main Street and beautiful old movie theater.

Bishop's Fruit Growers, established in 1871, is in Guilford, and so is Pepper's—the General Store for

Groton.

Miniature golf course, Clinton.

Animals. The New England Country Store, in Branford, sells "the world's best apple pie." The Totem Pole, "a Native American trading post," is on 1 southbound in Branford, across the road from a multiplex theater.

A trolley that serves as a tourist information center is on 1 northbound, in front of the Holiday Inn, in East Haven. The road runs alongside I-95, then exits into New Haven. On Columbus Avenue (U.S. 1), near Howard Street, a garden grows.

———

New Haven is the home of Yale University, but it could also be called the City of Gardens. In an ambitious citywide program, nearly seventy gardens have been planted by residents and community groups. Last year, New Haven was named an All-American City, "and the garden program was a big part of that," according to Sylvia Dorsey, of the New Haven Land Trust.

"Every kid in New Haven is gardening," Dorsey says. "We have so many gardens."

The garden on Columbus Avenue is special. "Please don't steal things from this garden," reads the sign in front of the Homeless Garden Project. Some of those who tend the crops live in the Columbus House shelter just down the street. The produce goes to soup kitchens at Columbus House and other shelters, or is sold at a downtown street market on Saturdays. Several specialty food shops get their vegetables from the half-acre plot on Columbus Avenue.

"This is the most interesting thing on Route 1 in Connecticut," Dorsey says proudly. "Definitely."

East Lyme.

Isn't there an alternate road we can use? Madison.

Mural, New Haven.

Crop selection may be a little haphazard—"this year, things just kind of got planted; the people who got involved didn't have much knowledge," she says—but the volunteers' hearts are in the right place.

Francis Beveridge and another worker are paid stipends to maintain the garden. Volunteers include Yale Divinity School students and minor offenders fulfilling court-mandated community service.

Beveridge, a blond native Canadian, was homeless himself when he came to New Haven.

"I was a resident of Columbus House," he says, shovel in hand. "I'm what you call a graduate. I went down the wrong road. I got into drugs. That took everything away, my apartment, my car. . . ."

This is the United Nations of gardens. Everything seems to grow here, from five kinds of tomatoes, string beans, sweet potatoes, cantaloupe, raspberries, and pumpkins to Swiss chard, basil, sorrel, marigolds, sunflowers, even chili peppers—Thai Dragon ("ten times the heat of a jalapeño," Beveridge says) and Scotch Bonnet ("fifty times the heat of a jalapeño").

"We had more tomatoes than we knew what to do with," Beveridge says. "We had a great garlic crop this year."

The choice of manure may have had something to do with that.

Sylvia Dorsey, who oversees the Homeless Garden Project.

The sign in front of the Homeless Garden Project, New Haven.

Enoch Lopez and Francis Beveridge, two of the gardeners who make the Homeless Garden Project grow.

"We have to give credit to those Yale polo horses," Beveridge explains.

Several local gardeners have small individual plots, including Enoch Lopez, who wears a big straw hat with a black band. He grows potatoes, tomatoes, collard greens, cilantro, and other crops.

"Put it in your milk," he says, holding a mint leaf between his fingers, "and your stomach feels good. Drink some at night, and you sleep good."

Beveridge and Dorsey decide that the following year they will probably grow less, concentrating on crops that sell well.

"We had a great harvest this year," Beveridge says, beaming. "We're going to be even bigger next year."

———

Lender's Restaurant and Deli is on U.S. 1 in Orange. Orange rivals Saugus, Massachusetts, in sheer commercial variety, but the road, with center turn lanes, is not as claustrophobic here. Milford is home to the Marine Invertebrate and Pet Center. In Bridgeport, U.S. 1 is, among other things, Barnum Avenue, named after all-American showman P. T. Barnum, who called Bridgeport home and served as the city's

Bridgeport.

mayor. At a pawnshop named Hock It to Me, you can get "cash in a flash."

There are several classic diners on 1 in Bridgeport—the Bridgeport Flyer, White's Family Diner. Across the street from White's, at Magic Carpet, is a stunning 1940s neon sign of a turbaned man riding the proverbial carpet.

At the traffic circle in Fairfield where 1 darts under I-95 in front of the Fairfield Lighting Center, a guy wearing a red, white, and blue bandanna is making hot dogs inside a white panel truck. But these are not ordinary hot dogs, and this is no ordinary hot dog man. It's the . . . SUPER DUPER WEENIE MAN, inside the SUPER DUPER WEENIE WAGON!

——

For Gary Zemola, it was love at first sight. In 1992, he was flipping through John Baeder's classic book *Diners* (Abrams, 1978) when he saw the hot dog wagon on page 47. At the time, Zemola was "fed up" with his job as chef at an Italian restaurant in South Norwalk. He took one look at the hot dog truck and suddenly realized his destiny in life. OK,

so maybe he just saw it as a better way to make a buck.

The truck, unused since 1985, was "disheveled, the windows cracked, the paint all faded," he recalls.

It was, amazingly, right in South Norwalk, on a waterfront lot. Zemola tracked down the owner, Neil Farans, who operated a Texaco station in Norwalk. Farans had purchased the wagon from its original owner, Robert Turner.

Zemola bought the wagon, gutted and rebuilt the interior, adding stainless steel, a new grill, and two Frialators he found in New York City's Bowery.

"The fry machines I had before were for Girl Scouts," he scoffs. "Then I got serious."

He had one goal in mind: "Make the most classic frickin' hot dogs anywhere."

The Super Duper Weenie Man would succeed only if he had the right stuff. He started buying his dogs from "two German guys" nearby.

"Beef and pork," Gary says in his raspy, Tom Waits–like voice. "All natural casing. And I don't fry them. I brush them with real butter. No fake butter, no Hollywood movie butter. And I steam my buns. Even the bacon—I do bacon strips. Bacon bits? What's that? To me, bacon bits is the scrap you sweep off the floor."

Bridgeport.

Gary Zemola outside his hot dog truck, Fairfield.

The Super Duper Weenie Wagon, Fairfield.

He decided to make his own relish instead of using a commercial brand. "The kind of shit," he explains, "that sits on the shelf for twenty years like a Twinkie. I call it nuclear green relish. You can die and 20,000 years from now someone can dig up that relish and still eat it."

His California dog combines chili, chopped onions, Monterey jack, hot pepper relish; while his New York dog comes with kraut, red onion, mustard, and hot relish. The New England hot dog includes kraut, bacon, mustard, sweet relish, and raw onions.

Unlike Alice's Restaurant, you cannot get anything you want at the Super Duper Weenie Wagon. For one, you cannot get a diet cola. Those who ask for it get Zemola Lecture Number One:

"Look around you. You're going to have a classic hot dog, classic relish, classic fries—and a Diet Coke? That's not going to save you! Go die at Joe's Salad Bar. There's no diet here!"

Tuesdays through Fridays, he sets up at the traffic circle; on Saturdays, he parks at Fairfield Green, in town.

"Saturdays are sick," he says. "Saturdays are twisted."

Translation: Saturdays are good for business.

In the winter, he makes his own soup—minestrone, beef stew, split pea, cream of broccoli, cauliflower cheddar, and other varieties. One night, a kid broke into his house and stole a quart of mushroom barley.

Customers jot down comments in the Super Duper Weenie Man's guestbook. There are the usual "nice buns" and "doggone good food," and then there are entries like this:

"Gary's food," wrote Rick Feola, "represents his own social angst and blatant disregard for the norm."

"It sucked," wrote Tom Ramos. "Shitty food, shitty music. Bad conversation. See you tomorrow."

The hot dog man hopes to open his own diner one day. He bought a vintage Silk City; it sits in a nearby lot.

"Everybody thinks the restaurant business is so hard," he says, his day over. "You know what's hard? The hours. Just keeping the quality. The real bottom line is passion. If you dig what you do, that's what counts. I don't care if you're making toothpicks."

———

Add one more to U.S. 1's list of honors: the Dunkin' Donuts capital of the world, at least in Connecticut. Dunkin' Donuts is as ubiquitous on 1 as McDonald's or Taco Bell. There are nearly forty Dunkin' Donuts on U.S. 1 in Connecticut, an astounding number considering there are only 119 miles of highway. There are better doughnut shops along 1—Honeydew Donuts and Bess Eaton shops throughout New England; Congdon's in Wells, Maine; and the incom-

parable Krispy Kreme (we'll visit the shop in Alexandria, Virginia), but for coffee, make mine Dunkin' Donuts. Real dark, two sugars, please.

———

Traffic jams along I-95 from New Haven to Stamford are a common occurrence. The reasons? Take your pick: a two-car accident, an overturned tractor-trailer, two overturned tractor-trailers, a toxic chemical spill, or something freaky, like a load of bananas on the road. U.S. 1, never more than a couple of miles from I-95 all the way through Connecticut, is often faster than the interstate. And, naturally, it's more interesting. Where else are you going to find the world's largest dairy store, anyway?

———

Stew Leonard Jr. scoots around his Disneyland of a supermarket, cup of coffee in his hand, acting part stock boy (rearranging the pot pies), part customer service rep ("Where do you have hamburger rolls?" a woman asks; "Here, let me show you," he replies), part motivational speaker ("Hey, Bob, I love you,"

Stew Leonard Jr. on the roof of his Norwalk superstore.

Fresh milk rolls off the line.
Stew Leonard's, Norwalk.

he tells one employee, "but this thing takes so slow; can we make it come out faster?"), even part El Exigente, sampling the beans in the coffee section at Stew Leonard's, world's largest dairy store.

"I was just thinking," he says to an employee, a phrase he would repeat many times as he makes his rounds this morning. He stops at the store's computerized cake decorating machine, where you can have a favorite photo scanned and reproduced on your cake. People are always asking how the machine works, how much does a cake cost, and so on; why not put up a board answering their questions?

More than one hundred thousand people shop every week at the Norwalk store, a Home Depot–sized place with immense quantities of your favorite ketchup, mustard, and breakfast cereal, and mooing cows, singing roosters, and a musical band of mechanized farm animals, known as Stew's Farm Fresh Five, who sing "Fresh Fresh Fresh."

It is that rare creature: a super-supermarket with personality. Fresh is the key. The store carries only a thousand or so different products—generally one brand of each item—unlike the fifteen to twenty thousand products at the average supermarket. The store eliminates the middleman, passing the savings on to customers.

The world's largest dairy store is also the world's largest in-store bakery, the world's largest single-store seller of orange juice, and the only supermarket on U.S. 1 with live barnyard animals out front. The wishing well at the entrance has gener-

If you get bored at Stew Leonard's, there really is something wrong with you.

The cowhead-decorated Clover Farms trucks were a preview of the theatrics to come at Stew Leonard's.

ated more than a million dollars for charity. In 1974, a customer named Colleen Blanchard sent in a picture of herself standing in front of St. Basil's Cathedral in Moscow with a Stew Leonard's bag in her hand. Soon photos from around the world began to arrive; they are displayed on a bulletin board at the entrance.

The store sells an array of prepared meals, from blackened Norwegian salmon to fresh shrimp scampi and chicken with herbs, made in the kitchen upstairs. Loaves of bread roll out of big ovens in the bakery department. The heady aroma of several dozen kinds of coffee wafts through the coffee section; the store roasts 200 tons of coffee beans a year.

Back in the ice-cold warehouse, Leonard runs into Scott Varanko, the produce manager. The store buys its produce direct—tomatoes from British Columbia, peppers from Holland, strawberries from California, blueberries from North Carolina. The two men figure how much corn the store sold over the Memo-

rial Day weekend. Let's see, 55 skids, 42 cases a skid, 48 ears per case—110,880 ears of corn.

"Not bad," Varanko says, "for a little family mom-and-pop."

That was a long time ago. Grandpa—Charles Leo Leonard—started bottling milk in Norwalk in 1924. He bought milk fresh from local farmers and

> "Damnable U.S. 1, the premier road of North America . . . Arterial highway poisoned with big blood count . . . Trucks, busses, dog-stands, gas pumps, Shore dinners, the horrors of New Rochelle, Port Chester, Greenwich . . . Endured because I know I will soon turn off . . ."
>
> Writer Christopher Morley, in the 1930s

delivered the bottles to customers in his Clover Farms trucks. By the 1950s, the yellow Clover Farms trucks were instantly recognizable: giant plastic cow heads stuck out from the front windshield. It was a preview of the theatrics to come.

Norwalk.

Stamford.

Charles's son, Stew Leonard Sr., dreamed of building a retail dairy store that would be a fun place to shop, and in 1969 the dream came true with the opening of the Norwalk store. The operation was praised in the 1982 bestseller *In Search of Excellence*, and the Reagan administration gave Stew Leonard Sr. the Presidential Award for Entrepreneurial Achievement. A Danbury, Connecticut, Stew Leonard's opened in 1991.

But the good times ended in 1993 when Stew Leonard Sr. and three company officials pleaded guilty to skimming more than 17 million dollars in sales from the Norwalk store. What became the largest criminal tax case in state history involved, according to the *New York Times*, "customized computer programs, destruction of records, and bags of money smuggled to the Caribbean." Stew Leonard Sr. spent almost four years in federal prison.

That's behind Stew Leonard Jr. now, and the future looks bright. A Yonkers, New York, Stew Leonard's opened in spring 1999. The company hopes to build another superstore in Connecticut.

Continuing his tour, Stew Jr. spots a package of gourmet salad that reads, "I'm in a new package but I'm the same weight." He crosses out "weight," and pencils in "amount," a word, he says, that will make more sense to people.

Regulars here include Paul Newman, Martha Stewart, Diana Ross, and Donna Summer.

Leonard makes a quick stop in his spacious, sky-lit office, decorated with photos of his wife and four daughters, and sayings from Dad ("Life is 10 percent what happens and 90 percent how you handle it") and Will Rogers ("Even if you're on the right track, you'll get run over if you just sit there").

Before long, though, he is down on the floor again, steering customers' carts, jotting down notes. He picks up a package, reads the wrapping, and circles the words "shelf life."

"People don't know shelf life," he says. "I was thinking . . ."

———

In only one state is U.S. 1 marked as something other than north and south. Through much of Connecticut, the road runs east and west, and is marked that way. It runs past Utopia ("The store with all the cool stuff"), Speedy Donuts, and barrel-roofed Swanky Frank's luncheonette in Norwalk, through Darien and into Stamford ("The City That Works").

Rippowam Diner, Stamford.

In Port Chester, U.S. 1, once more Main Street, runs past the old Lifesavers plant (which is being converted to condominiums), Video Latino, and the Nimble Thimble Market. No more confusing "east-west" signs now; we're on the Boston Post Road, a modern-day reminder of the colonial stage route that linked the thirteen colonies. Welcome to New York. Rye, Mamaroneck (a Nathan's Famous with a windmill on the roof is on 1), Larchmont (The Woodpecker Shop), New Rochelle (IGA Meateria and Noodle on One). U.S. 1 dips into New York City just below the Hutchinson River Parkway. In the Bronx, the highway runs the gantlet of maybe the greatest concentration of auto repair shops in the nation. Not for nothing all the "Tires Fixed" signs; this is one of U.S. 1's bumpiest, most potholed sections. Just past the Bronx River Parkway, U.S. 1 becomes Fordham Road. See the woods and fields on your left? People say New York City's a zoo. Well, on this stretch of 1, it really is.

NEW YORK

The Bronx, one of five boroughs of the city, was named for Jonas Bronck or Brounck, who in 1638 built the first manor house N. of the Harlem River. When in 1639 the Dutch West India Co. sold land here the area was called Broncksland, of which the present borough name is a corruption. . . . This approach to New York City is dismal and uninteresting. Gas stations, auto junk yards and diners and third-rate roadhouses line the highway. Weedy lots sprawl to the backdoors of private homes and apartment houses.

—*U.S. One, Maine to Florida*, American Guide Series, 1938

Doesn't sound like the WPA writer had a high opinion of diners. Even today, gas stations, junkyards, and, yes, diners, line U.S. 1's approach to the city, but the weedy lots have been asphalted over, with grocery stores, hair salons, video stores, and discount clothing emporiums taking their place. It is a lively, even riotous, stretch of road. Among the businesses: Good Deed Realty, the Food Temple, Fidel's Bar, and Top Tomato, with a giant inflatable tomato on the roof. Don't miss the great Post Rd. sign atop the building at Boston Road and Fenton Avenue.

The highway darts left under the El tracks and passes under the Bronx River Parkway. The New York Botanical Garden is on your right, and on the left, almost hidden in a copse of trees, is a magnif-

icent green gate. There are many unlikely sights along U.S. 1, but the 265-acre expanse beyond that gate may be the unlikeliest of all.

——

There may be bigger, better-kept, and more spectacular zoos, but there is only one Bronx Zoo, which celebrated its 100th anniversary in 1999. It comprises savanna, lowlands, and the 40-million-dollar Congo Gorilla Forest—and is surrounded by high-rise apartments and bodegas. The Bronx Zoo is the nation's biggest urban zoo, but does not immediately come to mind when one thinks of New York City's top tourist attractions.

How did Ogden Nash put it? "The Bronx? / No thonx!"

The Bronx.

The Bronx.

The zoo is operated by the Wildlife Conservation Society, which also directs Wildlife Conservation International. The organization, formed in 1895 as the New York Zoological Society, counted wealthy sportsmen, including Theodore Roosevelt, among its members. Their collection of 843 beasts, birds, and reptiles became, four years later, the Bronx Zoo. The original reptile house is still here, and so is the Taj Mahal–like Keith W. Johnson Zoo Center, a k a the Elephant House, a Beaux-Arts structure that

opened in 1907. The original aviary, built in 1899–1900 and known as "The Great Flying Cage," collapsed during a severe storm about ten years ago. The current six-story-high Russell B. Aitken Aviary opened in May 1997.

At the turn of the century, zoo animals were no more than prisoners, and their keepers had little clue how to take care of them. One zoo fed its gorilla sausages and beer; shortly after the Philadelphia Zoo opened in 1874, a sloth was poked to death with canes and umbrellas by zoo visitors who couldn't understand why sloths were acting like, well, sloths.

Undoubtedly the strangest and most embarrassing chapter in the zoo's rich history was that of Ota Benga, a Belgian Congo pygmy who became the bizarre star attraction of the Monkey House in 1906.

The story went that Ota's wife and family had been slaughtered by forces trying to conscript pygmies to harvest rubber for Belgian colonists. The story seemed to get better as soon as Ota hit these shores. This is how the *New York Daily Tribune* described his wife's death: "One day when Ota returned from hunting he learned that she has passed quietly away just before luncheon and that there was not so much as a spare rib for him."

Ota was put on display in the zoo's primate cage. Zookeepers scattered bones around the cage as if to suggest a cannibal had just eaten. When Ota was freed for walks on the grounds, keepers would chase and poke him, or spray him with a hose so he would leap for the crowd's amusement.

The Colored Baptist Ministers Conference angrily protested, but zoo director William Temple Hornaday didn't see what the fuss was about. "We are taking excellent care of the little fellow," he said. "He has one of the best rooms in the primate house."

The protests mounted, however, and Ota Benga was freed from his cage after several weeks. The pygmy was turned over to the Howard Colored Orphan Asylum in Brooklyn, where he learned the alphabet and became a minor celebrity.

Then he disappeared from public view. He turned up as a farmhand in Virginia and then went to live in the woods near a black seminary in Lynchburg.

"Later, when all the tourists leave, let's go down and bother the baboons." Bronx Zoo.

His best friends were two small boys who would go into the woods with him and hunt—not for elephant but squirrels. When Ota spoke, the boys would later recall, there were tears in his eyes. He told them he wanted to go home.

In July 1916, Ota Benga shot himself through the heart. He is buried in an unmarked grave in Lynchburg.

In many ways, the Bronx Zoo, the world's largest when it opened a hundred years ago, has been a pioneer. It was the first zoo to construct a predator-prey exhibit in an open setting. Lions and antelope roam an African veldt as real as the one in Tanzania; luckily for the antelope, the two are separated by moats. It was also the first with a World of Darkness exhibit. And it's the only zoo in the world with captive hoatzins (a South American bird).

It probably wasn't a first, but in 1983, the zoo started selling its manure—Zoo Doo—through mail order and retail. You could even buy Zoo Doo at Bloomingdale's! The manure came from giraffes, hippos, snakes, deer, ostriches and all the birds—basically, from anything that wasn't a meat-eater. Carnivores' manure was considered too acidic. The operation was actually run by the Bronx Frontier

Long-necked resident, Bronx Zoo.

Development Corporation, a nonprofit community service group.

The zoo's medical facilities are considered among the world's best. Each year, 15 percent of the zoo's 4,200 animals will die of old age, disease, or wounds. The multimillion-dollar medical center includes an operating room and hospital ward, where ailing animals—a porcupine with an upset stomach, for example—wait their turns.

Tissues from every resident animal since the 1930s have been taken and saved. The Bronx Zoo's first medical records date to 1902, when Dr. W. Reid Blair, ministering to a listless and depressed gibbon, prescribed one and a half ounces of blackberry brandy twice daily.

> "We are parlously like hens, and nowhere does the fact show so vividly as along Interstate Highway No. 1."
>
> an Gordon and Cora Gordon,
> On Wandering Wheels, Dodd, Mead, 1928

Brandy is no longer on the menu, nor is the high-cholesterol meat-and-eggs diet that was standard zoo fare for many years. Ellen Dierenfeld, the zoo's chief nutritionist, can take credit for that; under her guidance, diets rich in vitamins, minerals, and fiber have been implemented: crickets for the toads, crushed crab shell for the anteaters, lots of leafy vegetables like kale and mustard greens for just about everyone.

The zoo's nutrition center plans the menus for animals not only at the Bronx Zoo but the Central Park Zoo, the Queens Zoo, the Prospect Park Zoo, and the New York Aquarium at Coney Island. The five facilities go through about 900 tons of hay, 350 tons of feeds and pellets, 200 tons of fish and shellfish, 50 tons of meat, 5 tons of fruits and veg-etables, and 1 ton of whole rodents and insects in a year.

Here's the daily diet for a white-fronted wallaby:

High-fiber herbivore pellets, 200 grams (2 cups)
Kale, 100 grams (7 leaves)
Timothy hay, 200 grams (one-third flake).

Cockroaches are a good source of protein and fiber; baby rats a good source of vitamin E.

But slipping healthy food into the diets of zoo animals is not easy, which is why Dierenfeld and her assistants must resort to trickery. Egg whites are popped into the microwave and then fed to animals in the hope they will think, "Oh, grubs."

But every week brings a new nutritional challenge, or another finicky eater.

"Right now," Dierenfeld says, showing me around the labs, "we have some concern about bird of paradise diets. And we're starting to see problems in some carnivorous animals that may be related to too much vitamin A in their diets. It's time to step back."

Much is still not known about captive animal diets and nutrition. "Every zoo in the world feeds crickets of different sizes, but no one is doing any analysis of the composition of the different sizes," Dierenfeld explains. "We're in a black hole here."

Dierenfeld, who grew up in Deep River, Iowa, always had pets—a skunk, a raccoon, and Jake the snake. Her dad and brother are both veterinarians. When Dierenfeld started at the Bronx Zoo in 1986, only three other zoos had full-time nutritionists.

The toughest animals to satisfy, on a dietary basis, are the browsers—Columbine and proboscis monkeys and rhinos, for example. Columbine monkeys in particular suffer from poor teeth, diarrhea, and what Dierenfeld calls "twisted guts."

If you interview a zoo nutritionist, schedule it well before lunch.

"I have a student at Manhattan College," Dierenfeld says, "grinding up stomachs of frogs and toads [for a study]." She smiles. "I don't do that anymore. I did my grinding up as a student."

Her work often takes her far afield from the Bronx. The nutritionist has traveled to Africa to study beetles in the diets of jackals, to China to study bamboo-munching by giant pandas on one trip, and tiger diets on another. She's done studies on pancake tortoises, which live in crevasses in Tanzania, and on the digestibility of fiber for hedgehogs. An ongoing study at the zoo is vitamin E deficiency in marmosets.

"I get yelled at by my colleagues—'there is no art to this, it is a science,'" she says. "I disagree vehemently. Zoo feeding is an art as well as a science."

The nutrition lab includes high-tech equipment—atomic spectrometer, muffle furnace, fat extraction machine—and cabinets full of samples only a zoo nutritionist would keep—grasses eaten by antelopes in Mongolia, fruits eaten by birds of paradise in Papua New Guinea. One packet is labeled "Before and after baboon," which sounds like something best left unexplored.

After lunch, Dierenfeld visits the World of Birds to check on some of her charges. There are chopped greens in pans for the Great Argus pheasants; blueberries, carrots, peas, and corn for the Montezuma oropendula; a similar fruit-and-vegetable mix for the Bolivian cock-of-the-rock.

The nutritionist peers through the glass at an iris lorikeet, which in the wild licks pollen and nectar from fruit blossoms, and also eats berries, seeds, and insects.

"Hmm," the nutritionist says, checking the multicolored bits and pieces in the bird's food pan. "Looks like something from our fruit salad."

Peter Franklin, the world's gabbiest cabby, outside the Market Diner in Manhattan.

———

No book on New York City streets would be complete without a chapter on the people who know them best. Cabdrivers may be rude, they may drive like maniacs, and sometimes they want to take you for a ride (unfortunately, not the one you intended), but if you want to know what's really going on in the Big Apple, they're the ones to ask. There are about thirteen thousand cabs and forty thousand cabdrivers in New York City; how would I find a good one to interview? Stand on a street corner with a big sign reading, "AUTHOR SEEKS CABBY FOR BOOK ABOUT BOSTON POST ROAD. NO PAY, BUT WILL BUY LUNCH." When I heard about the Gabby Cabby, I knew I had found my man.

Peter Franklin says more people—300 million in the average month—have heard his voice than any other person in the world. So why have you never heard of him? If you lived in Botswana, Afghanistan, or Macao, you probably would have. Franklin is the Gabby Cabby. Fifteen years ago, a reporter for the BBC, Douglas Campbell, hopped into Franklin's cab and told him he wanted to go to Brooklyn. On the way, Franklin told him a few stories, like the one about the guy who shot his car on the Brooklyn Bridge. True story. His car had stalled on the span.

The guy got out, lifted the hood, and started pulling wires every which way. Nothing happened. The guy started cursing at his car. Drivers behind him blasted their horns. The guy pulled out a gun and started shooting his car. Kept firing away until he ran out of bullets. The car was now really dead. Murder on the Brooklyn Bridge.

The BBC reporter, Campbell, loved the story and the other ones Franklin told on the way to Brooklyn. They had plenty of time; traffic in New York City moves so slow, Franklin likes to say, that if you want to run someone over you have to get out of your car to do it. Campbell asked Franklin if he wanted to be on the radio. Ask a New York City cabdriver to do what he does best—talk—and get paid for it? Fuhgeddaboutit.

About 150 million people in fifty-one countries heard Franklin's chat with Campbell. The Gabby Cabby was born. Franklin calls himself "New York City's last English-speaking cabdriver." Which, of course, is not true, even if it seems sometimes that all New York cabbies are more fluent in about thirty languages other than English.

Franklin now does about forty live broadcasts—from his cab, from the cab company garage, even, on occasion, from his shower and bathtub—for radio stations from Dubuque to Delhi. He cracks some jokes; he tells some of his True Tales; he even offers insight into world affairs.

"I'm the only person who's heard on mainland China and Taiwan," he claims.

Franklin doesn't forget to tell his listeners that when they're in the Big Apple, they should take a personalized Gabby Cabby tour. "This is not some quickie tour of the city," he says. "We will go through all the ethnic areas—Chinatown, Little Italy, Black Harlem, Spanish Harlem. We will see the rich and filthy rich. We will even go to the South Bronx."

The Bronx: The tire and tire flat-fixing capital of the world.

Once, he took two South Africans on a tour. When they drove through Harlem, the Gabby Cabby stuck his head out the window and yelled, "Two white South Africans in the cab, two white South Africans in the cab!"

"I know everybody up there," he says, laughing. "I can do this."

So what's the Gabby Cabby got to do with U.S. 1? The first thing he said when we first talked was, "I hate Route 1 with a passion!" Actually, he didn't hate it so much as avoid it; traffic often moved slower than on the Major Deegan Expressway at rush hour, and that's pretty slow. Deep down, though, he loves the road. When he takes people on a Gabby Cabby tour through the Bronx, he tells them U.S. 1 is a "famous" road, like Route 66. "I'll give them a little schmaltz," he says. He'll say some of his best childhood memories lie along the Post Road. Franklin grew up in the Bronx. The first McDonald's he ever visited was on U.S. 1. His favorite ice cream shop was on Fordham Road—also U.S. 1.

Neighborhood mural, the Bronx.

Mural, the Bronx.

When he and his buddies would go to the movies on Saturday night in Stamford—"it was our equivalent of *Saturday Night Fever*," he says—they would take U.S. 1, not 95. He got his very first ticket as a cabdriver at the corner of Webster Avenue and Fordham Road—U.S. 1.

U.S. 1 may be a disaster—"if I'm going to Rye or Mamaroneck, no way in hell I'd go up Route 1"— but for the Gabby Cabby it's a disaster that comes with some nostalgia attached.

"I was in love with a girl named Marilyn Laron who lived in the Bronx," the City College graduate recalls. "One day she told me she was going to marry Allen Funt. Which she did!"

Franklin got over it. He met his future wife, Lalina, soon after moving from the Bronx to his first bachelor pad on West Forty-sixth Street in Manhattan. "She was hanging outside the building," he says. "Her dad was a big shot for the U.N. or something."

They have three children—Nicholas, who's at West Point; Catharine; and Alexi. Every Saturday, the family holds a Gabby Cabby staff meeting, where they go over Franklin's radio station shtick for the coming week. The cabdriver's Web site is gabbycabby.com.

The Geneva, Switzerland, fire department celebrated its 500th anniversary this year, and asked the Gabby Cabby to help them do it. He brought along some New York City firefighters.

Franklin has turned down Letterman and Leno, and there are no plans for Gabby Cabby T-shirts or coffee mugs. "My basic motto," he says, "is don't fall for your own bullshit."

If any group has an image problem, it's New York City cabdrivers. They are often portrayed as rude and crude—if not crooks. But how many cities now require their cabdrivers to go through charm school, as New York City does? The *Philadelphia Daily News* compared cabbies in the City of Brotherly Love and the Big Apple. The paper's conclusion: "Manhattan's cabs are cleaner, cheaper, and we get leftovers."

Franklin thinks a movie based on his adventures "would be one of the funniest movies of all time." His casting choice for the Gabby Cabby: John Travolta. No, make that Adam Sandler.

Franklin revels in his celebrity, even if it most of it can be found overseas. He drove a yellow cab on a nine-week tour of Ireland as part of a promotional tour sponsored by Goodfellas, a pizza company. "This country literally stopped to see me," he says. "There were lines at shopping centers."

How long will he keep driving? "Until I'm dead," he replies. "I'm going to be buried in my cab."

Best part about being a cabdriver? The freedom, he says. The money ain't bad either. "If you know what you're doing, on the average day you can make a couple hundred bucks, easy."

It's also kept him sane and reasonably well adjusted.

"If I wasn't as normal as I am," he says, smiling, "I think I would be an unbelievable snot."

———

U.S. 1, now Fordham Road, runs past Fordham University, makes a left onto Webster Avenue, a colorful, chaotic stretch of road jammed with ethnic restaurants, tire flat-fixing places, Saroop & Sons slaughterhouse, Botanica religious supply store, 99¢ World, Home Boy 2000, 3 Way Fried Chicken Restaurant, and other colorfully named businesses.

The highway joins I-95 for the short run to the great George Washington Bridge, which opened on October 24, 1931. The toll for "pleasure vehicles" was fifty cents; pedestrians were charged a nickel. Now pedestrians are free, but the passenger car toll has risen considerably.

Twenty-two miles from Port Chester, where U.S. 1 enters New York, the highway crosses into New Jersey.

NEW JERSEY

US 1 in this state, designed to speed the heavy traffic flow between New York and Philadelphia, avoids most urban congestion and cross traffic. It bypasses the center of every major city. Because the road runs for miles without a turn and carries more traffic than any other state highway, many New Jersey residents avoid it. Those who prefer scenery to speed, and historic landmarks to traffic circles, turn off at Elizabeth to State 27, an alternate route to Trenton; but the motorist who likes to test his skill on a modern highway, and is cautious enough to avoid trouble with the State Police, should follow US 1.

—*U.S. One, Maine to Florida*, American Guide Series, 1938

You have no idea how it pains me to make the following statement: If you ranked the fourteen states U.S. 1 passes through in terms of scenery and local flavor, New Jersey, my native state, would rank a very dead last. The WPA guide made note of the "long straight path of concrete" of U.S. 1 through the Garden State that confronted the driver in the 1930s. That still holds true today. "Hills," the guide added, "are rare." Even the "farms, woodlands, and nurseries" that existed in the 1930s from Linden south to Trenton are nearly all gone, replaced by shopping malls, hotels, and office parks.

"A region of smokestacks and marshes, of a few skyscrapers and many tenements, of patterns in steel rails and confusion in garbage dumps," is how the WPA guide described the highway's passage through North Jersey.

And yet the Pulaski Skyway, which carries U.S. 1 from Newark to Jersey City, is one of the most exciting and visceral 3.5 miles of road anywhere. U.S. 1 twists through Palisades Park and Ridgefield, and, in Jersey City, becomes Tonnelle Avenue, a concrete alley of car repair garages, hubcap dealers, abandoned warehouses, hot-sheet motels, and the likes of S & M Deli and King Louie's Sports Bar. The White Mana, a diner that resembles a bricked-over flying saucer, came from the 1939 New York World's Fair. Weekdays, Tonnelle Avenue is clogged with car and truck traffic; on muggy days, you almost need supplemental oxygen.

Twenty-five bucks a night? What a deal! Jersey City.

The Lincoln Tunnel Motel and the Skyway Motel offer day rates. Just down the road are the Captivating Lady Bridal Center and Istanbul Bar & Grill. The road tops a bumpy rise and suddenly you are on the Pulaski Skyway, soaring over an industrial wasteland worthy of Hieronymus Bosch: belching smokestacks, abandoned warehouses, container ship depots, truck terminals, power plants, junkyards, drawbridges, marshes, barrels, drums, and high-tension lines. It is quintessential New Jersey, and not New Jersey at all.

> "We bowled along the Holland Tunnel and came out, on the New Jersey side, on to the most magnificent and awe-inspiring road I have ever seen. For miles and miles it is lifted clean above the ground on a great ramp of concrete and iron, and there is room for at least six lanes of traffic!"
>
> Early impression of the Pulaski Skyway quoted in John Jakle, *The Tourist: Travel in Twentieth-Century North America*, University of Nebraska Press, 1985

When the Skyway opened in 1932, it was hailed as "the most beautiful bridge in the world" and "the outstanding highway engineering achievement in history."

Named after Revolutionary War hero Casimir Pulaski, the project was the occasion of a bloody labor battle. When Jersey City Mayor Frank "Boss" Hague awarded the contract to a non-union firm, political and labor war broke out. The ironworkers union called a strike. There were pitched battles between workers on the meadows below.

After a non-union worker was killed, Hague had twenty-one unionists indicted for murder. They were eventually cleared, but Hague declared war on what he called "racketeer" labor leaders, ordering a police crackdown that still evokes bitter memories in U.S. labor circles.

"We don't give our cops nightsticks for ornaments," Hague said.

> George Washington Bridge:
> "The sweetest, cleanest piece of engineering in the United States, supported, if at all, by sky hooks."
>
> Phil Strong, *Holiday* magazine, September 1952

Today, no one talks anymore about the Skyway's symbolic or practical significance. More than forty thousand cars—trucks, banned from the Skyway, must use Business U.S. 1 below—cross it every day, but it is largely a local road. The Skyway, which guides the traveler safely through an industrial hell unparalleled in the world, is no longer the world's highest elevated highway nor the longest continuous truss span. But it is as dramatic and beautiful as ever, its jet-black superstructure soaring high over polluted meadows, the Turnpike, and, it seems, all of the not-so-Garden State.

It is, and will forever be, my favorite New Jersey bridge, and road.

———

U.S. 1 in New Jersey, just like the highway overall, was not built at one time. In Linden, for example, the state took what was then, and still is, Edgar Road, and widened it by sixty feet, incorporating it as part of U.S. 1. Other local roads were similarly

Let's Go to Dutchland!

The Dutchland,
circa 1940, Elizabeth.

incorporated, and new sections of highway built, and in September 1930 U.S. 1—it then ran from Jersey City to Trenton—was opened in its entirety in New Jersey for the first time. It was immediately a traffic nightmare. A page-one story in the *(Elizabeth) Daily Journal* carried a warning from then-mayor Thomas Williams: "Thirteen deaths have occurred on the state highway since the first of the year. Most of these deaths are directly attributable to speeding by motorists. We cannot afford to have this stretch of highway as a free-for-all speedway."

In the 1930s, the segment of U.S. 1 through Newark and Elizabeth was called the busiest highway in the world; on one June day in 1937, more than one hundred thousand vehicles traveled it. Today, much of the 65-mile stretch of U.S. 1 in New Jersey is one of two things—bland or ugly—but the highway has a rich if not eccentric history in the Garden State.

The country's first cloverleaf was built at the intersection of Routes 1 and 9 and Route 35, in Woodbridge. *U.S. 1*, a Central New Jersey–based

community newspaper started by Richard Rein in 1984, is named after the road. U.S. 1 even had its own comic strip back in the 1980s. The main characters of Marvel Comics' *US 1* included Papa Wheelie, Wide Load Annie, Taryn (Taryn down the Highway) O'Connell, and Ulysses Solomon Archer, a tall, handsome trucker who could tune in CB transmissions through a metal plate in his head, the result of a near-tragic accident. *US 1*, the comic book, grew out of U.S. 1, Tyco's electric toy-truck line. Originally, the name for the truck line had been a tossup between U.S. 1 and Route 66. Despite its revered place in American highway legend, Route 66, the contender from the Midwest, lost out to U.S. 1, the East Coast upstart. "We figured that Route 66 wouldn't mean much to a five-, six-, seven-year-old," a Tyco executive said at the time. The comic book lasted twelve issues.

U.S. 1 through New Jersey may look dull, but there's a lot going on in those 65 miles. The main truck entrance to Tosco Bayway, the incredible profusion of pipe, stacks, and storage tanks that for

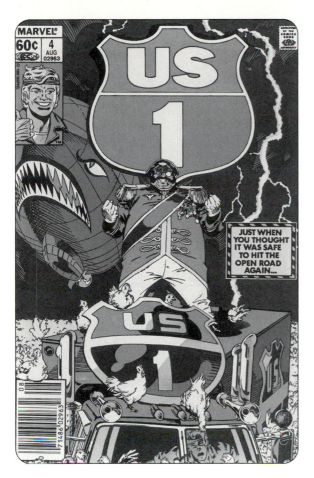

Marvel Comics' *US 1* comic book
appeared in the early 1980s.

including the U.S. Steel plant on U.S. 1. Nearby was a military airfield. Von Gart was out there one day looking through his binoculars when the police pulled up.

"What are you doing?" one cop asked. "I am looking for a brewery," von Gart replied. It would have been a good answer, except that von Gart delivered it in his customary thick German accent. He was arrested for espionage and spent three days in the city jail.

The company bought and leveled the U.S. Steel plant, opening its Newark brewery on July 3, 1951. There were several breweries in the area—Ballantine, Krueger's, the Elizabeth Rising Sun Brewery, Pabst, Hadlock's, and Liebmann, which brewed Rheingold. Over the years, one by one closed. Only the King of Beers remains.

Steve McCormick, the plant manager, is former assistant plant manager at Budweiser's St. Louis brewery. The St. Louis plant is twice as big as Newark, but Newark makes more regular Bud than any brewery in the world. The brewery produces 100 million cases of beer a year; 80 percent of that is Budweiser, the remainder Bud Light, Busch, Busch Light, Natural Light, Michelob, and Michelob Light.

The brewery, directly across U.S. 1 from Newark International Airport, cranks out 400,000 gallons of beer every year, which leave in some 250 trucks destined for wholesalers in six states. Production for Puerto Rico is being shifted to Newark; the finished product will be shipped in container ships from Port Newark.

The twelve-story-high main building is topped by a neon eagle fifty-two feet in diameter, made by Artkraft Strauss, responsible for many of the Times Square "spectaculars" in the 1920s and 1930s. From U.S. 1 north, the word "Budweiser" on the brick facade appears horizontally; from U.S. 1 south, it

many is the stereotypical New Jersey landmark, is on U.S. 1 (even though it is best viewed from the Turnpike). And more of the world's best-selling brand of beer is brewed on U.S. 1 in New Jersey than anywhere else in the world.

———

In the mid-1940s, as war raged overseas, August Busch sent a trusted aide, Paul von Gart, to check out potential brewery sites in the New York metropolitan area. The company Eberhard Anheuser started in 1860 (his daughter, Lily, would marry a young brewery supplier named Adolphus Busch) was prosperous. Von Gart checked out several locations,

A view of U.S. 1 from atop
the Budweiser brewery roof.

The open-air observation deck on the thirteenth floor offers a great, if vertiginous, view over U.S. 1. Behind the brewery is City Cemetery, a potter's field which was quietly and illegally turned into an industrial storage yard in the sixties and is now a city dump, according to the *(Newark) Star-Ledger*. Nearly twenty thousand people are buried beneath piles of dirt, construction debris, old tires, and household trash. When Elsie Lascurain discovered her father was buried there, the eighty-four-year-old Newark resident sued the city, demanding the return of her father's remains and a proper resting place for the thousands of others buried in the cemetery.

My knees wobbling from the dizzying view, I snap a few quick photos and follow Guindon back downstairs.

Beer making sounds like weird science: Lauter tubs and Schoene tanks, wort and chip beer, here at a boil, there at freezing temperatures.

The packaging lines are a wonder to watch, as cans and bottles are quickly shuttled from the side, like fast-merging highway traffic, into empty cardboard packs.

appears vertically. They were built that way to orient pilots flying in and out of Newark Airport.

Richard Guindon, the plant's environmental health and safety manager, takes me on a tour. Brewing beer is a complex process; the control room has more consoles, gauges, and buttons than a nuclear power plant. The process starts with barley malt, corn, and rice, shipped from Idaho and the Dakotas in train cars, and hops, trucked in from the Midwest and Washington State. The corn and rice are milled into an almost powdery substance.

We ride a freight elevator to the twelfth floor and climb one flight of stairs. "Are you afraid of heights?" asks Guindon, popping open the door leading to the roof.

The pyramid-shaped motel is New Jersey's contribution to hotel style. Rahway.

A 100-microcurie radiation source—"it's about the same you get from your television," according to Guindon—checks for missing or defective bottles. The "born-on" date is stamped on the cartons.

Twelve-packs are palletized and shrink-wrapped by a steel-tentacled machine appropriately called a Muller Octopus.

"We have some amazing technology in this plant, and all we do is make beer," Guindon says.

An army of buzzing forklifts delivers the beer to all those waiting trucks (some beer is shipped by train), and that's how Bud ends up on store shelves—and in your refrigerator.

More than 900 employees at the Newark brewery—150 brewers; 180 electricians, pipefitters,

The well-known Landmark Inn, Woodbridge, was reduced to rubble in 1998 to make way for construction.

machinists, and other skilled craftsmen; 150 administrative and clerical help; and 450 in packaging and shipping—make it all possible.

Back in his office overlooking U.S. 1, McCormick points out that Anheuser-Busch has invested nearly 700 million dollars into the facility in the past dozen years.

"We have a lot of confidence [in] being here in the future," he says.

———

U.S. 1, called the Straight Highway in the 1920s and 1930s, runs true to its name to Trenton. The stretch from Newark International Airport to New Brunswick is jammed with high- and low-end commerce, from massive malls (Woodbridge Center and Menlo Park Mall) to Dinettes Beautiful, Cadillac Plastic Outlet Store, and Transmission Land.

Tosco Bayway, which resembles some futuristic lost city with its tangle of towers, tanks, and stacks, is a breathtaking sight at night. Flames shoot from the tops of columns; bright lights illuminate the vast complex. The refinery opened in 1909, the chemical plant in 1919. One of the refinery's earliest efforts was kerosene for lamps. The chemical

New Jersey's strangest-looking diner. The Luna Bell, Woodbridge.

Princeton Cabins, 1920s, Clarksville.

plant's production of isopropyl alcohol in the 1920s marked the beginning of the U.S. petrochemical industry.

Today, Bayway makes more than three hundred different products, everything from motor fuel additives for Pennzoil and Castrol to polyisobutylene, the chewy part of chewing gum. Every day the refinery produces 200,000 barrels of "feedstock," crude oil chemically upgraded into gasoline, heating oil, and jet and diesel fuel. Jet-fuel pipelines run from Bayway to Newark International Airport and by a connecting line to John F. Kennedy International Airport.

The Bayway Circle, in Elizabeth, is one of New Jersey's vanishing circles; the state Department of Transportation plans to phase out all but a few circles (mostly in South Jersey) in the next ten or so years. A Chevy plant is on 1 in Linden; a Ford plant is on 1 in Edison. The Luna Bell, on 1 northbound in Woodbridge, is New Jersey's only medieval-style diner. Its roof rises and falls like a bell curve; a squat chimney curves gnomishly to the right like

something out of a fairy tale. The diner was once a Chock Full o' Nuts.

Just down the road, in Edison, is Frank's Italian Hotdogs, where Pat Martin has been dispensing good, plentiful food and homespun wisdom for twenty-five years. Her Italian hot dog—two hot dogs, peppers, onions, a big helping of potatoes, all shoveled into pizza bread—is not a normal dog, it's Cujo.

Martin got so tired of people asking for directions—on- and off-ramps for Route 440 and the Garden State Parkway are nearby—that she put this sign on the window: DIRECTIONS TO CUSTOMERS ONLY! PLEASE DO NOT ASK IF NOT A CUSTOMER.

The highway continues south, past the Ford plant and Big Joe's Fuel Stop in Edison, a WalMart and mini-mall built on the site of the former North Brunswick Drive-In, the old-time Valley Garage and Central Jersey Islamic Mosque in South Brunswick, past corporate parks and a million places with "Princeton" in their names (none accurate because neither Princeton Borough nor Princeton Township touches U.S. 1), before reaching the toll bridge—the only one on U.S. 1—to Morrisville, Pennsylvania. "Trenton Makes, the World Takes," reads the neon sign on the smaller "free bridge" to Morrisville.

The New Jersey capital was once home to the Lenox Pottery Works and Champale Malt Liquor. Its best-known business these days is a highly successful minor league baseball team—the Trenton Thunder.

PENNSYLVANIA

Between the western bank of the Delaware River and the Maryland Line, US 1 pursues a southwesterly course across the undulating terrain of Bucks County, through the city of Philadelphia, and over the section of highway known as the Baltimore Pike. . . . Many of the Quaker homesteads were utilized as stations of the "underground railroad," by which fugitive slaves were protected and aided in their flight northward. . . . South of Kennett Square US 1 dips down through excellent farming country.

—*U.S. One, Maine to Florida*, American Guide Series, 1938

In the 1930s, when the WPA guides appeared, U.S. 1 ran through the heart of Philadelphia, turning from Roosevelt Boulevard onto Broad Street and into downtown, circling City Hall, then turning west on Walnut Street to Baltimore Avenue (Baltimore Pike), proceeding through Morton, Swarthmore, and Media.

Today, the highway misses downtown entirely. It follows Roosevelt Boulevard along the city's backbone, past men selling soft pretzels on the grassy medians, Crown Cork and Seal Company, the former Whitman's Chocolates (closed in 1993) and current Nabisco factories, the Shriners Hospital, Pep Boy stores and car dealerships, crossing high over the Schuylkill River and becoming City Avenue.

Saint Joseph's University is on 1, and so is the Twelve Caesars banquet hall (HAPPY? ENGAGED? CALL 879-4000). A sign you'll only see in Philly: HISTORIC TREE. Diners, bowling alleys, Chinese restaurants, and hardware stores line the blue-collar highway—now State Road—for the beginning of its winding, leisurely run toward the Maryland state line.

Anyone who gets mail has gotten mail from The Franklin Mint, the people who bring you all those Precision Model die-cast cars and trucks, Limited Edition Heirloom Dolls, Official Colt .45 Peacemaker Collector Knives, and "the only exact reproduction" of Jackie O's famous faux pearls. One newspaper's description of the items available

Roosevelt Boulevard, Philadelphia.

through the Mint (where operators truly are standing by twenty-four hours a day): "Things that have no function, no purpose, other than to just be." Yeah, but you've got to have them anyway.

> "Without question, Route 1 is one great democratic movie you won't see on a major interstate. . . . Geographically speaking, with the exception of a desert or volcano, Route 1 has nearly everything. . . . Route 1 is an argument for a real there, a hearty ribbon of life, a bounty of people living in beauty and junk, all covered by a slow, old shadow. It is no escape route. It is a low-amp rural road that happens to go through the urban clangor of New York, Philadelphia, Baltimore, Newark, and Washington, D.C."

David Holstrom, *Christian Science Monitor*, November 1991

The Franklin Mint is the leading player in the ten-billion-dollar "instant collectibles" industry. The company was started by Joseph Segel, who as a kid growing up in West Philadelphia made business cards on his small printing press. In 1964,

two events caught his attention: news of Douglas MacArthur's death and a *Time* magazine photo of people lining up to buy silver dollars at the U.S. Mint.

Segel started the National Commemorative Society; its first issuance was a six-dollar MacArthur medal. Segel then created his own mint, General Numismatics, to make high-quality medals. GN was transformed into the Franklin Mint. In 1986, Segel struck gold again, beginning a home-shopping channel that would soon supplant the Home Shopping Network as king of the televised direct-marketing hill: QVC. The channel—QVC stands for Quality, Value, and Convenience—logged 100 million phone calls in 1998 (a rate of two per second).

Why was the Franklin Mint thus named? Ben Franklin, according to the Direct Marketing Association, issued the nation's first catalog and its first mail-order guarantee. In 1744, he printed a catalog listing 644 used books he wanted to sell. According to Michael Rozansky, writing in the *Philadelphia Inquirer Magazine*, Franklin announced he would sell the books on April 11 at the post office, which he ran from his house on Market Street. His guarantee: "Those persons that live remote, by sending their orders and money to said B. Franklin, may depend on the same justice as if present."

Franklin Mint corporate headquarters, and the Franklin Mint Museum, are on 1. Several miles south, the highway makes a sharp curve known as Dead Man's Hill. Babe Ruth once flipped over his Packard here, injuring himself, his wife, and three New York Yankees teammates. In recent years, at least fifteen people have died in the twisting stretch of U.S. 1 in Chester Heights. Five high school

Philadelphia.

girls were killed in January 1999 when their car slammed into a tree. Roadside memorials and wooden crosses are a common sight along Dead Man's Hill.

———

7-Eleven may rule the convenience store universe, but Wawa, headquartered on U.S. 1, qualifies as a major planet, with more than five hundred stores in Pennsylvania, Delaware, Maryland, New Jersey, Connecticut, and, more recently, Virginia, as the convenience-store chain starts its inexorable march south.

Wawa's early history reads like Stew Leonard's. But where the latter parlayed its dairy business beginning into "the world's largest dairy store," the

A roadside memorial,
Roosevelt Boulevard, Philadelphia.

other metamorphosed into one of the country's largest convenience-store chains—stocked with its own milk.

In 1902, George Wood, owner of a textile mill in Millville, New Jersey, opened a small milk plant in Wawa that specialized in the processing and delivery of "doctor-certified" milk. "Health inspectors would come out and check the cows—this is before pasteurization," says Richard D. Wood Jr., George Wood's great-grandson and Wawa's president and CEO.

"This is a snappy product for the time," adds company historian Mariah Thompson. "Not everyone is getting home-delivered milk in 1906."

"Take no chances with dirty milk!" went one ad campaign.

Wawa is a Lenni Lenape word for "goose in flight." "And in flocks / The wild goose Wawa" is a line from Longfellow's "Song of Hiawatha."

In 1929, the company built a modern dairy processing plant on Baltimore Pike (U.S. 1) in Wawa. In 1964, Grahame Wood, George's grandson, opened the first Wawa food market in Folsom, Pennsylvania, which still stands.

"By the late fifties, the handwriting was on the wall," Thompson explains. "Supermarkets were making great inroads on the home delivery milk business. And the textile business had gone south between the wars."

By 1972, Wawa had 100 stores. Today, Wawa is a billion-dollar company, selling six million cups of coffee and two million hoagies and sandwiches each month at its convenience stores.

Wawa corporate headquarters, on 1, is named Red Roof, after George Wood's original house, which was torn down around 1910 to build the present imposing stone structure, with its warm,

Philadelphia.

inviting lobby, decorated with archival photos of the company's manufacturing and dairy origins. The company has closed older, unprofitable stores, and is shifting toward 5,000-square-foot-plus "superstores," many with rows of gas pumps outside. Unlike other convenience-store chains, all Wawa stores are company-owned.

In 1996, the company sued a convenience store named HAHA south of Allentown, Pennsylvania, claiming the name was too similar. Some derided Big Brother for going after the little mom-and-pop. HAHA was owned by George Haaf, who said the name was not a takeoff on Wawa but a contraction of his last name and his wife's last name. HAHA did not get the last laugh; a judge ruled HAHA had to change its name.

One lobby display mentions a store Richard D. Wood and partner William Abbott opened on Market Street in Philadelphia. Delinquent accounts were always an unpleasant task; at one point Wood and Abbott hired a young lawyer from Springfield, Illinois, by the name of Abraham Lincoln.

———

U.S. 1, the fast food, car wash, strip mall, liquor store, go-go bar, hubcap dealer, multiplex theater, and roadside motel capital of the nation, adds one more title in Kennett Square: Mushroom Capital of the World.

South of Wawa, the highway runs through Chadds Ford—Andrew Wyeth country. The American Christmas Museum is on 1, but our next step is another museum, devoted to the mycological wonders of the "perfect food."

Pennsylvania's number-one business is agriculture, and its number-one cash crop is mushrooms. Within a 25-mile radius of Kennett Square are eighty growers, who produce nearly 50 percent of the state's annual output of 350 million pounds.

Corporate secrets literally take root in the rolling countryside; security checkpoints discourage uninvited visitors to local mushroom farms. But there are no secrets at the Mushroom Museum, which will tell you everything you wanted to know about the portabello, pom-pom, puffball, bluefoot, red lobster, and white hen-of-the-woods.

The building doubles as a country store, where you can buy fresh mushrooms, marinated mushrooms, and miscellaneous food and craft items. Pay $1.25 admission to enter the museum itself, an informative journey through the underground world of the mushroom.

According to a display, it's the "perfect food," number one in vitamin B complex and phosphorus and number two in protein and total minerals among all vegetables. You can sit on mushroom-shaped cushions and read about the fungus that the pharaohs believed was created by lightning bolts from heaven because it would grow, almost like magic, overnight.

Kennett Square's origins as a mushroom hotbed can be traced to J. B. Swayne, son of a carnation grower, who experimented by growing mushrooms under his father's greenhouse benches. In the 1930s, William W. Phillips was one of the first to pioneer year-round production. Today, Phillips Mushrooms Farms is the largest grower of specialty mushrooms—portabello, shiitake, maitake, enoke, oyster, crimini—in the country, and it runs the Mushroom Museum.

America is crazy about mushrooms. Consumption increased from 100 million pounds in 1960 to 200 million pounds in 1970 to 400 million pounds in 1980. It is now more than 600 million pounds. Eighty percent of chefs surveyed by the National Restaurant Association in 1997 picked mushrooms first among the top twenty "chic" foods.

Mushroom growing begins with compost, which may include corncobs, hay, straw, and stable manure (what, there's unstable manure?). Water, gypsum, and nitrates are added to start fermentation and fiber breakdown. Thirty percent of the total mushroom crop is sold fresh; the rest is processed.

The social event of the year in mushroom country is the Mushroom Festival every September. The festival includes a parade, mushroom farm tours, and the National Mushroom Judging Contest.

The store is stocked with mushrooms in every shape, size, and configuration—mushroom powder, mushroom chowder, mushrooms au jus, Mad-about-Mushroom Soup, and Wild Willy's Mushroom Madness gourmet spread. "I must be a mushroom," says one sign. "Everybody keeps me in the dark and feeds me bullshit." You can also buy a T-shirt that says "Shiitake happens." For a direct mail catalog, call 1-800-AH-FUNGI.

Store manager Marlene Giancola's favorite mushrooms? The crimini, which she sautés, and the portabello, which she stuffs.

There are even children's books, all of which have something to do with mushrooms. Naturally, the selection includes *Alice's Adventures in Wonderland*. You remember the line: "One side will make you grow taller and the other side will make you grow shorter."

U.S. 1 runs another 20 miles in Pennsylvania, a lonely, quiet stretch dotted with farms and silos. Several trailer parks come into view, and a sign by the side of the road announces: THIS IS THE MASON-DIXON LINE.

This is where Maryland, and the American South, begin.

MARYLAND

US 1 is one of two main routes between Philadelphia and Baltimore. The other, US 13–40, is less scenic and has heavier truck traffic though somewhat greater historic interest. US 1 traverses rolling country, skirting streams in deep valleys, wending along high tablelands, and overlooking fertile and well-cultivated fields. Dairying is a means of livelihood. . . . At 9.4 miles is the village of Conowingo (Indian, at the falls), principally made up of filling stations and roadside restaurants.

—*U.S. One, Maine to Florida*, American Guide Series, 1938

Signs for Spready Oak Road and Love Run Road, Liquorland ("Cut Rate Whiskey") and Hillybilly Sports are sprinkled along the road. The McDonalds—don't know if they're old—have a farm on U.S. 1 here. The road squeezes between concrete dividers on a bridge over the wide Susquehanna River. The road surface is so low it almost seems we are riding the waves. We're not on a bridge but a dam—the Conowingo Dam, completed by the Philadelphia Electric Company (PECO) in 1928.

The Susquehanna River, at 420 miles, is one of the longest rivers on the East Coast, but its shoals and rapids have long made it impossible for bigger boats to navigate. The Maryland Canal, completed in 1810, was one of the earliest in the country. But the coming of the railroad would spell its decline and eventual death.

Dam tours, as one might imagine, are not a real frequent occurrence on the East Coast, so I jumped at the chance to tour the Conowingo. Don Laskey turned out to be an informative, and funny, guide.

"A dam is a pile of rocks," he says. "Build that pile high enough and wide enough and you have a dam."

Technically, Chesapeake Bay starts right here, at the dam's base. The Susquehanna begins in Cooperstown, New York. The Indians called this spot Conowingo—"at the falls."

The first power plant on this site, in 1894, was a Susquehanna Water and Electric station built to run a paper mill on the other side of the river.

"It was a financial disaster," Laskey explains. "It cost 52 million dollars in 1928 dollars. In today's dollars that would be 20 billion."

PECO began construction on the dam on March 7, 1926. There were two separate work camps of 2,000 men each, with their own police and fire departments. The bridge carrying the Baltimore Turnpike over the river was blown up. Huge coffer dams were built to divert the river. Millions of cubic yards of earth and rock were excavated. Nearly 700,000 cubic yards of concrete were used. The 4,632-foot-long dam, 105 feet tall at the roadbed, had seven twenty-seven-ton turbines and fifty-two spill gates. The plant went on line March 1, 1928.

"When it was built," Laskey says, "it was the biggest power plant in the world."

A 1962 expansion project more than doubled generating capacity, from 253,000 kilowatts to 512,000 kilowatts.

Outside, he points out the massive transformers— "220,000 volts on those wires"—that have to be

Warning sign in front of Conowingo Dam.

regularly blasted with firehoses to remove "bird poop."

Back inside, we walk past various warning signs ("Caution, unguarded rotating shafts") and stand on a catwalk above a huge rotating shaft—a turbine—

Conowingo Dam, Conowingo.

Baltimore.

that looks like something out of *Journey to the Center of the Earth*.

"This thing's been running for seventy years," Laskey shouts above the deafening roar. "We've had one failure in all those years."

In 1994, PECO pulled off what the tour guide calls "the biggest fish lift in North America." The company caught 100,000-plus American shad trying to get upstream to spawn and shipped them by truck to Harrisburg, Pennsylvania, where they were released.

"It cost us about five hundred dollars a fish to move them upstream," Laskey says, smiling. "No one's taken that much interest in *my* sex life."

———

RV camps and signs for "Pit Beef" start appearing on the road to Perry Hall. Bel Air, the Harford County seat, should be called Car City USA, with as many dealerships per square mile as any community along U.S. 1. If haggling with your salesperson wears you out, you can always stop at the Serenity Club, on the highway's southbound side.

Perry Hall is the beginning of an 80-mile-long commercial strip that ends or, more accurately, takes a brief rest stop in Dumfries, Virginia, south of Washington, D.C. Fast-food chains, multiplex theaters, electronics stores, and enough strip malls to reach to the outer edges of the galaxy and back line the road to the nation's capital.

Baltimore.

Great Big Dog Wash is on the highway in Perry Hall. U.S. 1 is now Belair Road. Signs announce Poor Little Rich Girl bridal shop, the Baltimore Dog Bakery, and Country Car Radio ("Crank It or Yank It"). Just before the red-trimmed Overlea Diner is a sign marking the Baltimore city limits.

> "Route 1 is in heavy use again not because anyone travels it as a major north-south highway ('I would estimate the number of people who do that at zero,' said [state Department of Transportation traffic forecaster Robert] Lambdin) but because development all along the highway has spurred great amounts of local traffic."

Baltimore Sun, November 9, 1986

———

Baltimore probably gets the worst rap, tourist-wise, of any major American city. The Inner Harbor is great, but the "other" Baltimore is worthy of exploration, and U.S. 1 is the road best taken. The attractions on the road are of a different kind: row houses, neighborhood murals, schools (including one named after Duke Ellington), barbershops, sidewalk preachers on Sunday, and colorfully named businesses (Soul City Carry-Out, Candy in the Hood, Pat's Million-Dollar Co-Op Laundry). "If animal trapped inside, call ———," advise signs on boarded-up buildings.

Jim and Eda Bass claim the "best crab cakes in town" at their log cabin–like restaurant on Wilkens Avenue, one of a half dozen streets (Belair Road, North Avenue, Monroe Street, Fulton Street, Wilkens Avenue, and Southwestern Boulevard) that U.S. 1 appropriates as it zig-zags through the city. If you intend to follow the highway through Baltimore, buy a detailed map; U.S. 1 in Baltimore, as in Providence and Washington, D.C., is poorly marked.

At 1601 North Avenue is one of the more remarkable stories, and attractions, along U.S. 1. It is the story of a dedicated man and woman who wanted to educate a younger generation that seemed out of touch with its culture and history. The story begins with a dead body sticking out of the hatchback of a car.

———

To the cops who pulled over Elmer and Joanne Martin that one night on the Beltway, it looked like a dead body, anyway.

Actually, it was Frederick Douglass, the abolitionist. Or a wax figure facsimile thereof. In 1983, the Martins—he a professor of social work at Morgan State, she the director of the tutorial program at Coppin State—opened a storefront wax museum

Joanne Martin, co-director,
Great Blacks in Wax Museum, Baltimore.

on Saratoga Street. They had four wax figures, made by a sculptor.

"We started the Baltimore layaway plan," Joanne recalls, laughing. "He'd take ten dollars, one hundred dollars, one thousand dollars, whatever we could afford at the time."

She and Elmer had met in graduate school in Atlanta. Elmer gave her a book by James Baldwin "to see if I would get through it," she says.

Their initial wax figures were Harriet Tubman, Mary McLeod Bethune, Nat Turner, and Douglass. The Martins would take them on the road for public presentations, which explains why they were stopped by the cops that night on the Beltway.

A student at Morgan State showed Elmer how to make figures out of chicken wire and papier-mâché, which saved them money—at the cost of realism.

"The [more frail] chicken wire figures would move when people walked past," Joanne says. "We told people we were experimenting with animation."

State Senator Clarence Blount sponsored a bill awarding the museum a $100,000 matching grant, "which to us was like a million dollars," but it was a struggle nonetheless. Joanne pawned her wedding ring to pay the rent. Salvation came in the form of $300,000 in grants and loans from the city, and the promise of space in a city-owned vacant fire station on North Avenue.

In 1983, with thirty-eight figures on display, the museum drew 10,000 visitors. In 1988, it drew 40,000. This year, the Great Blacks in Wax Museum will draw close to 200,000 people.

"It's interesting," says museum executive director John Jones. "Some people come in here and spend hours, others go through like Luke Skywalker."

This is no carnival sideshow. Joanne and Elmer's 120 figures are amazingly lifelike and dressed in

Shirley Chisholm figure,
Great Blacks in Wax Museum, Baltimore.

period costumes. There's aviator Bessie Coleman, sitting in a mock airplane above the lobby. Queen Hatshepsut of Egypt, the first woman in recorded history to preside over a nation. Crispus Attucks, the first American to die in the Revolutionary War. Henry "Box" Brown, a slave who had himself shipped to Philadelphia in a box. A white-gloved Billie Holiday, in a splendid black dress with a white flowery bow. Bill Pickett, who invented the rodeo sport of bull-dogging. Malcolm X and Elijah Mohammed, Nelson Mandela and Steve Biko, James Baldwin and Richard Wright, Joe Louis and Jackie Robinson.

More contemporary figures include Reginald Lewis, who founded TLC Beatrice International Holdings, the largest black-owned business in the world, and Mary Carter Smith, an elementary school-teacher who in 1983 became Maryland's official *griot*, or storyteller.

The museum's aim is not only to show black heroes, but to tell the "hidden history" of black Americans.

"There were people of African American descent on the Lewis and Clark expedition; there were blacks on Columbus's ship, as navigators," Jones explains.

> "Today we revere the restored colonial heritage of Williamsburg. It is easily conceivable that, two hundred years from now, the culture represented by Route 1 will be equally revered."
>
> Peter H. Smith, director of a "commercial archaeology" tour of U.S. 1 from Washington, D.C., to Baltimore

The museum also shows the horrors of the black experience. Down in the hold of a replica slave ship, one can hear taped screams and moans, the clanking of irons and the almost nauseating sloshing of water. In the corner is the wax figure of a naked black woman, her breasts horribly streaked with whip marks.

On display is an excerpt from the 1738 journal of a slave ship officer:

> We whipped them . . . until chunks of flesh tore apart and fell off. Once they were bleeding from the lashes, we rubbed the wounds with cannon powder, lemon juice, and brine of pepper. After four days of such punishment the last of them died. The heads were cut off to show to their comrades who believed that a severed head could never return to Africa. We made all the other slaves kiss these heads.

And yet the museum's real horror is downstairs, past a sign strongly advising that parents not let children under twelve view the exhibit within. "The Struggle against Lynching: Lessons for Today" chronicles the history of lynching, in all its gruesomeness. Archival photos of hanged men and charred, smoking bodies line the walls.

A diorama re-creates an atrocity that draws shocked gasps from visitors. A woman hangs from a tree, her legs chopped off, a gaping hole in her stomach. Her name was Mary Haynes. Her husband was hanged after the farmer who owed him wages was found dead. A group of men then chopped off Mary Haynes's legs, cut open her womb, pulled out her unborn baby, and stomped on it. Then they sewed two cats inside her belly and took bets to see which one clawed its way outside first.

"This is unreal," whispers one museum visitor, here with his nine-year-old son.

Lynchings, according to the display, often were festive occasions. Potato salad and lemonade would be served.

Upstairs, Joanne Martin sits on a chair in the former fire station auditorium and talks about her museum's present and future. She now works here full-time. Friends "scour the city" for clothing that might fit a particular figure. The city has pledged 3 million dollars to renovate buildings on either side of the museum, which itself is undergoing an expansion.

Three-fourths of the museum's Maryland visitors come from outside Baltimore, and 53 percent of all visitors come from outside Maryland.

"We've gotten a lot of press, but we're still one of the city's best-kept secrets," she says.

Nation of Islam leader Louis Farrakhan visited one day with an entourage. He was not happy when he saw the wax figure of Elijah Mohammed, who was wearing a necktie. He never wore a necktie, Farrakhan said, because of the strangling danger it posed.

You don't have to stay at a fancy hotel. Fulton's Cabins, Pembroke, Maine.

Red's Eats in Wiscasset, Maine, is known for its lobster rolls.

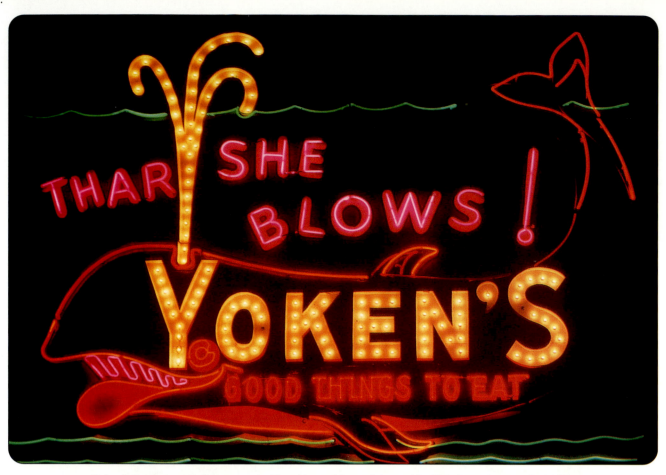

Yoken's Restaurant in Portsmouth, New Hampshire, celebrated its fiftieth anniversary in 1997.

Portsmouth,
New Hampshire.

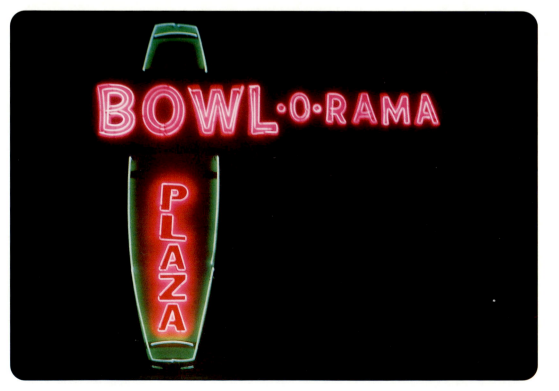

Two classic rides light up the night at the Topsfield Fair, Massachusetts.

Enjoying the rides at the Topsfield Fair.

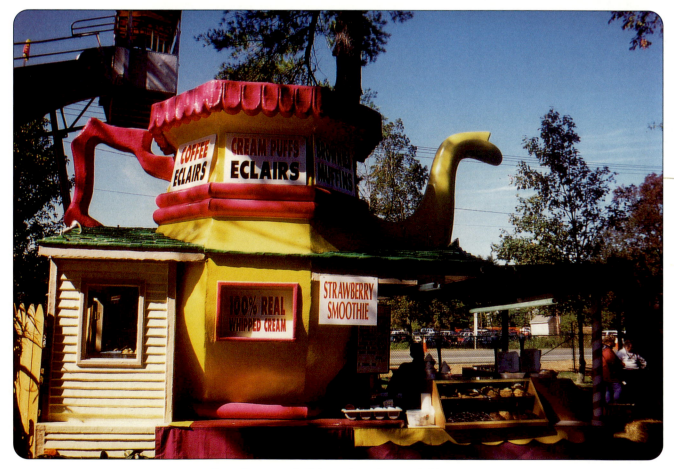

One of many colorful stands at the Topsfield Fair.

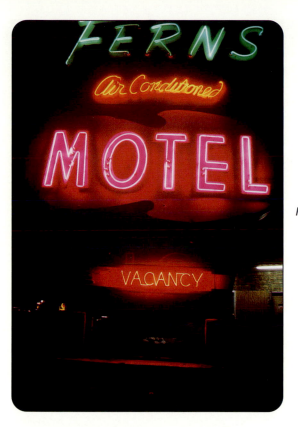

Psycho material, but a great sign. Saugus, Massachusetts.

Border Cafe, a Mexican restaurant, Saugus, Massachusetts.

Maybe the most wondrous of all U.S. 1's sights: The Hilltop Steak House, Saugus, Massachusetts.

The Farm Fresh Five
perform regularly
at Stew Leonard's,
Norwalk,
Connecticut.

Old Lyme, Connecticut.

The Bronx Zoo's Butterfly Zone is a place of multicolored beauty.

Webster Avenue,
the Bronx.

For many, the Tosco Bayway plant is typical New Jersey.

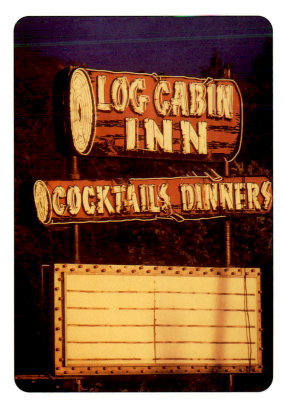

No longer there: The Log Cabin Inn and its eye-catching sign were just north of the Granite Run Mall, Media, Pennsylvania.

Mural,
Baltimore,
Maryland.

Mural,
Baltimore,
Maryland.

The Little Hotel, Henderson, North Carolina.

The splendid Raleigh Road Drive-In screen, Henderson, North Carolina.

Camp Mackall, North Carolina.

Pit crew member, North Carolina Motor Speedway, Rockingham.

Wallace, South Carolina.

Railroad crossing, Patrick, South Carolina.

A place of quiet beauty. Carolina Sandhills National Wildlife Refuge, McBee, South Carolina.

Columbia, South Carolina.

Clearwater,
South Carolina.

Okefenokee Swamp, Georgia.

"Service with a Hop!" advertised the legendary Green Frog on U.S. 1 in Waycross, Georgia.
The restaurant's specialties included chicken dinners, seafood, steaks, and, of course, frog's legs.
(Courtesy of Larry Cultrera)

Okefenokee National Wildlife Refuge.

Is there any spookier spot than Okefenokee Swamp?

Wall, Last Resort Bar. Port Orange, Florida.

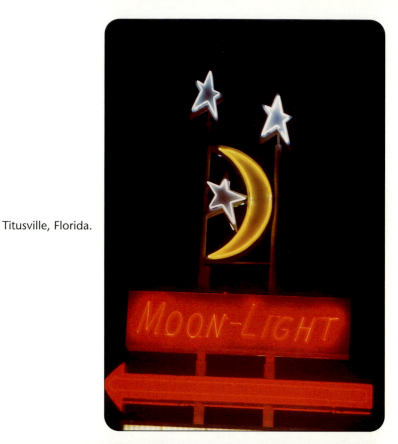

Titusville, Florida.

Cocoa, Florida.

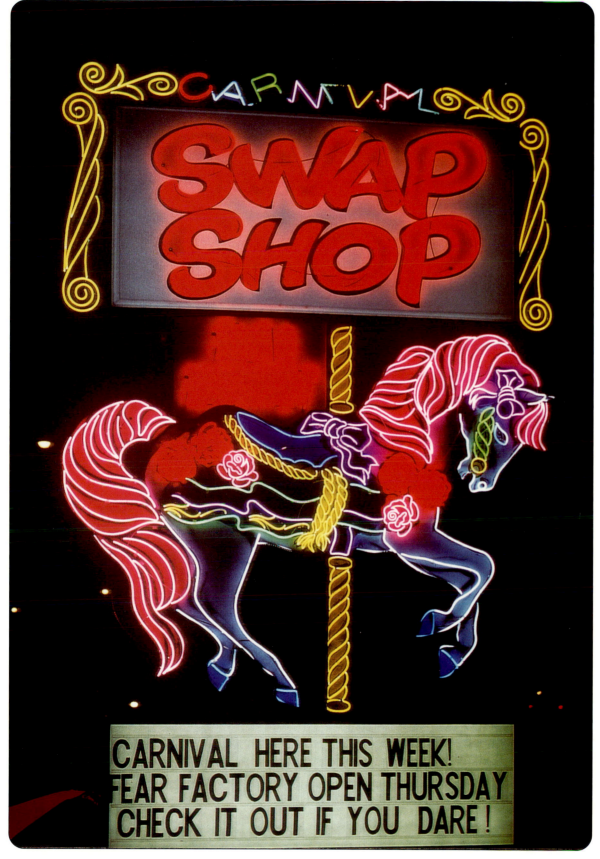

Rockledge, Florida.

Fort
Pierce,
Florida.

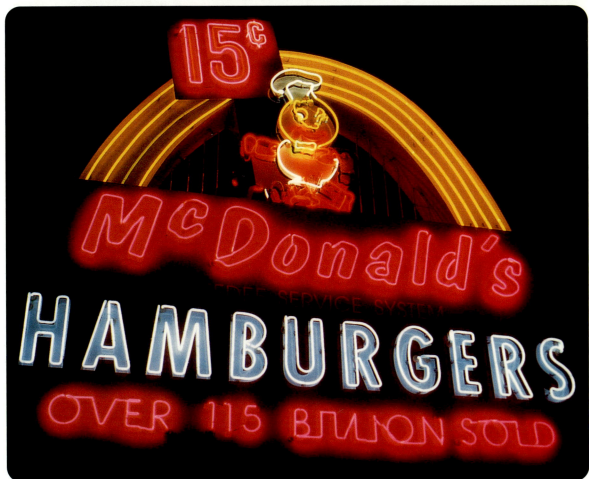

Maybe the greatest McDonald's sign of all. Stuart, Florida.

West Palm Beach, Florida.

Hypoluxo, Florida.

Boynton Beach, Florida.

Pompano Beach, Florida.

Fort Lauderdale, Florida.

Hollywood, Florida.

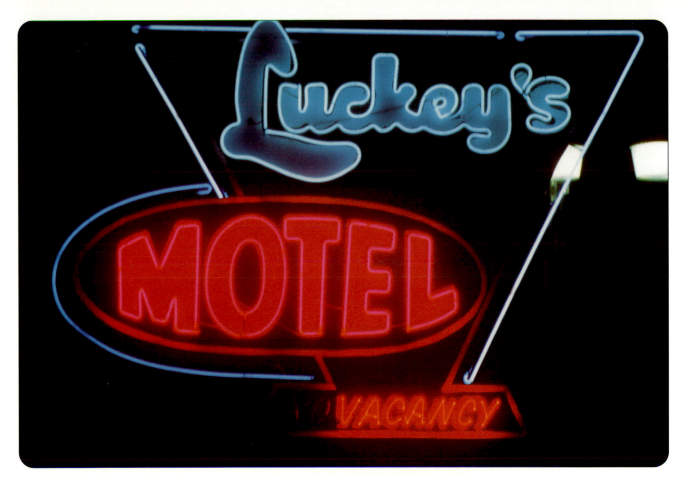

Dania, Florida.

Dania, Florida.

Brickell Avenue, Miami, Florida.

Jumping for joy at the Dolphin Research Center, Grassy Key, Florida.

Marathon,
Florida.

The most soothing stretch of highway anywhere. Overseas Highway, the Florida Keys.

Key West, Florida.

Key West, Florida.

"They not only chastised us about it, they went out and bought a bow tie and watched us put it on," Joanne says, smiling slightly.

The city asked the Martins to consider moving near the Inner Harbor, but they said no. A 22-million-dollar, mostly state-funded African American history museum is scheduled to open in the Inner Harbor in 2001.

"We don't think we'd survive in the Inner Harbor," Joanne says. "We'd have to change, not them. Would [tourists] want to come into a slave ship? We'd have to turn it into the Good Ship Lollipop."

The museum has come a long way from the humble storefront on Saratoga Street in 1983. Asked if she would have done anything differently, Joanne replies, "I wouldn't change a thing, even the struggle."

On a wall downstairs are the words from Sterling A. Brown's haunting poem "Old Lem."

> They got the lawyers
> They got the jury rolls
> They got the law
> They don't come by ones
> They got the sheriffs
> They got the deputies
> They don't come by twos
> They got the shotguns
> They got the rope
> We git the justice
> in the end
> And they come by tens
> They burn us when we dogs
> They burn us when we men
> They come by tens . . .

————

U.S. 1 continues its dash through the hurly-burly of the Baltimore-Washington corridor. In its heyday, U.S. 1 was known as "Bloody Mary" for the large number of accidents, and "Billboard Lane" for the glut of signs. In 1932, a Mrs. Edward McKeon from

Arbutus.

Baltimore, prominent in civic work, drove the 83.2 miles from Bel Air to Washington and counted 1,099 billboards. By the early fifties, the number had topped 5,000. Roadside businesses jammed every available square foot. One account described the highway as the "midway of America, a sort of flying carnival." After the repeal of Prohibition, speakeasies on U.S. 1 pulled up their blinds and called themselves restaurants and bars. One was built like a Mississippi side-wheeler, another like a Western dude ranch. "The atmosphere," one motorist observed, "is more alcoholic than bucolic."

Accidents were so frequent that the *Baltimore Sun* described U.S. 1 as "an abattoir for automobiles and humans." When I-95 was built, traffic on Route 1 was reduced as much as 50 percent.

> "Towns like Elk Ridge, Md., dot the landscape along U.S. 1, once a main highway on the East Coast."
>
> *Houston Chronicle*, January 1992

Some have argued that the beginning of the interstate spelled U.S. 1's death. It's hard to see how. The road is busier than ever; its easy access to I-95 and the beltways (I-495 and I-695) make it more commercially attractive than ever. You can't build on the interstate; you can on Route 1.

Eugene L. Meyer, in *Maryland Lost and Found* (Johns Hopkins University Press, 1986), colorfully evokes the roadside motels and tourist courts that sprang up along the highway in the 1930s and

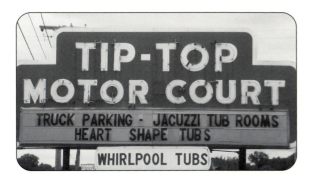

Elk Ridge.

1940s—the Del Haven White House Cottages in Berwyn; the Cedar Motel in Laurel, whose six-dollar room rate in the late seventies made it the cheapest hotel between Baltimore and the nation's capital; and the Valencia Motel, which was literally cut in half by a road bypass project, forcing maids to dash across the highway so they could clean all the rooms.

The Tip-Top Motor Court, mentioned in Meyer's book, is still on U.S. 1 in Elk Ridge. Just south, on one of the highway's few open stretches in the Baltimore-Washington corridor, is one of those refreshingly out-of-date businesses, like lemonade stands and single-screen movie theaters, that somehow manage to survive in an age of chains and superstores and glitz. Welcome to U.S. 1, the hubcap capital of the world.

———

At the corner of U.S. 1 and Kit Kat Road in Jessup, across the highway from Sunny's Warehouse Clearance Center, Flea Market World, and Duke's Famous Delly, is a roadside shack where hubcaps are lashed to the fence and a sign offers this bit of advice: "Don't go around with your nuts showing."

Words to live by if you're a hubcap dealer.

Sorry, *wheel covering* dealer.

"There are very few hubcaps made anymore," says Dan Selke, co-owner of Hubcap City. "The hubcap was something you snapped over the lugs. Now you got wheels, locking wire covers, center caps. A few trucks out there still have hubcaps."

A lot of older cars out there still have hubcaps, which is why Hubcap City and Hubcap World and Hubcap Man and all the other hubcap dealers around the country manage to survive, if not thrive.

"Guy in a Rolls-Royce came in earlier today," says Selke, a friendly, bearded man in a grease-stained white T-shirt. "He needed wheels for his Corniche." The hubcap man smiled. "Life's a bitch."

Life's good for this hubcap man, who opened for business fifteen years ago. There are three Hubcap City locations—on the "boulevard"—U.S. 1—in Jessup and Overlea, and on Crain Highway in Glen Burnie.

"We started out with fifty-eight hubcaps his grandfather," Selke says, motioning to partner Sam Coates, "gave to my wife. We would go to different junkyards, give them a price for what they had. Our first sale here was to a guy from New Jersey. It was out of pity. The guy saw Sam, me, the wife, three kids." He smiled. "We had a lot of pity sales that winter."

The hubcap man now has more than thirty thousand hubcaps or wheel coverings, and the roadside shack with the sloping floor is being modernized.

In the thirties, the shack was a gas station known as Dorsey's Garage. Coates's grandfather then started selling tires here.

"You dig six feet under that road right there," says Coates, waving his hand at U.S. 1, "and you'll find pine trees they brought from western Maryland, and oyster shells and clamshells from the Eastern Shore they used to build the road."

"You got a lot of homespun businesses along Route 1," Selke adds. "There are a lot of nooks and crannies on Route 1."

Hubcap City, Jessup.

Hubcap
City,
Jessup.

One of those nooks and crannies is Daniel's, a restaurant-bar on 1 in Elk Ridge, a few miles north, which is one of two open-air bars right on U.S. 1 (the other is the Green Parrot in Key West). Bikers love Daniel's; there's motorcycle-only parking out front.

"You want good food, good value, go in there, ask for Ma, the owner," Coates says. "She's got a twenty-two-ounce steak for something like $12.95. It's a real nice cut. When you're done, she'll ask you, 'You still hungry?'"

The hubcap man is now "dressing up" the shack, putting in a new—straight—floor, cabinets, and displays for his hubcaps.

"The customers now are looking for something different than they were ten years ago," he says. "I'm

Laurel.

Carole Mitchell and Alice Miles,
The Little Tavern, Laurel.

Still life, The Little Tavern, Laurel.

tired of people mistaking me for the junkyard down the street. I take that as an insult."

———

Laurel, 8 miles south, is the epicenter of the Baltimore-Washington metro corridor. U.S. 1, a divided highway through Laurel, is chock-a-block with chain and franchise operations. In 1972, George Wallace was shot in front of the Laurel Shopping Center on U.S. 1. A little A-frame building across the street from the Tastee Diner, though, gets our attention. Inside, truck driver Bud Brown and local James "Shorty" Love are talking about their favorite truckstops. Waitress Alice Miles and manager Carole Mitchell are behind the counter. A customer sitting at a table in the corner has just polished off nine

Laurel.

hamburgers. Don't worry, they're small burgers—Little Tavern burgers.

"Believe it or not, a Little Tavern burger tastes best at 2:30 in the morning," Miles says. "A lot of the guys used to call them death balls; I don't know why."

The burgers are good, and bet you can't eat just one, although you'd have to be real hungry to go for nine.

The Little Tavern in Laurel, which looks like a miniature roadside Swiss chalet, was opened by Marshall Devore in 1938, according to Miles. It was part of a fifty-eight-restaurant chain, started by a Mr. Duncan in 1927. They were called Little Taverns, but they were never bars. Today, there are four

Beltsville.

Little Taverns between Baltimore and Washington, D.C. A former Little Tavern on U.S. 1 in College Park, across from the University of Maryland, is a pizzeria.

"There used to be more of these than McDonald's," claims regular Leonard Shapiro.

"Back in the fifties this was just a sleepy little town that was supported mostly by the racetrack," says Walter Rau of Laurel. "Before they built 395 and 95, everything was on this road."

"I used to sit out here with the U.S. marshals, watch for people," says Morton Marlow, a former cop. "North, south, this was the only way you could come."

Today, U.S. 1 is far from the only way, but the highway is as busy as ever.

"When Miss Alice started here, you know how they made deliveries?" Bud Brown asks.

"No, how?" someone says.

"Horse and buggy," Brown replies.

"I'm going to get you for that," Miss Alice vows.

A NINE-INCH WORM CRAWLED OUT OF MY NOSE.

Four miles south of Laurel on U.S. 1 is a marker commemorating Samuel Morse and the first telegram. "What hath God wrought" passed over the wires here on a line of poles along the B & O Railroad on May 24, 1844.

Two miles farther south, on the northbound side, is the National Agricultural Library, part of the Beltsville National Agricultural Research Center. The center sprawls over 7,000 acres along U.S. 1. It is home to scientists, researchers, laboratories (the FBI and CIA have space here), and several of the Agricultural Research Service's national collections. We're not talking the National Corn on the Cob Collection, but the National Rhizobium Collection, the National Seed Herbarium, and the National Fungus Collection.

My favorite national collection is housed in Building 1180, a low-slung structure nestled in a hollow. The offices are in the basement, which is somehow appropriate, considering the nature of the beast inside. Want to see a mange-ridden cat head floating in formaldehyde, a twenty-five-foot-long tapeworm, or a parasite-infested dog heart? This is the place.

Exactly what would possess a man to seek the curatorship of the National Parasite Collection? For J. Ralph Lichtenfels, a bearded, white-haired man of sixty, it started when he was a student at Indiana University in Pennsylvania. He had his mind set on becoming a science teacher.

Some college students study baroque art; in one biology class, Lichtenfels studied road kill. If the road didn't cooperate, Lichtenfels and classmates would head to nearby woods "with a .22 and girlfriends" and shoot squirrels, possums, or raccoons,

Ralph Lichtenfels, curator, National Parasite Collection, Beltsville.

bring them back to the lab, "open them up," and remove the parasites for further study.

While doing his graduate work at the University of Maryland, Lichtenfels became acquainted with the National Parasite Collection, established in 1892 by Department of Agriculture scientists Charles Stiles and Albert Hassall. The two bequeathed their samples to the government upon their deaths.

Parasites, who spend their lives looking for free room and board, get no respect, and deservedly so. But they're everywhere, often in places we'd rather not have them be. Of the more than 1.5 million forms of life counted so far, according to *National Geographic* magazine, parasites outnumber independent-living species by at least two to one.

Parasites include tapeworms, lice, ticks, protozoans, nematodes, and trematodes. They range in size from one one-thousandth of a micron to whale tapeworms 100 feet long. Hookworms suck the blood of a billion people a year, killing up to a hundred thousand. Schistosomes infect 200 million people a year.

The world's number-one parasitic killer, though, is malaria, which infects 500 million people a year and kills 2 million, mostly in Africa. In 1993, parasites infiltrated Milwaukee's water supply and caused nearly four hundred thousand cases of intestinal illness. Worms and other creatures living in large animals cause about 2 billion dollars annually in losses to U.S. agriculture.

"Nematodes are so numerous that if every part of the world were to disappear, except for them, you could still see the outline of the Earth," Nathan Cobb, an early USDA researcher, once said.

The National Parasite Collection numbers more than a hundred thousand samples or lots, each of which may have thousands of specimens; the collection receives a thousand new samples every year. Physicians, veterinarians, and scientists make use of the collection either in person or through loan. The collection's specialty is helminths, a fancy name for parasitic worms.

"It is not ivory tower science; it has a very practical side," says Lichtenfels, the eighth curator in the

Did I show you my cat's head?
National Parasite Collection, Beltsville.

collection's history and former president of the American Society of Parasitology.

His office is located in a twisting, narrow warren of rooms that would be a perfect setting for a movie about, well, giant parasitic worms. The lunchroom doubles as the computer room. Lichtenfels's desk is piled high with reports with such titles as "Comparative morphology of *Osteragia mossi* and *Ostertagia dikmansi* from *Odocoileus virginianus* and comments on other *Ostertagia* from the Cervidae." In one corner are a spider plant and a poster describing the peculiar joys of a parasitologist:

> I can misspell big words and no one will know the difference.
> I get to visit disease-infested places.

And you get to bring back parasitic wonders lurking in the local water and food. A researcher here was sitting at her desk when a nine-inch worm crawled out of her nose. She had picked up parasitic eggs from food while doing work in Egypt.

At first glance, the collection itself looks like your local library, with its floor-to-ceiling shelves. But the shelves are filled not with classics and mystery novels but tapeworms, ringworms, pinworms, and other nasties.

"Hookworm in sheep intestine," reads one label. "Modular worm in sheep colon," says another. "Double-pored tapeworm in dog intestine." "Large-mouthed bowel worm in sheep." "Thorn-headed worm in pig intestine."

"This shows heartworm in a dog," says Lichtenfels, holding a jar of what looks like spaghetti and a rather large meatball, except upon closer inspection the spaghetti is parasitic worms, and the meatball is a dog's heart.

The samples are kept in preserving fluid. Explosion-proof lights and heat sensors line the ceiling and walls.

A coiled strand of brownish filament—a twenty-five-foot tapeworm—floats in a jar of fluid. But that's nothing. Tapeworms as long as sixty-six feet have been found in people. And get this: tapeworms can spend their entire lives in your intestines, absorbing nutrients through tiny moving fingers called microvilli that cover their body.

Another jar contains 174 "mostly immature" tapeworms found in the stomach of one Allen Young, twenty-two months old, of Flackey Creek, Kentucky, in 1930.

The grossest item here, though, is the mangy cat head, floating eerily and disembodied in a jar of fluid. Floating quite well, thank you; the specimen is more than one hundred years old.

There are two-hour public tours of the National Agricultural Research Center, but they don't include the National Parasite Collection. However, you can call the lab (301-504-8483) and arrange a tour.

"Parasites are fascinating to the public because they're hidden and mysterious," Lichtenfels says.

Yeah, and they have the habit of crawling out of your nose at the most inopportune times.

———

U.S. 1 negotiates a phalanx of adult bookstores, pawnshops, and check-cashing places before reaching College Park and the University of Maryland. Plato's Diner is here, and so is the laundromat Soaps ("He who is in you is greater than he who is in the world," says a message painted on the window). Hyattsville is next, and then Brentwood; U.S. 1 becomes Rhode Island Avenue, absolutely the rockiest, most potholed stretch of U.S. 1 anywhere. If you have been using a map to follow the highway to this point, throw it away. It's not going to help. Welcome to Washington, D.C., where U.S. 1 becomes . . . the Twilight Zone.

DISTRICT
OF COLUMBIA

We can walk down the little hill toward Constitution Avenue, where shines, white and superb at a distance, the imperial facade of government offices, which shows another kind of pride, which long ago replaced republican simplicity. It is a bold person indeed who does not cower before that front; there is no place on (relatively) dry land where one can sympathize more easily with the feelings of an Eskimo paddling a kayak under the overhang of a Greenland glacier. The columnar massif along Constitution Avenue . . . is intended to impress. Like the other artificial cities created to be capitals, ours was meant to be awesome.

—*Washington, D.C.: A Guide to the Nation's Capital,* American Guide Series, 1942

Telephone conversation with librarian in the Washingtonian section at the Martin Luther King Memorial Library, February 17, 1998:

"Do you know what streets make up Route 1 in D.C.?"

"Hmm, I don't know." (Pause.) "Rhode Island Avenue," she says confidently.

"Aren't there other streets?"

"There are other streets? Let me take a look at a map." She looks over a map. "The first indication I have on the map is that it becomes Sixth Street. Let me put you on hold again. . . . OK. What we're seeing is that it's Rhode Island Avenue and New York Avenue, which are parallel. Then it becomes Fourteenth Avenue. According to this, at Rhode Island Avenue, it just stops, then it turns onto Sixth Avenue."

"Is it ever Constitution Avenue?"

"No. Well, yes. I'd say it is. It's Sixth, at one point it looks like Eighth, and then it's a little bit of Constitution from Eighth to Fourteenth and then it becomes Fourteenth Street."

"I'm not sure there are any street signs."

"I'm not sure we have any more information than you. You seem to have tracked this already."

———

Nowhere on the entire highway, with the exception of Providence, Rhode Island, is U.S. 1 more poorly marked than in the District of Columbia.

A disgrace. District of Columbia.

U.S. 1 is, at one point, Constitution Avenue—between Ninth and Fourteenth streets. Or maybe it's Sixth and Fourteenth streets. U.S. 1 signs direct you to turn from Sixth Avenue to L Street to Ninth Street to Constitution Avenue. Yet the Michelin Central Washington, D.C., street map, the most detailed road map available, clearly shows U.S. 1 coming down Sixth Street all the way to Constitution, without ever turning on L Street or Ninth Street. A map inside the excellent *Access Guide to Washington, D.C.* shows U.S. 1 continuing on Fourteenth Street north of Constitution Avenue, when it most certainly does not.

U.S. 1 is not marked at all on Constitution Avenue, home of one of the greatest concentrations of monumental buildings in the world, although there is a U.S. 1/50 sign on Sixth and Pennsylvania directing you north.

What, you ask, is the big deal? It's the nation's capital! America's Main Street can't be adequately marked by a few simple street signs?

This is U.S. 1's course through Washington, D.C., from the northern city limits: Rhode Island Avenue to Sixth Street to L Street to Ninth Street to Constitution Avenue to Fourteenth Street to the George Mason Memorial Bridge over the Potomac River into Arlington, Virginia (northbound from Arlington into the District, 1 follows the Arland D. Williams Jr. Memorial Bridge over the Potomac).

This is just a sample of what's on or along U.S. 1 in the nation's capital: Chinatown, the National Museum of American Art, the Martin Luther King Memorial Library, FBI headquarters, the National Archives, the National Museum of Natural History, the National Museum of American History, the Interstate Commerce Commission, the U.S. Holocaust Memorial Museum, the Department of Agriculture, the Bureau of Engraving and Printing, and the Jefferson Memorial.

The Star-Spangled Banner is on U.S. 1, on display inside the National Museum of American History. And don't forget the Professional Coffee Shop and Uncle Boolie's Southern Cuisine. All that, and more, are on U.S. 1, although you'd never know it.

———

Richard Weingroff's office on Seventh Street S.W. is easy enough to find, but then again, he's not on U.S. 1. Weingroff, a writer and unofficial historian at the Federal Highway Administration, is the only person in this book not on 1, but he's in here because he knows the road's history as well as anyone.

This is a good time for a history lesson, because we've almost reached the halfway point on our 2,450-mile journey to Key West (the highway's length is erroneously put as anywhere from 2,209 miles—on the sign in Fort Kent—to 2,500 miles).

"One of the myths is that U.S. 1 is the first highway," Weingroff says. "It is not. It received the number 1 when highways were numbered in the 1920s."

U.S. 1's history begins in colonial America. The Boston Post Road in Massachusetts, Rhode Island, Connecticut, and New York is the best-known segment of a road that eventually became the nation's first interstate highway, connecting all thirteen original colonies except for Delaware (to this day, U.S. 1 bypasses Delaware). The road connected New York; Princeton, New Jersey; and Philadelphia, which served as the nation's earliest capitals, and Washington, D.C., the final choice.

The best concise history of U.S. 1 can be found in a U.S Department of Agriculture press release dated October 9, 1927. The route of the King's Highway, the Post Road, and, later, U.S. 1, was no accident. The roads followed the "fall line," the farthest point a ship in colonial times could travel upriver before reaching rapids, at which point cargo had to be transferred to wagons. The transfer points soon became communities, villages, then cities. And in the absence of a connecting waterway, a road grew to link the cities along the fall line.

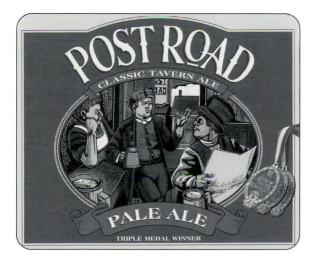

A beer with some highway history.

This physical fact influenced the locations of Trenton, New Jersey; Philadelphia; Baltimore; Washington, D.C.; Richmond, Virginia; Raleigh, North Carolina; Columbia, South Carolina; and Augusta, Georgia, all situated at the head of navigation on their respective rivers.

The road that is now U.S. 1 began as a trail in the mid-1600s. Blazed trees marked the way. Crude bridges spanned ravines. Canoe ferries helped people and goods across the wider rivers.

By the end of the seventeenth century, travel by horseback and pack horse between Boston, New York, and Philadelphia was common. The first common carrier service was established in New Jersey, along what would later become U.S. 1.

But the road was rough going for human and beast. In 1704, a Boston schoolteacher named Sarah Kemble Knight journeyed along the Post Road to New York. She was so rattled by the experience she composed this poem after returning home:

> Through many toils and many frights,
> I have returned, poor Sarah Knights,
> Over great rocks and many stones,
> God has preserved from fractured bones.

Regular stage service between New York and Philadelphia was in place by 1732. The journey took five days. The "Flying Machine," an ornate and brilliantly colored coach introduced in 1771, reduced the trip to two days.

Foreign visitors, explains Douglas Waitley in *Roads of Destiny* (Robert B. Luce, Inc., 1970) were shocked at the condition of American roads and coaches. One complained: "You are fully exposed to inclement weather and soaked as if you were out of doors. You are crushed, shaken, thrown out, bumped in a manner that cannot adequately be described. . . . It is not unusual to see the coaches shattered, the passengers crippled, and the horses drowned."

One of the first tasks confronting Benjamin Franklin after being put in charge of the nation's postal system in 1751 was resolving customer complaints about mailing charges by the mile. No one knew the exact distance to anywhere. So Franklin invented an odometer, rigged it to his carriage, and on a ten-week tour of New England, measured every inch of the Boston Post Road's three branches. Workers then installed mile markers at the proper places.

By the turn of the nineteenth century, turnpikes started to appear. Toll roads had originated in medieval England; turnpikes were metal bars inserted into a gate to keep people from entering until they paid the toll.

> "The ugliest, most-traveled, deadliest, and most historic highway in this region."
>
> *Washington Times Herald*, April 22, 1940

The early toll roads in this country, built by turnpike companies operating under public charters, appeared in virtually every state. Between 1792 and 1810, more than 150 turnpike companies were chartered in New England alone.

Tolls at the time, according to Alice Fleming in *Highways into History* (St. Martin's Press, 1971), ranged from twenty-five cents for a four-wheeled carriage drawn by two horses to three cents a dozen for a herd of pigs. Not everyone appreciated tolls. Travelers outwitted the turnpike companies by bypassing the main road and opening up smaller roads, called shunpikes, which skirted the toll gates.

Road conditions changed hardly at all over the nineteenth century, but the automobile would revolutionize American travel. Freewheeling Americans took to the highway by the millions in the 1920s. The number of registered private automobiles was 8,000 in 1900. By 1910, it had reached 458,000; by 1920, eight million; by 1930, 23 million.

Motorists, as John Jakle points out in *The Tourist* (University of Nebraska Press, 1985), organized and lobbied for better roads. The Lincoln Highway Association, formed in 1913, brought together motorists, manufacturers, and road builders in a grand promotional scheme to mark a transcontinental highway, from New York City to San Francisco, honoring Abraham Lincoln.

The Lincoln Highway spawned many imitators: The Jefferson Highway from Winnipeg to New Orleans, the Quebec-Miami International Highway, the Old Spanish Trail from St. Augustine to San Diego, and others. The Dixie Highway was promoted by the Chattanooga Automobile Club to capture Miami-bound traffic in Tennessee. Branches running from Illinois and Michigan met at Chattanooga, only to split again into roads serving east and west Florida. The Midget Map of the Transcontinental Trails of the United States, circa 1923, shows a crazy-quilt of interlocking and parallel highways: the Atlantic Highway (which ran parallel to the route of present-day U.S. 1), the Pikes Peak Ocean-to-Ocean Highway, the Black and Yellow Turnpike, the Lone Star Route, the Lone Star Trail, etc.

The named highways, many of which served a valuable purpose in the 1910s, became a chaotic, often redundant system of roads in the 1920s. AAA President Thomas Henry and Ernest Smith, the auto club's general manager, drove their Cadillac on a ninety-six-hour cross-country journey from Washington, D.C., to San Francisco in September 1925. Smith and Henry had little difficulty finding their way to western Utah, where a sign signaled the parting of the Lincoln Highway (New York City to San Francisco) and the Victory Highway (New York City to San Francisco via Baltimore). Turning right onto the Victory, the two soon came to a hill. "Six roads led over the top," Smith would later recall, "and each road was worse than the other." He walked ahead a half mile to make sure they got on the right road. Even then, it was no picnic. "For the next two hours we pitched and tossed, dropping into chuckholes and raising clouds of dust," he said.

Order needed to be imposed, and it came in the form of the U.S. numbered highway system. At the time, the U.S. Bureau of Public Roads (BPR), now the Federal Highway Administration, was part of the Department of Agriculture. The state highway agencies, therefore, asked the secretary of agriculture to help develop a system of identifying and marking the nation's main interstate roads. In 1925, the secretary appointed the Joint Board on Interstate Highways, which included three federal officials and twenty-one state highway officials. Names, the board concluded, had to go. The interstate roads would be numbered. But how?

Edwin James of the Bureau of Public Roads, a member of the Joint Board, had a plan. "The U.S. is about twice as wide as it is from north to south, and with this I saw a complete pattern of just what I wished," James wrote to a friend. "It stares one in the face, it is so simple and so adjustable. With north-south roads numbered odd from east to west and east-west roads numbered even from north to south, you at once start a simple, systematic, complete, expansible pattern."

Accordingly, James's proposed "Route No. 1" would be the first route along the Atlantic Ocean side of the United States, following as much as possible the old "fall line" roads. The committee accepted James's plan and drew up a map of one-, two-, and three-digit U.S. routes.

One myth about U.S. 1 is that it is our "first highway." The highway was designated on November 11, 1926, along with all the original routes of the U.S. numbered system. And it's not a federal highway; U.S. 1, like the other numbered highways, followed existing state and local roads, "linked in a system for the benefit of the traveling public," according to Weingroff, "but still owned and operated by the states."

Initially, the numbered highway system received mixed reviews. The *Tombstone (Ariz.) Epitaph* welcomed the change, calling named-highway boosters "blood-suckers who have sat in their swivel chairs and milked the public for funds." But the *Lexington (Ky.) Herald* mourned the passing of an era: "The traveler may shed tears as he drives the Lincoln Highway or dream dreams as he speeds over the Jefferson Highway, but how can he get a 'kick' out of 46 or 55 or 33 or 21?"

Route 66, where you could get your kicks, was born at the same time as U.S. 1 and the other original U.S. numbered routes. As the route of the migrants fleeing the Dust Bowl (depicted in John Steinbeck's *The Grapes of Wrath* and John Ford's movie version), as celebrated in the song "Route 66" by Bobby Troup, and as the setting of a popular TV show, *Route 66*, in the early 1960s, the highway would become the nation's most famous numbered highway. But with all that, it was bypassed by the Interstate Highway System in the 1950s, and has since been decommissioned as a U.S. numbered highway.

"By comparison," Weingroff says, "Route 1 has an even longer history and its cultural touchstones, but it can't meet the book, song, and movie test." He added, "Route 66 also has in its favor the fact that it no longer exists as a U.S. highway. There's a lot more nostalgia for something that doesn't exist except in our memory—and in the many remaining stretches of old highway we can search out on our vacations. Route 1 is a current and vibrant highway. We aren't nostalgic for a road we use every day. It remains an economic lifeline throughout its length, but it has its share of potholes and congestion, too."

———

U.S. 1 makes a graceful sweep past the Jefferson Memorial, then crosses the Potomac into Virginia. The road, now the Jefferson Davis Highway, plunges through the hotel/office tower canyons of Crystal City, passes National Airport, and rolls into Alexandria as Henry Street (southbound—northbound 1 is Patrick Street). Blue and White Carry-Out, a little neighborhood luncheonette, is on the highway, and so is the Washington Speakers Bureau, in case you want to book someone for your next meeting.

Five minutes later, I pull into a coffee shop on U.S. 1—now Richmond Parkway—to speak with the people who give grease a good—no, great—name. It's time for Hot Doughnuts Now!

VIRGINIA

US 1 between Fredericksburg and Washington more or less follows an Indian trail established long before the Europeans penetrated the country. Because it provided the shortest route along the Virginia bank of the Potomac River, colonists persisted in using it despite the mire, difficult fords, and other obstacles that drew their curses. . . . John Marshall spoke feelingly of miring his horse, and Thomas Jefferson bemoaned the fact that the best speed he could make was three miles an hour. Testy John Randolph of Roanoke likened the Chopowamsic Swamp to the Serbonian bog that swallowed the unwary forever.

—*U.S. One, Maine to Florida*, American Guide Series, 1938

The United States may be the land of the free but not quite the home of the doughnut. We eat billions of doughnuts a year, but Canada, with one-tenth the population of the United States, has twice as many doughnut shops.

The Krispy Kreme people are trying to remedy the situation. If a greasy, glazed ball of fried dough gives you indigestion, proceed immediately to the next section.

"When Krispy Kremes are hot, they are to other doughnuts what angels are to people," the writer Roy Blount Jr. once said. "They're not crispy-creamy so much as right out on the cusp between chewy and molten. Kind of like fried nectar puffed up with yeast. No *ugh* in these doughnuts, unless you eat five."

The Krispy Kreme outside Washington, marked by a splendid sign with two crown-topped K's above the company name and the trademark red neon "Hot Doughnuts Now" sign, has delivered greasy glazed joy since 1962. It is known as the Alexandria Krispy Kreme, but the store is actually in Fairfax County.

"Granville Hampton and I were the first ones in the door when they opened," claims Lewis Allen, sitting on one of the green stools.

He remembers when a Krispy Kreme was a nickel and a cup of coffee ten cents. The donuts are now

Doughnut assembly line, Krispy Kreme, Alexandria.

fifty-eight cents each, although a dozen glazed are $3.96, and if you buy two dozen, you get a dollar off.

This is not just a doughnut shop; it is a twenty-four-hour-a-day, seven-day-a-week doughnut factory. About thirteen hundred doughnuts an hour pop off each of two lines, destined for supermarkets, convenience stores, and gas stations in Virginia, Maryland, and the nation's capital.

"Only one day a year this plant is shut down, and that's Christmas," says manager Johnny Handy. "And I'm not going to lie to you, because the retail shuts down but there's still production."

Krispy Kreme was started by Vernon Rudolph, who bought a doughnut shop in Paducah, Kentucky, from a Frenchman named Joe LeBeau. Rudolph acquired the company's assets, the Krispy Kreme name, and the rights to a secret yeast-raised doughnut recipe that LeBeau had created in New Orleans.

Rudolph moved the operation to Nashville; he and other family members opened shops in Charleston, West Virginia, and Atlanta, Georgia. In 1937, Rudolph decided to leave the family business and strike out on his own. He and two partners left Nashville in a 1936 Pontiac, with two hundred dollars in cash, several pieces of doughnut-making equipment, and the secret recipe. The three ended up in

Winston-Salem, North Carolina, which in the late 1930s was becoming an economic hub in the Southeast, with tobacco, textiles, and other industries.

Rudolph and partners rented a building across from Salem College, removed the back seat of the Pontiac, and installed a delivery rack. They installed the back seat in the doughnut shop, using it as a bed when they worked fifteen-to-twenty-hour days. They charged five cents for two doughnuts, twenty-five cents a dozen. In 1937, Joe Louis was heavyweight champ, Amelia Earhart disappeared over the Pacific Ocean, the Golden Gate Bridge was completed, and a popular song proclaimed you could live on doughnuts and coffee if you were in love.

The first Krispy Kremes rolled off the line on July 13, 1937. The operation was strictly wholesale; when people stopped by the Winston-Salem shop and asked for hot doughnuts, Rudolph cut a hole in the shop's wall through which doughnuts could be sold. It was the beginning of Krispy Kreme's window service.

Jerry Shriver, writing an account of a sixteen-stop, thirty-six-hour fast-food tour of Columbus, Ohio, for *USA Today*, called the Krispy Kreme drive-through window "the most perfectly realized creation in the history of Western Civilization."

Son Q. Che, assistant manager of the Alexandria, Virginia, Krispy Kreme, gave me a tour of the Willie Wonka–like doughnut factory. The process begins with dry mix, prepared in Winston-Salem and shipped to individual stores. The dough is mixed with water for fourteen minutes. The doughnuts-to-be then "relax" for ten minutes. Then they're baked for twenty-two minutes at 350 degrees in a floor-to-ceiling glass-enclosed oven.

Then comes a bath—fifty seconds on each side, no more, no less—in a tub filled with hot vegetable shortening. The glazed doughnuts pass through a streaming wall of melted sugar that reminds one of a waterfall—or car wash. The final step in the dough-nut's long journey to your mouth: a forty-five-minute ride on an overhead conveyor, which you can watch through a glass window as you sit at the counter.

"The sight of all those doughnuts marching solemnly to their fates makes me proud to be an American," Nora Ephron wrote.

Adolph Levitt, a Russian émigré, is credited with the first doughnut machine, which he introduced in his Harlem bakery in 1920.

Who put the hole in the doughnut? The Dutch brought *olykoeks*—oily cakes—to the New World, but it was Elizabeth Gregory, a ship captain's mother, who took deep-fried dough, put hazelnuts or walnuts in the middle, and called them doughnuts. Hanson Gregory suggested to his mom that she put a hole in the middle of the fried cakes to ensure they would be fully cooked.

By 1931, Levitt's machines, as David A. Taylor explained in *Smithsonian* magazine, were earning him 25 million dollars a year. At the 1934 World's Fair in Chicago, doughnuts were billed as "the food hit of the Century of Progress." Singer Cindy Hutchins's mother remembered buying them after seeing movies at a Washington, D.C., theater. Along with the doughnuts came a slip of paper with these words: "As you go through life, make this your goal: Watch the doughnut, not the hole."

Millions of people today heed that advice. Krispy Kreme, headquartered in Winston-Salem, sells more than one billion doughnuts a year; every ten minutes the company makes enough doughnuts to make a stack as high as the Empire State Building. In 1976, Beatrice Foods bought

The wall of glaze, Krispy Kreme, Alexandria.

Alexandria.

Krispy Kreme; in 1981, a group of franchisees bought it back.

The most famous Krispy Kreme fan was Elvis Presley; it is said he demanded a dozen jelly-filled be kept on hand at all times at Graceland. A 1950s Krispy Kreme Ring King Jr. machine is in the Smith-sonian. In *Driving Miss Daisy*, Morgan Freeman tells Jessica Tandy: "Here's your Krispy Kremes, Miss Daisy."

Dunkin' Donuts, with stores in twice as many states and in thirty-seven countries, sells five times as many doughnuts as Krispy Kreme. But Dunkin' Donuts' chocolate-frosted, jelly, and sugar-raised have not inspired the poetry that Vernon Rudolph's doughnuts have.

Krispy Kreme launched its Yankee invasion in 1994 with a drive-through shop in Indianapolis. The 135-store, 20-state chain is slowly marching north, with shops in Wilmington, Delaware; New York City (including Penn Station); and Scranton, Pennsylvania.

"I hope that New York's acceptance of Krispy Kremes is not ironic," Blount says. "Southern food in New York is often served up in quotation marks. For instance, at a restaurant called Live Bait. Like life, a hot Krispy Kreme goes by so fast that if your tongue's in your cheek, you miss something."

"The Appalachian love child of the soufflé and croissant," is how Melissa Schorr described the Original Glazed in *GQ* magazine. "As warm as a

Dumfries.

Fairfax County.

June night in Tennessee, as sweet as a blonde belle, it tumbles effortlessly to the bottom of your stomach."

The doughnut show must always go on. Johnny Handy says there's a plumber on staff, and the store's maintenance shop is equipped "with any type of motor that can fail here." Handy says he gives thirty dozen doughnuts a day to a local social worker, who distributes them to homeless shelters in the area on his own time.

"I like this place," says Lewis Allen, nursing a cup of coffee at the counter. "It's like my second home."

———

Mike Keck, who lives right behind the Krispy Kreme, collects memories. A lot of them involve U.S. 1. Keck runs an antique book and back-issue magazine service called Out of the Past. His living room is filled floor-to-ceiling with boxes; he has more than one million magazines. He talks about Richmond Highway's colorful history in Fairfax County. The Penn-Daw Motel on 1, he says, was the first motor court to advertise in *American Motorist* magazine. Arthur Godfrey would often eat there. A Mrs. Robertson sold Hybla Valley fruitcake from her home on the highway.

"She maintained people drove for hundreds of miles for her fruitcake," Keck, sixty-six, says. "She said there were billboards from Maine to Florida for Hybla Valley Fruitcake."

The landmarks on this stretch of U.S. 1 included the Dixie Pig Barbecue and the Totem Pole Motor Lodge. The Loew's Drive-In in Mount Vernon reportedly had the largest screen in the world. An amusement park along the highway was called Kiddie City.

All of the above are gone, most recently the Dixie Pig, whose cupola, at least, was saved by the local firehouse.

Several years ago, Keck proposed a Museum of the American Roadside on U.S. 1. It would be kind of a retro Williamsburg, filled with half-scale replicas of diners, gas stations, and such long-gone highway marvels as giant coffeepots, milk bottles, and shoes, in which shops would be housed.

"Everybody likes to trash Route 1, but it's the best-known highway in the country," Keck argues.

Woodbridge.

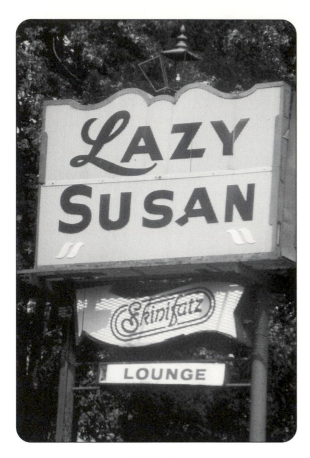

Colchester.

"It is a piece of American history, and is worthy of preserving before it is all gone."

The museum, which would be built on the site of the former Woodley-Nightingale trailer park, would cost about 5 million dollars. The Smithsonian has told Keck it would be happy to donate items, but Keck has been unable to find anyone willing to finance and build the museum.

"Everybody wants to save three hundred years ago, but nobody wants to save forty, fifty years ago," he says.

———

Fort Belvoir, headquarters of the Army Corps of Engineers, is along U.S. 1, and so is the main gate to Quantico Marine Corps base. In Dumfries, "Vir-

ginia's Oldest Town," Confederate Court intersects U.S. 1. Dumfries to Stafford, and then on to Ashland, is one of the highway's more scenic stretches. The Greyhound bus depot is on 1 in Fredericksburg, which marks the beginning of what could be called the Trailer Park Belt. Mobile homes now appear with increasing frequency all the way to the Florida state line. Spotsylvania, just south of Fredericksburg, is a mobile home builder's empire, with four manufacturers side by side on 1. Hart's What Not is on 1 in Cedon, while Get It 'n Git, a convenience store, is on 1 in Ladysmith.

It is pretty country, but the ghosts of the Civil War still seem to haunt the roadside. The highway from Fredericksburg south to Petersburg "runs through the heart of an area that has seen more bloodshed than any other on the North American continent," according to the WPA guide.

Civil war markers start popping up, and one could get a concise history of America's bloodiest conflict by reading the markers on U.S. 1 through Virginia and the Carolinas.

In the hamlet of Ruther Glen, halfway between Ladysmith and Ashland, is a reminder of another painful past. About a half mile south of the sign for Buzzard's Bottom Road is a metal Coca-Cola sign in a field on the highway's southbound side, next to

Great name for a convenience store. Ladysmith.

A reminder of the Jim Crow era: faded Beverly's Grill sign, Ruther Glen.

Beverly's Grill. Under "Coca-Cola" are the words "For Colored."

In the forties, it was attached to the screen-doored luncheonette. The sign was later painted over, but the top coat wore off, reviving the original message. Richmond's Valentine Museum wanted to buy the sign for an exhibit on the Jim Crow era, according to the *Washington Post*, but Josephine Beverly Jones, who owns Beverly's Grill, said no. "We plan to keep it as a landmark," Jones said.

General stores, dairy farms, and thrift shops line the highway to Ashland. The Snow White Inn and the faded marquee for the old Rose Bowl Drive-In are on U.S. 1 just south of Ashland.

The highway becomes Brook Road, slips past I-95, makes a left onto Azalea, a fast right on Chamberlayne, passing Mohammed's University of

Old drive-in sign near Ashland.

Ashland.

Islam as it heads into downtown Richmond. At the corner of Belvidere (U.S. 1) and Canal, alongside the Downtown Expressway, is a three-story red brick building with a blue-and-green sign and an eye-catching name.

——

The whole world has not been against the Daily Planet; it just seems that way. The homeless center opened in the mid-eighties, and quickly became a political football no one wanted to touch. In fact, for the first twelve years of its existence it operated illegally; not until 1997 did the City Council vote to give the Daily Planet the permit it needed to keep operating.

Proposals over the years would have relocated the shelter to other, more remote sites downtown or to the city's outskirts, but they were vehemently opposed by residents and businessmen.

"We're all functioning people," one resident said at a town meeting. "You are proposing to move into our neighborhood dysfunctional people. How in the world can you do that to us?"

"This is an enterprise zone," a Brook Road businessman said. "What the hell are you thinking of?"

Somehow, the Daily Planet survived and grew as it tried to meet an increasing demand for food,

James Price, the Daily Planet's director.

Daily Planet headquarters, Richmond.

shelter, and medical care for the city's indigent population.

"We've had instances where people wound up here in front of our door and nobody knows how they got here," James E. Price said of the Bunkhouse, a shelter for the mentally ill that is part of the Daily Planet.

Price is Daily Planet's director. A former schoolteacher and principal, he served as the assistant state education commissioner before retiring at the age of fifty-three. He was looking for consulting work when he read that something called the Daily Planet was seeking a director.

"I didn't know what it was," he says, sitting in his bare-floored, poorly lit office in a building wedged behind a Domino's Pizza on Belvidere and Grace. Battered file cabinets are in one corner. There is no name plaque on Price's desk, just his name typed on a piece of paper inside an orange plastic sleeve.

When Price took over the Daily Planet in February 1995, the shelter was ministering to 300–400 people a day.

"I couldn't believe that many people were homeless," he recalls.

This year, through its various programs, the Daily Planet will serve about thirty thousand people—85 percent men, 15 percent women; 84 percent black, 15 percent white, 1 percent Hispanic. About 50 percent of the total, according to Price, have "some sort of addiction problem."

Each day, about two hundred people eat breakfast at Canal Street (the Freedom House, a separate organization, serves dinner). Many of those standing outside the building in the morning are waiting to be hired for one-day contracting, painting, or roofing jobs. A clinic provides medical care to about two thousand people a year. Counseling is available at a drop-in center. Those with mental disabilities can get yard maintenance and janitorial jobs through the Rainbow program.

For all this, the Daily Planet received about sixty thousand dollars from the city budget last year, and has been unsuccessful in attracting state funding, although it did receive 1.2 million dollars in federal Housing and Urban Development aid. The Daily Planet's 2.2-million-dollar annual budget comes

Richmond.

from government grants, community donations, and the United Way.

"They allow these people out of [a state institution], they get on the street, they're homeless. Who gets them? We get them," Price says. "We feed them, we bunk them, we provide counseling. But we can't get the state's money.

"We ask the city to give us thirty-four thousand dollars more to make this transition," he says of a planned expansion in the Grace Street building, "and they say no. We do the city a favor, in my opinion. I think we're an asset to them."

"The city government's failure on the homeless question has been shameful," the *Richmond Times-*

Richmond.

Bellwood.

Arnette's drive-in restaurant, 1940s, Colonial Heights.

Dispatch editorialized. "The city contributes [this year] just $61,000 to the Planet's operations—a pitifully paltry sum. So the city is getting the Planet's services for next to nothing, and this while jerking the Planet around as to where it might move."

Corporate support of the Planet has been sparse. The Reynolds Foundation, Circuit City Foundation, and the United Parcel Service Foundation, among others, have given grants, but the Planet has not been able to attract "that big corporate donor," Price says.

The center has been offered a lot of money—to get out of downtown. An anonymous donor said he would donate 1 million dollars if the Daily Planet moved to a site owned by Virginia Commonwealth University on Seventeenth Street, near the city jail.

"I don't see enough appreciation for what we're trying to do," Price says.

Inside the Canal Street building, Jeff Toller is making his morning rounds. Toller, a former Pinkerton's security guard, is the Daily Planet's director of nutrition and employment.

He shows me the clinic, the laundry and shower rooms, and kitchen. The community living room, just inside the main entrance, has cracked tile floors and cinder-block walls. An old upright piano stands in the corner. A man in his fifties sits on a couch with his walker in front of him, staring out the window.

"We're supposed to be closed between eleven and one, but in the winter, when it's really cold, we stay open," Toller explains. "And when it's hot and humid out and you can't walk to the corner without staggering, we stay open."

Price, who plans to retire for good soon, is confident the Daily Planet is finally on solid ground.

"We've come a long way," he says, smiling.

"Once we renovate this building and the food program gets established on Canal Street, the city should be proud."

———

Bullets, on 1 southbound in Richmond, may not be a politically correct name, but the drive-through's neon-lit exterior is fabulous at night. The Jefferson Davis Motel and the Traffic Jam Lounge come up later, on the southbound side. A rocket looks ready to blast off in front of Hull Street Outlet on 1 in Richmond.

Need a wheel cover? Lot of Hubcaps should have it. Bonnie's Burgers on the Pike is on 1 south, across from the Snow White Motel. The Bellwood Manor, a vintage motor court—now abandoned and weed-overgrown—is on the northbound side.

In Colonial Heights, just past Mutual Termite Control and the Shooting Gallery (All Pistols on Sale. UZI, 9 mm), but just before the Martin Luther King Bridge and Petersburg, is a tractor-trailer parked in front of an auto parts store. Painted on both sides of the trailer, for all to see, is this provocative message: ABOLISH THE CORPS OF ENGINEERS.

Calvin L. Meadows put the message up. Cal has never been one to mince his words.

A quick glance at the window signs at Cal's Auto Parts tells you all you need to know about the man inside:

> In God We Trust—not the Supreme Court.
>
> America—Love it or Leave it.
>
> We believe in workfare, not welfare.
>
> No one with arresting powers allowed on property without identifying themselves first.

And the most appropriate one:

> Enter at Your Own Risk.

"We opened in 1990," Cal says of his business, which is part auto supply store, part scrap yard,

Cal Meadows, owner of Cal's Auto Parts, Colonial Heights.

No truer words were ever spoken. Cal's Auto Parts, Colonial Heights.

and part pawnshop. He sells everything from chainsaws and guns to Nintendos and jukeboxes. He's a bail bondsman, too.

"The next year we had the EPA down," Cal continues. "We were audited by the IRS. The state environmental people came in. The ATF [Bureau of Alcohol, Tobacco, and Firearms]. The state police came down, checked every car in the yard. I asked

Cal's Auto Parts, Colonial Heights.

them, 'Anyone else you want to send down?' The Army Corps of Engineers put in all these regulations. The Army Corpse of Engineers, I call them. It's a nice dead body of government. They didn't want me to lease the land. I did. They came down." He smiles. "There were words."

It's not clear where Cal's problems started, or who he ticked off first, but his business has been investigated, probed—some would say targeted—by what seems like every governmental agency within a hundred miles. Cal speaks his mind, and sometimes people don't appreciate it.

"I'm not the dummy in the bunch," he says emphatically. His glasses are perched on his bald head. "The Constitution says no army has jurisdiction over civilians except in time of war. And this is not war. Read your Constitution."

"Rush Limbaugh," says a Cal's regular, "has nothing on Cal."

Cal writes letters to legislators and judges decrying "reprobate sluggards" who have more rights than "honest and forthright laborers." He says democracy has been replaced by socialism, "where you are better off if you don't work and don't care." He had his own radio show on a station in nearby Hopewell.

"I suggested at the last Colonial Heights meeting that we put the Ten Commandments up in the schools, or in the courthouse or even in the municipal building, and received no response whatsoever," he wrote in one letter to the editor. "What does this kind of reaction tell you?"

Cal halfheartedly ran for city council one year—"he put a few signs up," says his son—and got 800 votes in a ten-candidate race (the winner had 2,300).

"I'm going to keep it up there as a nice big billboard for them," he says of his anti–Engineers message. "You don't have to like me, you just have to respect me."

"I can't imagine a little businessman getting the attention we have gotten here," says his thirty-

Petersburg.

Petersburg.

DeWitt.

eight-year-old son, James. "They've tried to set us up. My God, there's nobody else to send. Problem is, if you stink, Daddy will tell you to go get some soap."

"I like a good stand," Cal says, "better than I like a fall."

Cal lost his son Robert in 1993. Cal doesn't bring the subject up; his son Jim does. "He had a bad heart," Jim explains. "He couldn't get a transplant and yet that governor of Pennsylvania got one, and he was in his sixties. My brother's wife was six months pregnant, and they had a small child."

But Cal is in good spirits today. "Here comes an old goat," he says, spotting his friend Jimmy Hawthorne. "Hey, old goat," he says as Hawthorne

steps inside, "what was the most exciting thing that ever happened along Route 1 besides you meeting a woman?"

Hawthorne smiles slyly. "That was it," he replies.

"Democrats are Welfare Pimps," reads another sign in the window. "North for VP, Schwarzkopf for Chief of Staff."

"A woman came in here one day and said, 'I'm going to give you a piece of my mind,'" Cal recalls. "I said, 'No, you won't, you don't have any pieces left.'"

———

U.S. 1 doesn't run a straight course in any of the cities it goes through, but nowhere is the highway's path more torturous than in Petersburg. The road goes like a broken field runner through town. As Third Street,

Meredithville.

Atlanta Downtown Hotel sign, near McKenney.

Buggs Island.

U.S. 1 is at its humblest—a narrow street, little more than an alley. But the Little Pig Barbecue is on 1 southbound in Petersburg, and if you run into any legal problems, you can always stop at Allen, Allen, Allen, and Allen downtown.

About 5 miles south of Petersburg is a marker titled "Where Hill Fell," a reference to the Confederate general A. P. Hill, one of Robert E. Lee's most trusted lieutenants. Hill, who did not know that Lee's line had been broken at last in the siege of Petersburg, rode right into a party of Union troops advancing on the city. He was forty. His was said to be the last name on both Lee's and Stonewall Jackson's lips before they died.

Just north of Dinwiddie, hundreds of wagon wheels and the sign "Wheel of Fortune" line the road in front of the Overton farm on 1 southbound. The highway from here to the North Carolina border—

through DeWitt (look for the Pet Ice Cream sign), McKenney, Sturgeonville, Warfield, Alberta, Meredithville—is beautiful, lonely, and forlorn, dotted with modest ranch homes, tiny post offices, rusting cars, and abandoned buildings. There is a cat crossing in Meredithville, the only one I've seen on the entire highway.

"When in Atlanta," says a faded billboard on the southbound side, "Visit the Downtown Hotel."

I-85 dogs U.S. 1 here, as I-95 does just about everywhere else. The road dips and climbs like a gentle roller coaster. The Hut Beauty Shop, located in a Quonset hut, is at the northern end of South Hill; the Horseshoe Restaurant, with its great old rusty sign, is in town. Look for the "Burnt Store Road" sign.

About 12 miles south of town, just before the bridge over Buggs Island Lake, is a sign for the Buggs Island Telephone Cooperative. Four miles past the Steel Bridge Mini-Mart, U.S. 1 crosses into North Carolina.

NORTH CAROLINA

Between the Virginia line and Raleigh, US 1 runs through rolling farm lands and occasional pine and oak forests. . . . In spring, wild flowers bloom in profusion by the roadside, the white blossoms of dogwood contrasting with the tightly closed lavender-to-purple buds of the Judas tree, while the ground beneath is carpeted with a tangle of honeysuckle vines. During the autumn, goldenrod, asters, and gentians flower against a background of brilliant red and tawny golden leaves.

—*U.S. One, Maine to Florida*, American Guide Series, 1938

U.S. 1 runs through Wise, with its tiny post office. Norlina, the next town, marks what the WPA guide called the state's "Black Belt," a region populated by descendants of slaves who toiled at antebellum plantations. "Paddyrollers" operated around Norlina—throughout the South, in fact—before the Civil War. Paddyrollers patrolled the roads looking for slaves who had escaped their owners, or free black men who had become "obnoxious or unruly," according to one account. Paddles were used as punishment on the slaves, who were forced to bend over barrels. Upon impact, the barrels would roll, thus the name "paddyrollers."

On the road to Henderson you'll find convenience stores named Smackers (not Smuckers!) and El Cheapo Gas. Tobacco Road? It intersects U.S. 1 in Middleburg. Henderson might be the geographical center of the Trailer Park Belt. Mobile home manufacturers hate the word "trailer." They don't even like "mobile home," preferring the more antiseptic "manufactured housing." Mobile home dealers line U.S. 1 in Henderson like flowers. Westwood, Freedom Homes, Ted Parker Home Sales, Goodson's Mobile Home Store, and Homeboy Housing, among others, are on the highway.

Henderson is unofficial capital of the Trailer Park State; Texas has more mobile homes, but North Carolina has the most per capita. There are 8 million mobile homes in the country; North Carolina has more than one million. One in sixteen Americans lives in a mobile home or "manufactured housing."

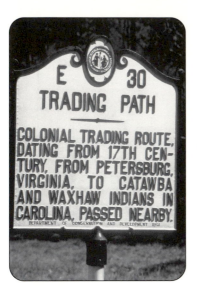

Norlina.

North of Henderson.

What did former Clinton advisor James Carville say about mobile homes? "Drag a hundred-dollar bill through a trailer park and there's no telling what you'll find." Carville is just the latest in a long line of trailer park bashers. J. Edgar Hoover called them "dens of vice and corruption, haunted by nomadic prostitutes, hardened criminals, white slavers, and promiscuous college students."

Susan Orlean began an article for *The New Yorker* this way: "A guy known as the Catman lived in Portland Meadows Mobile Home Park for a while; he had a hundred cats and a mouse-colored trailer, which he parked in Space 19, near a knobby maple tree." Among the community's residents were "a man who hated everyone and used a battery-powered bullhorn for normal conversation," "a phony blind

Middleburg.

priest with a Great Dane seeing-eye dog," and a man who claimed to be Mikhail Gorbachev's cousin.

Fact is, mobile homes are a comfortable, inexpensive alternative, especially for young couples, to "normal" homes. According to the 1990 U.S. Census, the average mobile home cost $27,800 new, the average new house $149,000.

Nearly 50 percent of mobile home residents are between the ages of twenty-five and forty-four; nearly a quarter are sixty-five and over. Twenty-five percent of all the homes built in the last twenty-five years in this country have rolled up to their sites on wheels. And "mobile" is not even an appropriate term; 95 percent of all mobile homes go from the factory to a site, never to be moved again.

Back in 1929, Arthur G. Sherman became the first large-scale producer of what were then called trailer coaches. In the late 1940s, the first house trailers were built. In 1955, Elmer Frey started building ten-foot-wide coaches; Frey is credited with coining the term "mobile home."

"A lot of us snotty folks who grew up in houses sneer at those who lived in homes on wheels," says Todd Kimmel, publisher of the superb magazine *Lost Highways*. "We shouldn't. Regular folks live in them."

Business U.S. 1,
Henderson.

Southern Culture on the Skids, the white-trash band whose albums have included *Dirt Track Date* and *Plastic Seat Sweat*, have written about trailer parks. Rick Miller, singer, guitarist, and banjo player for the Skids, grew up in Henderson. One of his songs is called "The Man That Wrestles the Bear," about a fellow who worked in a mobile home factory in Henderson with Miller's father. Every year, the fellow would try to wrestle the bear at the county fair—and get his butt kicked.

Henderson is a colorful crossroads community. A vintage Bull Durham sign is splashed across the side of a building on Business U.S. 1 downtown. The Little Hotel, which is actually quite grand, is at the corner of U.S. 1 and Route 158 (Garnett Street).

It's getting dark, though, and we have a movie to catch. Round up the lawn chairs, honey, we're going to the drive-in!

———

At a hotel in Henderson, I ask the clerk how to get to the drive-in. "There's no drive-in here," she says.

"You sure?" I ask. "There was one here the last time I was through." "That hasn't been open in a long time," she replies. "The closest one is in Raleigh."

Well, the drive-in is less than 2 miles from the hotel, and it definitely is open. OK, so maybe it isn't showing the greatest double-bill in the history of American cinema—*Woo* and *Species II*—but who goes to a drive-in to see the movie?

Well, me, for one, because I'm by myself.

"It's the perfect drive-in movie," Jeff Brand says of *Species II*. "Plenty of naked women and things bursting out of people's stomachs."

The wisecracking Brand drives a VW Beetle and runs the projector at the Raleigh Road Drive-In, on Business U.S. 1. Beth Lyles, whose father, N.T., bought the drive-in in 1977, is the owner. There's none of that fancy automated, computerized, digital operation you get at the local impersonal multiplex.

The Raleigh Road Drive-In is one of only three operating U.S. 1 drive-ins. (The Big Mo Drive-In in Monetta, South Carolina, opened in spring 1999.) The reels come in big tin cans and are loaded by

Jeff Brand is the wisecracking projectionist at the Raleigh Road Drive-In.

hand. *Titanic* came in twelve reels, and Brand had to load every one himself.

There is nothing like parking in the front row of a drive-in (or better yet, the back row) and watching a great monster movie like *Godzilla* (the original, without Raymond Burr) or a classic road movie like *Cannonball Run*, or even an awful movie like *Species II*, which, like the original *Species*, has one redeeming quality: the main character is a curvy blonde alien. You don't get those much in movies anymore.

"The alien DNA has infected us," one character says in *Species II*. "It's time we infected them!"

"There's a kid who lives next door who runs around in the parking lot in a cape as soon as the movie starts," Brand warns me.

Sure enough, there he is, dashing between the cars, a spectral figure in flowing cape.

The drive-in opened July 15, 1949. The first movie was *Ali Baba and the Forty Thieves*. It was called the Moonglow Outdoor Theatre; the words are barely visible today on the spectacular ochre-colored outdoor screen on U.S. 1. Admission was forty cents;

children under twelve in cars were free. "Walk-ins" were forty cents, too.

"Dress as you please . . . perfect vision from either the front or back seats of your car," went an ad in the local newspaper.

The world's first drive-in was the Automobile Movie Theater, in Pennsauken, New Jersey (not Camden, as most accounts would have it). Richard Hollingshead, sales manager of Whiz Auto Products Company, came up with the idea. He mounted a 1928 Kodak projector on his Model A Ford and hung a screen on a large maple tree in his backyard. Hollingshead and his cousin W. W. Smith opened their drive-in on June 6, 1933. A sign out front read:

Drive-in Theater
World's First
Sit in Your Car
See and Hear Movies
25 cents per car
25 cents per person
3 or more persons one dollar

The Automobile Movie Theater featured a playground and concession stand, which would become staples of drive-ins everywhere. The Saco Drive-In, on U.S. 1 in Maine, which opened in July 1939, was one of the earliest drive-ins. Some, like the Panther Drive-In in Lufkin, Texas, had room for 3,000 cars.

In 1948, Edward Brown, a former navy pilot, opened the first Fly-In Drive-In Theater, in New Jersey. (A first-rate Web site devoted to drive-ins can be found at www.driveintheater.com.)

"In the fifties, the drive-in was the hottest thing going in America," says Don Sanders, author, with his wife, Susan, of *The American Drive-In Movie Theatre* (Motorbooks Publishing, 1997). "Porter Waggoner and Patsy Cline did music shows at drive-ins. Buddy Holly got his start at the Sky-Vue Drive-In at Lamesa, Texas. It's still there."

One time, patrons at a Miller, South Dakota, drive-in were halfway through the movie when a tornado tore through the area, sending the screen flying. The storm passed, leaving stunned moviegoers facing a screen that was no longer there. The movie they had been watching? *On a Clear Day You Can See Forever.*

By the mid-1960s, the handwriting was on the big screen. Skyrocketing land values, increasing development, changing lifestyles, television, and, later, cable TV and the VCR, made Saturday nights at the drive-in a fading memory. In 1981 there were 3,354 drive-ins (and 12,291 indoor theaters) in the United States; by 1994 there were 850 drive-ins (and 24,789 indoor theaters, most of them with multiple screens).

At the Raleigh Road Drive-In, car speakers are available, but only in Row 6; everyone else must turn on a radio. The drive-in is open year-round. "Some years we don't even get any snow," Beth says. Many patrons still call it the Moonglow.

Inside the bunkerlike projection room, Brand tells me about a nudist colony once located just off U.S. 1 in Kittrell, south of Henderson. It was called the Middle of Nowhere Naturist Colony. Brand wrote about his search for the nudist colony in *Crinkum Crankum,* the North Vance High School literary arts magazine; Brand was editor-in-chief in 1998.

N. T. Lyles passed away in 1991. Beth, a librarian in town, now runs the show. She has no intention of letting that big screen go dark, as it has in many states. Today, there are about six hundred drive-ins left; New Jersey, birthplace of the drive-in, lost its last one in 1991.

"I'd like to do an all-night program," Beth says, joining us in the projection room around midnight. "But Vicky in the snack bar would kill me."

No, I didn't stop in. Franklinton.

———

The 40-mile ride to Raleigh is dotted with trailer parks, Baptist churches, car repair garages. A sign in Franklinton advertises "Massage—All Girl Staff." "County Line Turkey Shoot," reads another.

Sprawling corporate complexes—Sprint's regional headquarters, Burlington Industries' Wake plant—share the road with New Touch Worship Center, Conduit Dentistry, and Insurance Authorities Furniture. The highway is Capital Boulevard in Wake Forest and Raleigh, the state capital. It piggybacks onto I-440 (the Beltline), splits, then joins Route 64.

Apex received its name in the 1870s when a surveying crew showed it to be the highest point

Want to go north and south at the same time?
In Sanford, you can.

Sanford.

(504 feet above sea level) on the railroad right-of-way between Norfolk and Sanford.

Signs for Old U.S. 1 between Raleigh and Sanford speak of a time the highway ran a different, although parallel, course. The road winds through the pines to Vass. Calvin and Hobbs Aluminum Company is on the northbound side, and so is a palm reader who promises to "solve all problems." "NRA = USA," announces a billboard in Dunrovin.

Southern Pines, a woodsy version of the densely packed commercial strips up and down U.S. 1, is a popular stop for the three highway essentials: gas-food-lodging. Biscuitville is here. The Cardinal Park-Motel, with its pretty, duck-filled lake, marks Pinebluff.

Dunrovin.

Camp Mackall.

Halfway between Pinebluff and Hoffman, the road makes a wide curve. Keep your eyes open or you'll miss the sign, on the northbound side, for "Special Forces Road." Down that road are tough soldiers, hellish obstacle courses, and the ghost of John Wayne.

———

"Fighting soldiers from the sky. . . ." Barry Sadler's "The Ballad of the Green Berets," the number-one song in 1966 for five weeks in a row, plays during the opening credits for *The Green Berets*, the only major film released during the Vietnam War that supported U.S. involvement.

John Wayne, who co-directed, plays Col. Mike Kirby, while David Janssen is the antiwar newspaper reporter who starts out condemning U.S. involvement in the war but ends up in the trenches passing mortar shells to soldiers.

It is not one of Wayne's better movies, and not a very good introduction, either, to the Special Forces, known as the Green Berets for their trademark caps.

"One can say, 'What's so remarkable about [jumping out of planes]?'" Aaron Bank says. "Conventional Airborne and Marine Recon do that. But Special Forces go beyond that. They operate deep in enemy territory, right into the enemy heartland, and for indefinite periods. Not for two or three days, but weeks, months, or longer, and they operate in those areas, when required, in civilian attire and in enemy uniform."

Chief Warrant Officer Douglas Caylor, Camp Mackall.

Bank, a retired army colonel and founder of the Special Forces, appears in the video *The Green Berets: Fighting Men Series* (Garuda Productions, 1993), a good introduction to the history and role of America's secret soldiers.

Who exactly are the Special Forces and what do they do? The answers can be found at the end of Special Forces Road, at Camp Mackall.

"This is not classified here," Jerry F. Clemons says by way of introduction. "Primarily what we do here is army Green Berets—Special Forces—training."

Clemons, who spent eleven years in the marines and eleven years in the army before becoming the first-ever civilian manager of Camp Mackall, sits behind his desk in a tiled-floor, bare-bones office. A brown vinyl couch is in the corner, next to a table covered with camo-colored cloth. A pair of black army boots stand at attention next to a bookshelf.

About two thousand Special Forces candidates pass through here every year. Soldiers come from army posts around the world, but they must be at least a sergeant if enlisted and at least a captain if an officer. The qualification begins with a twenty-one-day "weed-out." Half of all candidates don't make it any further.

"They do a lot of physical things," Clemons explains. "I don't want to say too much because they don't want young soldiers knowing what to expect before they get here. They are guaranteed four hours of uninterrupted sleep a day, but they never know when those four hours will be. They eat MREs [meals ready-to-eat]. They can go through the mess hall, but they can't eat in the mess hall; they eat their meals outdoors."

No TVs, VCRs, or microwaves are allowed in the barracks. No linens are supplied with the metal bunk beds. No overnight passes or furloughs allowed. No alcohol is available in the PX; no alcohol can be brought on base.

"Going into a barracks at Fort Bragg is like going into a Howard Johnson's," Clemons says. "Not here."

Soldier, Camp Mackall.

The "physical things" include an encounter with Nasty Nick. NN is an obstacle course named after Special Forces Col. James "Nick" Rowe, who spent five years as a POW in Vietnam and later headed the army's Survival, Evasion, Resistance, and Escape (SERE) training program.

The obstacle course, which winds through a picturesque grove of pine trees, looks like it was designed during the Inquisition.

Soldiers leap from stump to stump (often on wet days; look out broken ankle); shimmy their way on ropes over rocks; crawl through dark, wet pipes; swing from bars; climb to the top of a pit using only their backs and legs; and in the ultimate test, climb a rope to the top of a platform, run across narrow boards, and then scale an A-frame ladder that gets increasingly smaller and abruptly ends at the top of a three-story-high net—over which you must climb and clamber down the other side. I got dizzy just looking at it.

"A lot of troops from Fort Bragg like to come out here and use it," Clemons says. "It's quite challenging."

In *Apocalypse Now*, Captain Willard (Martin Sheen) is in awe of Kurtz (Marlon Brando) after reading he went through SF training at age thirty-

Jerry Clemons, manager, Camp Mackall.

eight: "I did it when I was nineteen. It damn near wasted me."

The Special Forces grew out of the Office of Strategic Services (OSS), which conducted counter-intelligence, commando, and guerrilla warfare missions during World War II. After the war, the agency's espionage activities were assigned to the CIA, while commando and guerrilla missions passed to Special Forces.

SF was not welcomed enthusiastically within the military at first. John F. Kennedy changed that. He was the first president to recognize the importance of counter-insurgency. On a visit to Fort Bragg, Kennedy was greeted by Special Forces troops purposely wearing their not-as-yet-military-approved green berets, adopted from the caps British commandos wore during World War II.

In *Fighting Men*, Lt. Gen. William P. Yarborough recalls it was quite an effort to find enough berets to go around for everyone in preparation for the president's visit.

"They came out of packs, they came out of dime stores, they came from all over the place," he says, smiling.

A soldier's got to do his laundry. Camp Mackall.

Kennedy saw Special Forces performing a counter-insurgency role in Southeast Asia, and it was the behind-enemy-lines missions by such groups as McCullough's Airborne Tigers that brought the Green Berets fame during Vietnam, and resulted in the movie, the hit song, and Robin Moore's best-seller, *The Green Berets*.

In 1980, Col. Charles Beckwith's Delta Force, composed largely of Special Forces troops, unsuccessfully tried to free hostages held in the American Embassy in Teheran. Delta Force, headquartered at Fort Bragg, trained at Camp Mackall.

The camp, which opened in March 1942 as Camp Hoffman, served as the home of the U.S. Airborne Command. It is named after Pvt. John Thomas Mackall, who in 1942 became one of the first American paratroopers to die in combat.

If you miss twenty-four hours of training at Mackall—sprained ankle, bad cold, whatever—you're out of here.

The base's tiny PX offers everything from aspirin, batteries, and camo-colored bungee cords to soda, snacks, and reading material (*Playboy's Voluptuous Vixens*, *Soldier of Fortune* magazine, and copies of *Five Years to Freedom*, an account of Nick Rowe's five years in captivity).

About nine hundred soldiers visit the twenty-four-hour medical clinic every month. Common ailments: blisters, sprained ankles, heat prostration. "No Whining," reads a placard on the wall. There is a snapshot of one soldier with a blister that covers practically his entire foot. Underneath the photo is the caption: "If your blister is worse than this one, we will consider a med drop."

Alpha, Fox, and Gulf companies handle Special Forces training here. Maj. Patrick Eberhart is Fox Company commander.

"There's a glorified Hollywood notion to what Special Forces does," the City Island, New York, native says. "Even within the army, people have that Rambo impression—you're going to put a bandanna on and run into the woods. The reality is quite different."

About three thousand Special Forces soldiers are currently based in thirty-five countries in everything from "counter-rev" (counter-revolutionary) to peacekeeping and medical missions.

If they survive the twenty-one-day "weed-out," candidates go through advanced weapons and demolitions training, small unit tactics, reconnaissance and night missions, and hand-to-hand fighting, among other subjects.

The course also includes Robin Sage, a sixteen-day exercise in which soldiers perform various missions in a 6,400-acre area, north and west of Mackall, that is transformed into a fictitious country known as the People's Republic of Pineland, complete with its own flag. Local towns and residents participate in Robin Sage, which is held four times a year.

> "An interminable monotony of signs, billboards, and ugly roadside slums, a veritable nightmare to the pleasure-seeking motorist. No need to describe it."
>
> Elizabeth B. Lawton and Walter Lawton, *Nature* magazine, May 1941

Special Forces school has three phases; those who finish phase three graduate, get their green berets, and head to Fort Bragg for foreign language training.

"Young soldiers come in, they think they're going to kick doors in," Eberhart says. "The whole purpose is to find people who will know what to do when they're in another country, on their own."

I want one of those Cheerios shirts. North Carolina Motor Speedway, Rockingham.

A lot of guys have gotten used to seeing this car in front of them. Jeff Gordon's car, North Carolina Motor Speedway.

Imagine a jet plane landing on your head. No, imagine a dozen jet planes landing on your head. One hundred thousand people around you are yelling their heads off, but you can't hear a thing because of the roaring in your ears that threatens to make your head explode.

"Are we having fun yet?" I wanted to scream, but it wouldn't have made any difference. There are two places where no one can hear you scream—outer space, and in the pit area at a NASCAR race. I thought it would be fun to see America's fastest-growing spectator sport up close and personal, and what better place than The Rock?

The Rock, as every NASCAR fan can tell you, is North Carolina Motor Speedway, located on U.S. 1 in Rockingham, about 10 miles south of Camp Mackall. Twice a year, The Rock hosts a Winston Cup race—the Goodwrench 400 in February and the AC Delco 400 in November.

Drivers are known not so much by their names as by their numbers—24, 3, 6, 88, 2, and so on. Any NASCAR fan can reel off the matching names quicker than the alphabet—Jeff Gordon, Dale Earn-hardt, Mark Martin, Dale Jarrett, Rusty Wallace. 10? That's Ricky Rudd. 17? Darrell Waltrip. 44? Kyle Petty, son of all-time great Richard Petty. There's Lake Speed (9), Hut Stricklin (8), Rick Mast (75), Bret Bodine (11), and in a great-name category all his own, Dick Trickle (90).

I love Dick Trickle. Trickle, of Wisconsin Rapids, Wisconsin, is the oldest active NASCAR driver never to have won a Winston Cup race. Oh, he's won plenty of times—1,200 races on shorter tracks in a thirty-five-year career—but he's never won a Winston Cup race, held nearly every weekend of the year from February to November.

The GM Goodwrench 400, North Carolina Motor Speedway.

North Carolina Motor Speedway.

Part of the problem is that Trickle didn't start full-time Winston Cup racing until he was forty-eight. Even then, in 1989, he was Rookie of the Year, finishing a career-best fifteenth in the overall standings. Maybe Number 90 would finally break through at The Rock, where he's always done well.

The pre-race atmosphere is fun, as fans check out souvenirs and memorabilia for sale in mobile trailers. Sales of NASCAR merchandise jumped from 80 million dollars in 1990 to 800-plus million dollars in 1998, and is expected to top 1 billion dollars in 1999.

Yes, races still attract a bunch of good ol' boys who just want to have fun, but NASCAR's audience goes far beyond the mobile-home-dwelling, Pabst Blue Ribbon–swilling stereotype. Thirty percent of

NASCAR fans make more than fifty thousand dollars a year; 55 percent have at least some college education—figures comparable to other major sports. A male-dominated spectator sport? Hardly. Women make up 40 percent of all fans.

NASCAR, which celebrated its fiftieth anniversary in 1998, was built, as Mike Hembree explained in *Inside NASCAR* magazine, on a foundation of sand and dirt. Men were driving cars at shocking speeds on Daytona's hard-packed beaches as early as 1902.

On winding backroads in the Carolinas and Georgia, moonshiners drove souped-up cars to deliver their product. They argued whose car was fastest, and as early as the 1930s settled those arguments on crude ovals cut into cow pastures.

In 1934, William Henry Getty "Big Bill" France, a driver and race promoter, moved to Daytona, where drivers had carved out a course that wound along the beach and the parallel asphalt of Highway A1A. Beach racing was wet and wild. Cars occasionally dashed into the surf and incoming tides sometimes ended races early.

In 1948, France became president of the newly formed National Association for Stock Car Automobile Racing, headquartered at 88 Main Street, Daytona Beach, just off U.S. 1. There were fifty-two sanctioned races that first year, but the first season

U.S. 1 Cruisin' Inn, Rockingham.

of real consequence came in 1949, when NASCAR began Strictly Stock racing—drivers using cars similar to the ones regular folks used on the road.

The first Strictly Stock race was held at Charlotte Speedway in North Carolina. Glenn Dunnaway crossed the finish line first, but his 1947 Ford, a converted moonshine hauler, was later declared illegal "because its springs had been enhanced in order to support heavy loads of liquor in the trunk," according to Hembree.

The first NASCAR premier-division champion, Red Bryon, earned 5,800 dollars; Jeff Gordon won 4.2 million dollars as Winston Cup champion in 1997—and nearly 6.2 million dollars in 1998.

Darlington Speedway, in Darlington, South Carolina, changed the face and future of NASCAR racing; in 1950, stock car racing's first 500-mile race, the Southern 500, was held at Darlington. The 1954 season saw the Grand National season's first road race, a 100-mile race in Linden, New Jersey, on a 2-mile course that included the runways of Linden Airport, located on U.S. 1.

In 1959, with the first running of the Daytona 500 (Lee Petty, father of Richard Petty, won by inches), NASCAR entered a new era of expansion. New tracks started popping up: Charlotte Motor Speedway, what are now Atlanta Motor Speedway and Bristol (Tenn.) Motor Speedway, and, in 1965, North Carolina Motor Speedway.

In 1967, Richard Petty, well on his way to becoming a NASCAR legend, won twenty-seven times out of forty-eight starts, including ten in a row. NASCAR's modern era began in 1972, with Winston signing on as series sponsor and Bill France Jr. succeeding his father as NASCAR president.

In 1976, Janet Guthrie became the first woman to compete in a modern-era NASCAR Winston Cup event. In 1981, ESPN televised its first NASCAR race,

the Atlanta Journal 500. Other networks came on board, giving the sport the national exposure it needed to grow beyond its southern roots.

Corporate America jumped on the NASCAR bandwagon, sponsoring drivers and races (the Jiffy Lube 300, the Miller Lite 400, the Food City 500) and offering NASCAR-licensed products. That accounts for the jumble of brand names found on race cars, and results in some cool-looking merchandise, including the red-and-yellow-striped Kellogg's Corn Flakes Racing Hendrick Motorsports Terry Labonte No. 5 jacket I bought at Labonte's trailer before the GM Goodwrench 400 at The Rock. NASCAR drivers, as L. Jon Wertheim explains in *Sports Illustrated*, are independent contractors funded by corporate sponsors; one consequence of this is that drivers own their image and cut their own merchandising and licensing deals.

Each Winston Cup race brings in some 60–80 million dollars to its host community, with average attendance ranging from 100,00 to 150,000. Some have derisively referred to it as "500 miles of left turns," but stock-car racing is the fastest-growing sport in the country. NASCAR annual revenues top 2 billion dollars; between 1990 and 1996, Winston Cup attendance increased 65 percent.

"We honestly feel that no sport has anything over NASCAR," Bill France Jr. says.

So you're going to attend your first NASCAR race? My advice: forget the cheap plastic earphones you can buy at the track, and instead invest in an official Winston Cup headphone-radio. You can hear the race, and keep your eardrums from shattering, especially if you're lucky (or unlucky) enough to be in the pits.

"And now, ladies and gentlemen," announcer Hill Overton proclaims, "the most exciting moment in professional sports. Gentlemen, start your engines."

A roar goes up from the crowd, and the cars blast down the 1,300-foot-long front straightaway. For the next three hours, the pits will be a scene of both frenzied activity and surreal calm, as crews change tires and other parts in record time, then scan the track like hawks, following their drivers around the 1.017-mile oval.

From the announcer, these magic words: "Dick Trickle is fourteenth."

The John Deere pit crew is next to the Skittles crew, which is next to the Gum-Out guys. Huge rolling toolboxes, TV monitors, and tires mark each space. Gasoline is stored in canisters that resemble workshop vacuums.

Here's Rusty Wallace dropping down to the inside of Mark Martin . . . Ricky Craven is sitting right behind them. . . . We've had some good racing in the first 162 laps at North Carolina Motor Speedway. . . .

RVs, motorhomes, even old school buses are packed around the infield, their rooftops offering prime race-viewing—and partying—seats.

Jeff Gordon a while ago was running in the thirty-first position. Well, he's done a little driving. He's now in the thirteenth position. . . .

Over the headphones, the crackling reports sound like dispatches from the front lines.

The noise along the banked turns is so loud, my headphones shake. After a few minutes there, I start to walk away and stagger slightly, my balance shot.

We just passed the halfway point. It's been a competitive race. Fifteen lead changes, ten different leaders, three cautions, average speed, 118.328. . . .

With 157 laps to go:

Ernie Irvan is trying to get the seventh spot from Dick Trickle. . . . Trickle is slipping away. . . .

A graphic flashes on the screen: Trickle, fifty-six years old. 230 races. 0 won.

The 42 car—Joe Nemechek—crashes into the wall on lap 272. By lap 282, the familiar 24—Jeff Gordon—is in second. By lap 290, he's in the lead.

Best seats in a noisy house. The GM Goodwrench 400, North Carolina Motor Speedway.

The race is a blur of brand names: Valvoline, Ford Credit, McDonald's, HotWheels, Cheerios, Kellogg's, Tide, Skittles, Citgo.

Dick Trickle's car has been retired for the day.

With twenty-seven laps to go, it's Gordon, Wallace, Bodine, Martin, Spencer.

I've been to a lot of races at The Rock, and this has been one of the best of them. Very entertaining . . .

There is a pile-up on the back straightaway. Six cars are involved.

This one's going to get physical before it's over.

Number 24—Jeff Gordon—barrels across the finish line, winning the Goodwrench 400 for the second year in a row (eight months later, he would win his third Winston Cup championship in four years).

"We took time to make some adjustments," Gordon says in the winner's circle after taking the obligatory swig of Pepsi, a team sponsor. "We went one way, it didn't work, we went the other way. The Good Lord blessed us today."

For Dick Trickle, there would be another day, someday. He ended 1998 still looking for his first Winston Cup win. He finished twenty-ninth in the Winston Cup final standings, with one top-ten finish. In 1997, he had two top-five finishes.

It wasn't a happy year. His nephew, Chris Trickle, a rising star on NASCAR's SouthWest tour (he had been voted most popular driver) died in March. He was shot in the head while driving to play tennis with a friend.

——

Downtown Rockingham is 10 miles south of The Rock. On the way are Sandy Bear Rottweilers and the Cruisin' Inn. The #1 Diner is just north of town. South of Rockingham, the highway passes farms and thick stands of pine. Suddenly, the road curves and a marker appears. Welcome to South Carolina.

SOUTH CAROLINA

US 1 traverses the central section of South Carolina, an area of deep sandy ridges with sparse and stunted vegetation. Short-leaf pine and blackjack oak are the chief trees. For years this was the most poverty-stricken section of the state, redeemed only by the fall-line cities and the few towns that were settled mainly as resorts. . . . The highway crosses the Big Pee Dee River, passing through an old covered bridge, the only one on US 1. Each piece of wood was cut and numbered, its place being determined in advance of the building.

—*U.S. One, Maine to Florida,* American Guide Series, 1938

The covered bridge over the Big Pee Dee River (named after an Indian tribe and said to have been the inspiration for Stephen Foster's "Way Down upon the Swanee River") is long gone, replaced by a steel span. A faded red-and-yellow sign for the Wallace Motel (Large Truck Parking/Waterbeds/In Room Phone) sprouts from bushes on the highway's northbound side.

Nearby is a historical marker on Sherman's March. On my last visit to tiny Wallace, a man and a woman stood on U.S. 1 holding a sign that read "Hungry In Need."

Cheraw, a pretty, tree-shaded town, is the home, according to the welcome sign, of Dizzy Gillespie. The term "lynch law" is said to have originated in Cheraw during revolutionary times. Col. Charles Lynch had been named judge advocate to serve at the court-martial of Gen. Nathaniel Greene. So arbitrary were some of Lynch's decisions, according to the WPA guide, that the expression came to denote the passing of sentence without trial. William Lynch, a contemporary of Charles who operated as a vigilante in Virginia, is also cited as the source of the term.

Welcome signs, a common sight along U.S. 1 from Maine to Florida, are not only informative (see endpapers) but often whimsical. The welcome sign to Patrick, 13 miles south of Cheraw, reads: "Home of the Pinestraw Festival. Squirrel and Bird Sanctuary." After Patrick, the highway enters a lost

Civil War marker, Wallace.

world of pine forest, rolling hills, and quiet beauty—Sandhills State Forest and Carolina Sandhills National Wildlife Refuge, two of the more remarkable, yet unknown, sights on U.S. 1.

——

Asked how many rangers work at the 45,000-acre Carolina Sandhills National Wildlife Refuge, Kay McCutcheon smiles.

"The Fish and Wildlife Service," she says, "is not into rangers."

That would be the National Park Service. The U.S. Fish and Wildlife Service, part of the Department of the Interior, is manager of the five hundred–plus national wildlife refuges, everything from Koyukuk/Nowitna National Wildlife Refuge in Alaska to the Rachel Carson National Wildlife Refuge in Wells, Maine.

The refuges include some well-known areas—Okefenokee NWR in Georgia, Chincoteague NWR in Virginia, and the Great Swamp NWR in New Jersey. But most are little known and not on the usual tourist itinerary. The refuges, however, offer a wide range of recreational activities—fishing, hiking, camping, boating, even hunting.

When land for the Carolina Sandhills National Wildlife Refuge was purchased by the federal government under the Resettlement Act, the soil was badly eroded and little wildlife was to be found. Accounts at the time referred to the area as a "biological desert." Efforts began immediately to restore the damaged, barren land to healthy, rich habitat for the plants and animals that once lived there.

Longleaf pine/wiregrass, the refuge's characteristic habitat, once covered more than 90 million acres from Texas to Virginia. Less than 2 million acres are left.

The biggest single piece is in the Carolina Sandhills NWR, which lies along the fall line separating the Piedmont Plateau from the Atlantic Coastal Plain. McCutcheon has worked at the refuge for nearly thirty years.

"To the average person, it doesn't look like much," she says in the refuge office, set on a rise overlooking a deep pine forest. "I like the fact that we have so many hidden treasures."

The refuge, which gets about 65,000 visitors a year, is home to many threatened and endangered species, including the pine barrens tree frog and southern bald eagle.

But the refuge's star resident is the red-cockaded woodpecker. In the 1970s, the refuge gained national attention because it was found to have the largest concentration of RCWs, as they are called, in the country.

Woodpeckers, naturally, need trees, and much of the prescribed burning in the refuge today is done for their benefit. The burning mimics the natural fires that historically burned through longleaf pine/wiregrass. The fires suppress the growth of hardwood trees, creating an open parklike habitat preferred by Woody and other plants and animals native to the ecosystem.

About 12,000–15,000 acres of refuge are burned every year, most of it by "aerial ignition." Ping pong ball–like dispensers filled with ammonium nitrate are dropped from airplanes, igniting upon contact with the ground.

The refuge is home to white bobtail deer, beaver ("doing real well, much to the chagrin of many people"), wild turkey ("they have made a real nice comeback here"), raccoon, otter, fox, bobcat, and many other animals. Great blue herons, egrets, red-tailed hawks, and northern harriers are commonly seen. Plants include pixie moss, three kinds of pitcher plant, and the pine barrens gentian, a "spectacular" cobalt-blue plant, McCutcheon says.

The Goat Man knew the Sandhills well. Chester McCartney was his name, and he and his wagon, led by a team of eighteen goats and festooned with pots, pans, license plates, and lanterns, was a frequent, if odd, sight along America's backroads in the thirties, forties, and fifties.

"There were quite a number of years where he was rambling up and down the highway," McCutcheon says of the Goat Man and U.S. 1.

"Line by line, crinkle by crinkle, the topography of an America which was is etched in the leather canvas of Chester McCartney's face," is how freelance writer Jerome Chandler described the Goat Man. "The face speaks eloquently of macadam roads—100,000 miles of them—and gently borne loads. He started out in Iowa in the '30s, his rich farm a victim of the Great Depression. The only things the bank left him were a couple of books—*Robinson Crusoe* and the Bible—and a herd of goats."

"I have been called crazy, stupid, ignorant, and many other uncomplimentary names," the Goat Man once said, "because of my way of life—herding a passel of smelly goats from Florida to Maine to Washington and California."

He and his goats made it to every state except Hawaii. By the late 1960s, the Goat Man had stopped wandering, settling into a rusting hulk of a yellow school bus in south Georgia. The Goat Man died in November 1998 in a Macon nursing home. He was ninety-seven.

The Goat Man would feel right at home on U.S. 1 through the Sandhills, because there are few stretches along the 2,450-mile highway that are as unspoiled and untraveled.

> "The romance of the road is no better expressed than by America's Number One Highway, U.S. 1."
>
> David A. Heller,
> *The Highway Magazine*, November 1951

No overnight camping is allowed in the refuge, but there is a 9-mile-long auto tour, three hiking trails, and fifteen to twenty ponds open for fishing. The lookout tower halfway through the auto tour is a great spot to pull over and do absolutely nothing. Wiregrass sways in the breeze; the faint call of a bird echoes in the distance. Chances are you'll have the tower, and what seems like the entire refuge, to yourself.

"The Sandhills gets under your skin," McCutcheon says. "You're out there, you can hear the pines, the wind blowing through them."

"Whispering pines?"

"Yes," she replies, her eyes lighting up. "Whispering pines."

———

Peach groves line the road to McBee. Bethune, 7 miles south, is home of the Chicken Strut, one of many lively, local festivals found along U.S. 1. In Cassatt, a big sign on the northbound side advertises the

No, I've never done the Chicken Strut. Bethune.

Michelle Wilson, manager, Hard Times Cafe, Cassatt.

Hard Times Cafe. Times aren't that hard in the Hard Times Cafe, but owner H. C. Robinson thought it would be an appropriate name.

"I retired from DuPont and already owned this building," he says, sitting in the cheery, two-room restaurant. "I wanted to open a restaurant. My wife said, 'Your first retirement check came in the mail.' I said, 'Don't cash it, frame it. It'll remind us when we hit hard times.'"

This was once Brown's Grocery. In the 1980s, it was a game room, with pool tables and poker machines. Hard Times opened in 1992. H.C.'s daughter, Michelle Wilson, runs the restaurant.

"Today, we have ham [with the all-you-can-eat daily lunchtime buffet]; tomorrow we have roast beef; Thursday we have pork chops; Friday we have fried catfish and salmon stew," Michelle says. "We have chicken every day. Everything's cooked in fatback, for the flavor. It's real country. A lot of people come in for the cornbread. We have fritters, biscuits." She smiles. "Country cooking."

Check out the Monday buffet selections—BBQ ribs, Salisbury steak, chicken, rice, mashed potatoes, black-eyed peas, string beans, yams, turnip greens, broccoli with cheese, cornbread.

Women rule this place. Geneva Paul is the cook; Martha Wilson, Michelle's mother-in-law, is the waitress; and Zulene Robinson, her eighty-four-year-old grandmother, comes in to help.

H.C., a big guy who looks like Kenny Rogers, worked at the DuPont plant in Lugoff, Kershaw County's largest employer. His wife, Annette, still works there.

"We opened up as a barbecue and dinner buffet place," H.C. recalls. "I did all the meat. Barbecue all day, barbecue all night. That was killing me.

"Fridays are our big days," he adds. "People come by for the catfish. Thursdays, we grill pork chops outside on the grill."

"People don't sometimes realize what is on this road," Michelle says later.

One of these days, she's going to find out herself.

"My friends kid me—'You've never been out of South Carolina!'" She laughs. "I've never been to Florida. Georgia? I was there overnight."

Camden.

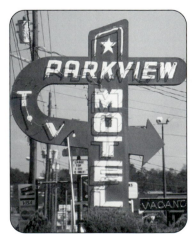

Lugoff.

There are clothing outlets, shoe outlets, furniture outlets, and handbag outlets, why not an Affordable Housing Outlet? There's one in Camden, oldest inland city in South Carolina.

"Free tickets to heaven. Details inside," says a sign outside a Baptist church. Sonics—"America's drive-in"—start appearing on U.S. 1. Elgin is Home of the Catfish Stomp, another one of the highway's small-town festivals. The Stomp, which includes a parade, carnival, and plenty of fried catfish and catfish stew, is held the first weekend of December.

Just south of Elgin, in Pontiac, a roadhouse sits on the highway's southbound side. Inside, it looks rough-and-tumble, but you're in good hands. The only letters on the sign outside are L, on one line, and I E F, on the next. I'm not sure what the I E F stand for, but the L stands for Larry. As in Larry's Redneck Bar.

Larry's Redneck Bar, Pontiac.

"My parents were two fine Christian people," says Larry Nelson. "They'd probably turn over in their graves if they knew I was running a beer joint."

Then again, they might approve if they saw the place. It's good ol' boy heaven, with NASCAR banners and Budweiser signs on the walls, poker machines in the main bar, pool tables in the side room, and the usual variety of pickled stuff in jars. But you don't have to be a redneck to love Larry's Redneck Bar.

"Why the name?" says Larry, who, like H. C. Robinson, worked at DuPont. "I spent the first twenty years trying to impress people; I spent the last twenty years having fun. I just decided, I'm going to do what I want to do. That to me is the definition of a redneck."

In the 1950s, the building housed a convenience store and gas station, owned by Frank Dial. Frank sold produce, bait and tackle, and beer. He died six years ago, and Larry, who had taken an early retirement from DuPont, bought the place.

"We got a lot of New York Yankees come in here," says Larry, and he doesn't mean the baseball team. "Pennsylvania Yankees, too. It's a conglomerate of people."

Dentsville.

"I got two degrees and a bunch of half degrees," says Bob, one regular.

"What's a half degree?"

"It's when you start on a degree and quit in midstream," he replies.

Larry has two cooks, both named Charlie, so he calls one Charlie and the other Charlie Charlie. Once a month, Larry does a barbecue and pig roast in the bar.

"I work for Iron and Steel," Bob proclaims. "I iron in the morning and steal at night."

At Larry's Redneck Bar, the entertainment comes free.

"Here comes the preacher!" someone yells.

"Here comes the damn preacher!" Carl Gambrell adds.

Sure enough, Doc, a retired highway patrolman and current justice of the peace, walks in. He's here for business and pleasure. He recently married two of the bar's regulars. There are papers to sign, so the three walk into the other room and spread the papers on the pool table.

"Parking for Confederates Only," announces a sign on the wall. "All others go back north."

"There are three rules in life," says another. "Shit happens. Shit happens often. And you got to get used to shit happening."

"I'm scared to leave, I'm scared to go home," says a regular at the bar. In his car are the pizza and the carton of milk his wife asked him to pick up. He bought them at 3:30 in the afternoon. It's now past nine.

Doc returns to the bar, his business concluded. He takes something out of his jacket pocket.

"This looks like an acorn, but I think it's one of those rubber nuts," he says, placing the nut on the bar. "It doesn't break."

Larry tries to smash it, but can't. The justice of the peace puts the nut on the bar and breaks it in two even pieces. It's a rubber nut, all right. Inside is a condom.

"Bunch of characters in here," Larry says, smiling.

———

When George Washington traveled in 1791 along what later became U.S. 1, he observed, "The whole road from Augusta to Columbia is a pine barren of the worst sort, being hilly as well as poor."

Columbia, founded in 1786, was one of the country's first planned communities; it was laid out with wide streets to prevent the spread of epidemics. U.S. 1 through the capital city and suburbs is one of the liveliest commercial stretches on the entire highway. Signs, billboards, and one-of-a-kind roadside businesses enliven the usual humdrum of fast-food franchises and national chain hotels.

Columbia.

One-stop shopping: fireworks, used cars, notary public. Columbia.

At a trailer-converted office at U.S. 1 and Parklane Road, you can find a notary public, used cars, and fireworks. Custom Sound is in the shape of a giant tape deck. "Trailers for rent," reads the Grand Motel's fabulous vintage sign, echoing Roger Miller's classic "King of the Road." Twenty-four-hour video arcades outnumber convenience stores.

"I'll buy anything except guns," announces the sign in front of Hursey's Trading Post. There's Dirty Boy Car Wash, and the 2 Close 4 Comfort Lounge.

U.S. 1 is Two Notch Road, then Millwood Avenue, Gervais Street, Meeting Street, and Augusta Highway. The state capitol is on the highway.

Main Street Pawn and Gun, Spirit of Life Church, and U.S. 1 Metro Flea Market are all on 1 in Lexington. Beyond Lexington, strawberries and peaches grow by the side of the road. Irrigation systems shoot water into the sandy soil. A business offers "Custom Processing—Beef Pork Deer Emu."

A sign indicating the road to Prosperity is in front of the Food Lion on 1 in Batesburg-Leesville.

Columbia.

Store mural, West Columbia.

"Trailers for sale or rent . . ."
Grand Motel, Columbia.

Batesburg.

Prosperity was once called Frog Level. Ridge Spring–Monetta High School might have the biggest front lawn of any high school in the country. Several miles south is Sand Hills Grocery, a k a The Monkey Store.

"The fellow who used to own it kept monkeys here," the manager says. "I'm the only one left."

"Welcome to Aiken, Proud Home of the Aiken High Hornets," says a welcome sign in the county seat. Want to order some takeout from Hog Heaven? Call 649-OINK.

South of Aiken, on U.S. 1's southbound side, is the Highway Holiness Church. Across the highway,

The former Monetta Drive-In reopened as The Big Mo Drive-In in spring 1999.

James Fulmer sells fireworks and tomatoes from his stand on U.S. 1 in Clearwater.

set up on a hill, is the Help St. John Holy Temple, a makeshift trailer church with "No Smoking—Holy Ground" signs outside.

A little red-and-white stand in front of the Rainbow Terrace Motel in Clearwater offers an interesting combination of goods: fireworks and tomatoes.

James Fulmer has been selling produce and fireworks on what he calls "the Number One Highway" for nine years. Apples, four for a dollar. Bananas, five for a dollar. Tomatoes, two dollars a basket. Pecans, two dollars a bag. Red onions, fifty cents a pound.

Sign south of Aiken.

"I've been in the fireworks business twenty-five years," says Fulmer, wearing a blue windbreaker and a Goodyear cap. My daddy sold produce. I ended up taking after him."

What sells better—the produce or the fireworks?

"Produce sells better in the summer," he replies. "Fireworks you have but two seasons—Christmas and Fourth of July."

Tomatoes, pecans, and bananas are in boxes out front. The fireworks are inside the little trailer— sparklers and firecrackers, Red Devils, Saturn missiles, and Bang Rockets.

Asked how long he's going to stay on Number One Highway, Fulmer, seventy-two, replies, "Rest of my life, as long as I live. I'm getting old. Ain't take no kind of medicine. I had colon cancer five years ago and they said it ain't come back.

"I'm in pretty good shape," he adds, smiling, "and I hope to stay that way."

About 4 miles later, the highway passes the former Tacky Tony's, with the two big replica M80s out front, then crosses the Savannah River into Georgia.

GEORGIA

In its 222.5-mile course in Georgia, US 1 S. of Augusta passes through only one town, Waycross, with a population exceeding 2,500. The highway traverses a rural section that is the locale of two outstanding works of modern fiction: Erskine Caldwell's novel, 'Tobacco Road,' from which the record-breaking play was adapted, and Caroline Miller's Pulitzer Prize novel of 1933, 'Lamb in His Bosom.' Charm and mellowed grace linger about the old homes, some of which date back almost to the Revolution, but more in evidence is the unpainted shack of the sharecropper, with sagging porch and paneless windows.

—*U.S. One, Maine to Florida*, American Guide Series, 1938

One of the few reminders of America's first successful motel chain stands on U.S. 1 northbound in Augusta. Well before Holiday Inns, Ramada Inns, and Howard Johnson's, Alamo Plaza Courts beckoned road-weary Americans. "Remember the Alamo Plaza," went the advertising for Edgar Lee Torrance's motel courts, modeled after the famous monument in his native Texas.

Torrance and his partner, Judge J. W. Bartlett, opened their first Alamo Plaza in Waco, Texas, in 1929. Singles were a dollar, doubles two dollars. "A Beautyrest Mattress on Every Bed, a Telephone in Every Room," proclaimed postcards. Alamo Plazas were distinguished by their white-stuccoed, bell-shaped false-front facades and drive-through registration buildings. Newspaper ads touted them as "The South's Finest Tourist Courts" and "America's Finest."

By 1960, thirty-four Alamo Plazas were scattered around the country, but the chain soon started to fall apart, victim of the interstate highway system and competition from new corporate giants like Holiday Inn, according to John Margolies, author of *Home away from Home: Motels in America* (Bulfinch Press, 1995). A few Alamo Plazas cling to life, "still stunning in their old-fashioned theatrical bravura," Margolies says.

In the 1920s, religious signs along the highway in Augusta startled motorists. "Because There is Wrath, Beware!" read one, the work of David Brinkman, a local evangelist.

Before there were Holiday Inns and Ramadas, there were Alamo Plaza Courts. Augusta.

Roadside signs today are less apocalyptic, but no less eye-catching. "Deer Processing RV Overnight Park" is the intriguing message on a sign on 1 in Wrens. The town was the boyhood home of Erskine Caldwell, author of *Tobacco Road* and *God's Little Acre*.

Tobacco Road did exist. It was a dirt road that ran along a ridge from northern Georgia to a point on the Savannah River below Augusta. Tobacco was hauled on mule-drawn carts over the road to the port, where it was loaded on boats.

John Deeres stand ready in a field at a tractor dealership in Louisville. Swainsboro is home to a Geor-

gia State Patrol barracks and Mom's Barbecue. The Suwanee Tourist Court in Wesley is a reminder of America's pre–motel-chain era. Lyons hosts the Southeast Georgia Soapbox Derby. Several miles south of Lyons is one of the more unusual intersections along the entire highway: U.S. 1 and Dasher Street.

Augusta.

Hot Doughnuts Now! Augusta.

Untitled, parking meters,
Augusta, Georgia.
From *North & South:*
Berenice Abbott's U.S. Route 1.
Courtesy of the Syracuse University
Art Collection.

The weather is frightful in the little town of Santa Claus, Georgia. Ominous black clouds roll overhead. The wind scatters paper across the road. Rain begins to pelt down.

Inside the Santa Claus Motel, though, it is warm and cozy. The smell of cats fills the air. Owner Stanley McDonald shuffles into the wood-paneled office to greet his visitor. A thunderous boom shakes the walls; lightning crackles somewhere nearby.

"I bought this place seven, eight years ago," says McDonald. "I bought it to get out of the big town. And I wanted something to piddle with."

The big town was Nashville, where he grew up. "Worked in a slaughterhouse, hardest work there is," he says.

Shady Grove Tourist Camp,
circa 1942, Lyons.

Santa Claus.

Santa Claus.

He's seventy-nine, and he's selling the motel. "This U.S. Highway One, it's gotten busier. The traffic has doubled, tripled since I've been here. It's picking up, but that don't make no difference to me. I just want to get out."

McDonald asks if I want to talk to the mayor of Santa Claus, and when I say sure, he calls him up.

"We've been a town since November 1941," says Bernard Harden, who lives on Dancer Street in Santa Claus, population 225.

The name can be traced to Calvin Green— "Farmer Green" as he was known—who had a pecan grove and country store on the highway.

"He started calling the place Santa Claus, more of a promotion than anything," explains Harden, a life insurance salesman who has five kids. "People called him Santa Claus. He had rosy cheeks. He looked the part."

There's at least one other Santa Claus in the country—Santa Claus, Indiana. Both towns do a nice business in answering or postmarking Christmas letters from children around the country. Santa Claus, Georgia, handles about ten thousand letters every Christmas. The town asked for its own post office, but was turned down; mail is handled in the Lyons post office.

All the streets in Santa Claus except one are Christmas-themed. There's Donner, Dasher, Prancer, Rudolph, and Reindeer streets—and Salem Boulevard, named for the original builder.

"When we order signs, we order two of them," Harden says. "We can't keep them up."

On Christmas Eve, all the streets are lined with candles. There's a big Christmas party at town hall, on Noel Street.

"I don't know any town, any size, that has a Christmas party and all the residents are invited," Harden says.

Thunder shakes the motel again; the rain comes down harder. A jolly-looking Santa smiles on the sign outside. Harden has been mayor since October 1985, but doesn't expect to stay in office forever.

"We've had maybe five mayors since the town was organized," he notes. "It's usually ten, fifteen years before people get tired of you."

———

The Edwin I. Hatch Nuclear Plant is along U.S. 1 north of Baxley, Georgia's "Nuclear City." The Oakdale Motel, on the highway's southbound side in Baxley, is an old-fashioned cabin motel, set back in the trees like the Maine Idyll. "Family owned and operated since 1934," the sign says. "We welcome room inspection."

The 45-mile stretch of U.S. 1 from Baxley to Waycross is scenic piney country. Used toys, clothes, and glassware are spread on tables in front of mobile homes. Logging trucks barrel down the road.

Alma ("Georgia's Blueberry Capital") is the seat of appropriately named Bacon County. Tenant

Baxley.

farmers raised pigs and hogs here in the 1930s and 1940s. Alma even has a Piggly Wiggly, right on U.S. 1. Yankees may not know Mr. Pig from Mr. Ed, but the Piggly Wiggly mascot/corporate symbol is a southern icon. There are 650 Piggly Wiggly supermarkets, most of them in the Deep South.

Piggly Wiggly was the nation's first self-service grocery store; Clarence Saunders opened the first one in Memphis in 1916. Before Piggly Wiggly came along, shoppers gave their orders to clerks, who gathered goods from store shelves.

Saunders—who was either "flamboyant and innovative" (according to Piggly Wiggly's official history) or "eccentric" (according to the *Wall Street Journal*)—let shoppers serve themselves. Out went the clerks, in came open shelves and shopping carts. The chain also says it was the first to provide checkout stands, first to price-mark every item in the store, and the first to use refrigerated cases.

Alma Exchange Bank, Alma.

Mystery still surrounds Saunders's choice of the giggle-provoking name. According to one story, he was sitting in a train when he noticed several little pigs struggling to get under a fence. Piggies wiggling . . . Piggly Wiggly!

The grocery store franchiser is trying to make itself over as a more energetic, streamlined operation, starting with Mr. Pig himself. The smiling porker, found on storefronts and corporate logos, lost some weight—about 12 percent—last year. Old Mr. Pig, in these cholesterol-obsessed times, was too fat. And he was scaring children. Enter the new Mr. Pig.

"He's a slimmer, more health-conscious pig," one Piggly Wiggly store manager said.

———

Fifteen miles south of Alma is Dixie Union, and the Highway One Church of God. The road to Waycross is lined with mobile homes, hardscrabble lots, and abandoned houses with broken-down couches on front lawns.

Waycross, the largest city in the largest county in the largest state east of the Mississippi, is gateway to nearby Okefenokee Swamp. The Holiday Inn north of town advertises "Swamp Packages." In the 1930s, the town was at the convergence of nine railroads and five highways, thus its name. Some

Waycross.

have argued that Waycross is short for "Way of the Cross," having been named by the early settlers, who were highly religious. "They go to church six times a week and six times on Sunday," one contemporary visitor observed.

Dixie Union.

Waycross.

Is any name on the American landscape more mysterious and alluring than Okefenokee Swamp? Owaquaphenoga, the Indians called it—"the land of trembling earth." The peat deposits that cover much of the swamp floor are so unstable that in spots one can cause nearby trees and bushes to tremble by stepping on them. Indians lived in the swamp as far back as 2500 B.C.E. The last tribe to call Okefenokee home were the Seminoles, who were driven out of the swamp into Florida in the 1850s.

> "U.S. 1 Highway claims to have many advantages over the others and the reasons given are as follows: Better hotel, motor court, and food accommodations; an excellent highway that is not as congested with trucks as the other; a highway that offers more comfort and safety in travel; by far the most things of interest to see along the route as you travel . . ."
>
> *American Motorist*, December 1952

Today, the 400,000-acre swamp is a National Wildlife Refuge, the third largest wilderness area east of the Mississippi.

Actually, there are two Okefenokee Swamps—the 396,000-acre Okefenokee National Wildlife Refuge and the 1,600-acre Okefenokee Swamp Park, a private, nonprofit attraction operating under a lease agreement with the U.S. Fish and Wildlife Service. The park is more tourist-friendly, with its easy hiking trails, open-air zoo, and maybe the best gift shop on all of U.S. 1 (gator heads, gator jerky, Okefenokee Swamp Cane Syrup).

However, the refuge, with its access to the swamp's core, lives up more to the Owaquaphenoga name. It's the kind of place a guy from, say, New York, can walk into one day and show up, a little worse for wear but alive, forty-one days later.

His name was Michael Goodell, a thirty-three-year-old prison guard from New York State. In February 1996, he parked his car in Stephen Foster State Park, inside the refuge's west entrance, and took a little hike. At one point, while trying to take a picture of a pileated woodpecker, he wandered off trail.

Way off trail, apparently. His car was found several days later in the parking lot, his canoe at nearby Billy's Island (named after Billy Bowlegs, a Seminole chief). For several days, 100 people searched the 8-square-mile Billy's Island with hounds, cadaver dogs, and a helicopter with infrared equipment.

"We had some of the best woodsmen, best tracking people on the ground, and the best tracking

Okefenokee Swamp.

Okefenokee
National Wildlife Refuge.

equipment in the air looking for him," Charlton County Sheriff Dobie Conner told a reporter. "I think it would have been impossible to have gotten by that."

The search was abandoned after a week, and Goodell was given up for dead. Forty-one days after he walked into the swamp, he walked out, much to the astonishment—and skepticism—of many.

"I'm not going to call anyone a liar," one tour guide said at the time, "but something is fishy about the whole thing."

When found, Goodell was dehydrated, cut and bruised, and 50 pounds lighter than the 300 pounds he went in as. He told police he lived on bugs, leaves, and berries, washed down with swamp water. He had a working cigarette lighter but didn't use it because it was against refuge rules due to the risk of starting a forest fire.

Temperatures dipped below freezing at least ten nights. Goodell said he wrapped himself in the thick vegetation to keep warm.

Many suggested it was just a publicity stunt for a book deal.

"Why would I put myself through all this pain for a book?" Goodell said at a press conference. "If you don't believe me, I don't care."

You don't need to go to such extremes to have an Okefenokee wilderness experience. The refuge includes the 9-mile-long Swamp Island Drive, a wildlife observation loop, 5 miles of hiking trails, seven overnight canoe stops, a 4,000-foot-long boardwalk into the swamp, and two observation towers.

"Everybody going into the swamp must sign in," explains park Public-Use Specialist Maggie O'Connell. "So if there's a car left in the parking lot at the end of the day, we know where to look."

First-time visitors approach the Okefenokee with some trepidation, and for good reason. The name alone sounds creepy. The movies have added to the mystique. Jean Renoir's first American feature was *Swamp Water*, with Dana Andrews and Walter Brennan. *Swamp Country*, a late sixties southern drive-in

Okefenokee Swamp.

"People have no idea what to expect when they get down here," says O'Connell, a native of Chicago. "They think it's a deep dark place." She laughs. "There are not going to be snakes hanging from trees ready to drop into your boat. And you're not going to be eaten by an alligator. We haven't had anyone eaten by an alligator, although there have been 'nips,' and those are employees who are out in the swamp more. We have black bears out there, but they do not eat visitors."

The refuge, a naturalist's dream, is home to 621 species of plants, plus 39 fish, 37 amphibian, 64 reptile, 235 bird, and 50 mammal species.

Humans, as usual, can't leave well enough alone. In the 1890s, a 12-mile-long canal was built in a failed attempt to drain the swamp. During the early 1900s, huge amounts of timber were cut down.

hit, told the story of a guy who gets blamed for a crime and escapes into the Okefenokee, where he survives attacks by gators, snakes, bears, and a mountain lion.

The reality, though, is something different.

In the Okefenokee, gators rule.

More than three hundred thousand people visit the refuge every year. About one hundred-twenty thousand visit Okefenokee Swamp Park, which includes a serpentarium; a bear observatory; an open-air zoo with turtles, otters, and gators; and the Walt Kelly Museum.

Kelly was the creator of the comic strip *Pogo*, set in the Okefenokee Swamp. The characters included Pogo (a possum), Howland Owl, Albert the Alligator, Churchy (a turtle), Beauregard Bugelboy (a hound dog), Sis Boombah (a chicken), Deacon Mushrat, and Moonshine Sonata (a frog).

Kelly had an ear for language and dialect and a love for words, bolstered by his work with the U.S. Army Foreign Language Unit during World War II. "He mixed Elizabethan English, French, and black dialects to create a poetic language that set the swamp apart," John A. Lent writes in the highly recommended *100 Years of American Newspaper Comics* (Gramercy Books, 1996).

Kelly's characters talked and argued constantly, parodying human dialogue. The cartoonist used puns, double-entendres, one-liners, and plays on words. The most quoted, Lent notes, was Pogo's sad observation upon the garbage-cluttered swamp: "We have met the enemy, and he is us."

Pogo was no ordinary comic strip; Kelly was merciless in his skewering of the high and mighty— J. Edgar Hoover, the John Birch Society, Richard Nixon, George Wallace, Senator Joseph McCarthy, and others. Kelly even did radio and television commentary for NBC during the 1956 Democratic National Convention. By the late 1950s, nearly six hundred newspapers carried *Pogo*. Kelly died in 1973.

The museum is a re-creation of his studio. Copies of *Life* and *Look* magazines are spread on the desk; a manual typewriter sits nearby. A massive copy of *Webster's International Dictionary* is perched on a wastepaper basket.

No visit would be complete without a boat ride into the swamp. The guides at Okefenokee Swamp Park alone are worth a stop. They all seem to be auditioning for a show on Comedy Central.

"This still produced five gallons a day, anywhere from 120 to 190 proof," says Rusty Tatum, pointing out an old moonshiner's haunt. "They called it Block and Tackle. If you drank it and walked a block, you could tackle anything."

It gets better.

"This water is almost 100 percent pure," he says, guiding the skiff down a creek. "Actually, it's 90 percent pure and 10 percent Gatorade."

Rusty, a raw-boned sixteen-year-old, lives in Waycross. "The edge of the swamp comes right up to the edge of my house," he says. This is his second week on the job. "It's a lot better than flipping hamburgers."

As a kid, he fished and hunted in the swamp. There were deer, wild hogs, black bears, bobcats.

We head deeper into the swamp. The vegetation thickens. The light has a gray, soupy cast. A red-tailed hawk swoops overhead.

"Look in the water," Rusty says. "I believe that's the gator we call Crazy."

Crazy, lounging on a bank, is mild-mannered today. About twenty thousand gators live in the swamp. They feed on catfish, snakes, raccoons, deer, "just about anything they can get their hands on," Rusty says.

Mosquitoes bad here in the summer?

"Oh yeah," he says eagerly, as if this is one of his favorite topics. "It's not just them, but what we call yellow flies. They will tear you up."

As we slide through a narrow slit between the trees, it begins to rain.

"The weather here is so crazy," Rusty explains. "The forecast can say no chance of rain and it can flood, or it can say 80 percent chance of rain and be sunny."

The Everglades, he says, has more birds, but the Okefenokee has more animals. Oscar is the biggest gator in the park—fifteen feet long, more than one thousand pounds.

"He has about forty females he mates with," Rusty explains. "He's the domineering boy gator around here. One day he walked out and set himself in front of the gift shop for three hours. They couldn't find anybody to go over there and tell him to move."

If you have a pet, it's a good idea to keep an eye on it here. "We've had people tie up their pets over there"—the guide points to a stream bank alongside the parking lot—"because they didn't want them to suffocate in the car. When they come back, all that's left is the leash. Pets are not allowed in the boats. Gators like dogs like we like steak."

Rusty sounds like a stand-up comic; Lamar Deal, another guide here, really is one. "When I do a show," he says, "I make this guarantee: If you don't laugh hard enough that you'll piss on yourself, *I'll piss on you.*"

His family goes back 150 years in the swamp. His mother and grandmother were born here. His aunt, Rachel Lyons, lives in a mobile home and runs a nearby restaurant called Blueberry Hill. "I was born and raised here, but I moved to Atlanta long enough to forget how to speak English," says Deal, standing in front of the weather-beaten shack that serves as the swamp guides' office.

What does he think about Goodell, the guy who was lost in the swamp for forty-one days?

"No way he was on that island," Deal says. "A person could get lost out there, but the particulars

Lamar Deal, the Okefenokee Swamp's stand-up comedian.

don't add up. My guess is that he was at the Holiday Inn."

He does well on the Georgia stand-up circuit. Competition can be fierce.

"There's a guy, Leonard Sharing, who may be the weirdest comedian in North America," Deal says. "His act consists of tap dancing and jokes in French. And we're in the mountains of Georgia now."

Being a comedian pays the bills, but being a tour guide is "the most fun job in the world."

Why is the swamp special?

"It was one of the first attempts to reclaim what human beings have torn up," he replies. "For me, it's a way to reclaim my ancestral home. And it's beautiful."

———

U.S. 1 runs straight and true through this, its wildest, most unpopulated stretch. Race Pond, 20 miles south of Waycross, derived its name from the horse track built around a pond by soldiers sent during the Seminole War to capture Indians hiding in the swamp. The Race Pond Trading Post is on the highway's southbound side.

Folkston, a smaller crossroads version of Waycross, is next. Mr. Dryclean is housed in a red caboose. The Okefenokee Festival is held in Folkston every October. The highway crosses the St. Marys River and takes in a stretch of motels, Indian trading posts, and roadside barbecue shacks. Welcome to Florida, the fourteenth and last state along U.S. 1.

FLORIDA

The northern part of this section of US 1 traverses much unimproved pine land, interrupted by occasional marshes and cypress hammocks. . . . Between Fort Pierce and Palm Beach the highway runs through a series of modest coast towns; between Palm Beach and Miami, Florida's Gold Coast, landscaped estates and many nurseries line the highway, and add to the floral beauty of the region. . . . The Overseas Highway is the only route running down over the curving chain of coral islands at the southern end of Florida. . . . The bridges are so long that at times it seems as though the route were running over the sea itself.

—*U.S. One, Maine to Florida*, American Guide Series, 1938

The 22-mile segment from the state line to the Jacksonville city limits is so unlike the stereotypical Florida you may wonder if you're in the right state. The initial landmarks include Mr. Pig, an abandoned barbecue shack; the State Line Bar; a sign advertising "Poor Boy's Mud Bog"; and the vintage Dixie Motel, in Hilliard.

A1A begins at the intersection with U.S. 1 in Callahan; the two highways will run parallel, A1A closer to the coast, toward Miami. A PBS special on A1A, part of the "Great Drives" series, was another in a long line of misguided stories about U.S. 1.

The program ascribes to A1A history and attractions that actually belong to U.S. 1. "The Florida Flagler developed," host Maria Conchita Alonso says, "follows A1A right down to the Keys." No, it doesn't. A1A stops in Miami Beach (and reappears, briefly, in Key West). Much of the program is devoted to the Keys, accessible by U.S. 1, not A1A. "A1A puts you in touch with the soul of Florida," the narrator says. At the end of the road, in Key West, Alonso says A1A is the road that took her there. No highway is more overlooked, or put down, than U.S. 1.

Within the Jacksonville city limits are Indian trading posts, old motels, and other reminders of the 1950s American roadside. A billboard advertises WORLD FAMOUS IMPROV TRAFFIC SCHOOL. "We mark them up just a little bit," a Toyota dealership proclaims. Mt. Vernon Motor Lodge ("for adults only") is followed by Crabs 4-U Seafood.

Boulogne.

Gray Gables.

U.S. 1 takes its usual big-city circuitous route through Jacksonville, following New Kings Road, the Twentieth Street Expressway, Main Street (J.W.'s Doghouse Bar is at Main and East Fourth), and Phillips Highway (home of The Joe Motel and Chopstick Charley's Restaurant). Downtown, the highway does a funny little jog along one side of 95, then the other.

The 43 miles from Jacksonville to St. Augustine, one could argue, is where modern Florida began. Henry Flagler, who either developed or doomed the Sunshine State, depending on whom you talk to, was one of John D. Rockefeller's closest business associates in the Standard Oil business.

In 1883, Flagler eyed Florida as a potential resort gold mine. He bought the railroad between Jacksonville and St. Augustine, and by buying up existing lines, extended his railroad all the way to Key West, building posh hotels along the way.

Florida didn't boom right away; when World War I started, Miami's population was just 6,000. Miami Beach was a sand spit reached only by motorboat. Postwar prosperity started the tourist flow. Then someone discovered the new El Dorado—the value of Florida real estate—"and the gold rush was on, with Miami as the shining goal," according to the WPA guide. People streamed in by train, steamer, car, on muleback, and on foot. Fortunes were made and lost, but the state's population jumped 50 percent between 1920 and 1930.

Keep putting up signs like this, maybe we will. Boulogne.

Roadside appliance dealer, Dinsmore.

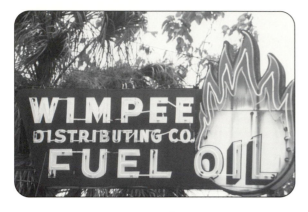

Jacksonville.

Only Joes can stay here? Jacksonville.

In St. Augustine, America's oldest city, U.S. 1 is Ponce de Leon Boulevard and parallels the San Sebastian River, while Business U.S. 1 is San Marco Avenue and runs past Castillo de San Marcos National Monument, America's oldest and best-preserved fortification. The Indian River Fruit Market—"Florida's largest fruit and gift market"—manages the neat trick of being on both U.S. 1 and Business 1. There's a WalMart on 1 in St. Augustine.

The most morbid little museum along U.S. 1—maybe in the country—once stood at the corner of San Marco Avenue and Williams Street. At Buddy Hough's Tragedy in U.S. History Museum, you could see the 1963 Lincoln Continental convertible John F. Kennedy rode in hours before he was assassinated in Dallas, the 1953 Chevy Lee Harvey Oswald used to drive to the Texas Book Depository, and the Ford ambulance that carried

Green Acres Motor Court, Jacksonville.

GREEN ACRES MOTOR COURT, JACKSONVILLE, FLA.
ON U. S. No. 1 AT SOUTH CITY LIMITS
50 WHITE BRICK COLONIAL TOURIST COTTAGES

6 780

the assassin to the hospital after he was shot by Jack Ruby.

Also on display were Oswald's bed, two pillows, and his chest of drawers—Oswald's landlady made Hough repair her porch roof as part of the deal.

Other items included the 1966 Buick 225 Electra—or what was left of it, anyway—that Jayne Mansfield was riding in when she was killed in an auto accident in June 1967—a crash that decapitated the buxom actress. Bonnie and Clyde's bullet-riddled getaway car. Elvis Presley's last will and testament. A worn, torn leather jacket that once belonged to James Dean.

Hours after the museum opened, local officials tried to shut it down, arguing that Hough, a liquid propane gas distributor, violated an ordinance prohibiting attractions unrelated to St. Augustine's history. (Ripley's Believe-It-or-Not Museum on Business U.S. 1, meanwhile, had a shrunken head and a two-headed cow on display.) Hough took the city to court; four and a half years and sixty thousand dollars in legal fees later, he won in Florida Supreme Court.

Hough died in 1996, and his widow decided to put the place up for auction. A Florida state representative bought the Jayne Mansfield car for an undisclosed amount. John Reznikoff of Stamford,

Just north of St. Augustine city limits.

Connecticut, bought the 1963 Lincoln Continental convertible for $17,500. Jeff Hutchinson of Jacksonville picked up the Bonnie and Clyde getaway car for just $1,900.

"Tragedy," Hough once said, "is what makes this country great."

> "America's number-one highway, the most heavily traveled and at the same time one of the most woefully inadequate."
>
> Wildred Owen of the Brookings Institution, in a talk at the Florida Highway Conference, 1950

The highway passes the seemingly endless Palm Coast development, goes through Bunnell (the Florida Agricultural Museum will be built north of town on U.S. 1), and runs past three of the more colorfully named hamlets on the highway: Korona, Favoretta, and National Gardens.

One mile south of Giant Recreation World, and just before Smiley's Tap, is a brown building that seems a perfect introduction to Florida. The interstates may have the official state welcome centers, but U.S. 1 has the headquarters of Hawaiian Tropic.

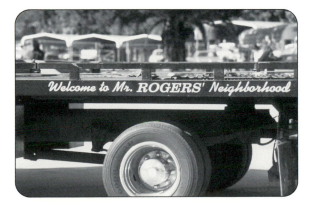

Bunnell.

"We're going to start in blowmolding," Karen Cox says cheerily as she begins my tour of Hawaiian Tropic's 240,000-square-foot Ormond Beach facility. The company's first tractor-trailer load of suntan lotion left the plant in 1974; today, the company is the second largest suncare manufacturer in the world, with twelve plants in five countries.

And to think it all started in a garbage can. Ron Rice, Hawaiian Tropic's party-loving, globe-trotting founder, says he would still be a chemistry teacher and part-time lifeguard in Daytona Beach if not for the trip he made to Hawaii in the early 1970s. While there, Rice noticed women on the beach using natural oils to protect their skin from the sun. Having looked in vain for a product that would protect his light complexion from the sun, he flew back to Florida determined to create a lotion that would let him achieve a tan worthy of a native Hawaiian.

With five hundred dollars borrowed from his father, Rice started a suntan lotion business in his garage, using a garbage can to mix his secret formula of coconut, avocado, and other natural oils. He bottled the lotion and sold it on the beach and at local pools.

"I had an old Ford Mustang the ocean had just eaten apart," he recalls. "I drove to pool decks and lifeguard stands to sell the lotion. I was obsessed."

Today, fifteen blowmolding machines at the Ormond Beach plant produce 35 million bottles of lotion a year, in forty-five shapes and sizes, for Hawaiian Tropic and other suncare companies.

There are bottle-cap machines, regrind machines, hot stamp machines, UV drying machines, all kinds of machines—whirring, pounding, and hissing in the factory. A room contains samples of all the company's domestic and international products. The biggest overseas market? Canada, of all places.

Hawaiian Tropic was the first U.S. suncare company to use tropical coconut/banana fragrance in lotions and oils, the first to introduce sunblocks without chemical sunscreens, and the first to place a higher-than-SPF-30 lotion in the U.S. mass market. About 350 people work at the Ormond Beach plant.

The garbage can Rice used to make his first batch of suntan lotion is silver-plated and sits in the living room of his 5.5-million-dollar estate in Daytona Beach. And he got rid of the Mustang. He now owns a 250,000-dollar Lamborghini, and an eighty-foot yacht, the *Princess Sterling*, named after his daughter.

"This is where we keep the raw materials. I call it the pantry," says Cox, entering a room that smells like a beach—or a beach with suntanned bodies on it. Containers are filled with moisturizers, aloe, menthol, fragrances, and denatured alcohol.

The next stop on the tour is the most grueling, torturous, and inhumane step in the suntan lotion manufacturing process.

Inside a secret laboratory behind the main building, two test subjects are being forced against their will to . . . sit in a hot tub and watch TV?

"We have four to five hundred subjects every year," says Sherriel Wallace, clinical technician in the company's SPF testing lab. "We're only allowed [by the FDA] to recruit certain skin types, certain age groups."

A testing session involves anywhere from eighty minutes to eight hours in the water. Lotion is applied to several spots on the back.

The tour over, Cox loads me down with The Girls of Hawaiian Tropic calendars, the Miss Hawaiian Tropic International beauty pageant video, and other essential items. She says Hawaiian Tropic's future is bright; the Ormond Beach facility had a major expansion in 1996 to meet increasing demand.

Holly Hill.

Daytona.

"Our growth," she says happily, "has been boomp, boomp, boomp."

――――

Trailer parks, motels, and roadhouses enliven the road through Ormond Beach, where John D. Rockefeller had his winter home, and Holly Hill. In Daytona Beach (named for Matthias Day of Ohio, who founded the city in 1871), U.S. 1 is Ridgewood Avenue.

During Bike Week, billed as the world's largest motorcycle event, bikes roar majestically down U.S. 1 in packs of twenty-five and more. The Banned Bookstore is on 1, and so are the National Cremation and Burial Society and the White Lady Motel. Biker bars line the highway from Ormond Beach north of Daytona to Port Orange south of it. I pick the one with the catchiest name, and it turns out to be the right choice, in more ways than one.

At least fifty Harleys are parked in a neat row in front of the Last Resort Bar. It's Bike Week, and the

The Riviera, circa 1942, Daytona Beach.

Al Bulling, owner,
Last Resort Bar,
Port Orange.

Aileen Wuorinos
was here.
Last Resort Bar.

biker bar, like its counterparts up and down the highway, is hosting a Bike Week outdoor party. There are shot specials, live bands, giveaways, vendors, the Human Bomb, all-girl cornstarch wrestling—you know, the usual.

Al Bulling, the Last Resort's Brooklyn-born and -raised owner, shows me around. "It's been a biker bar the last twenty years," says Bulling, who wears orange-tinted glasses. "You remember Aileen Wuornos? She was arrested right here."

Aileen Wuornos. The FBI called her America's first female serial killer. A prostitute who was convicted and sentenced to die for the shooting deaths of seven men—an electronics repair shop owner, a heavy equipment operator, a rodeo worker, a merchant marine-turned-missionary, a sausage delivery man, an ex–Alabama police chief, and a former security guard. She said it was in self-defense.

"Well, I came here to confess to murder," she told police in a videotaped confession. "Most of 'em

either were gonna start to beat me up or were gonna screw me in the ass and they'd get rough with me. So I'd fight 'em and I'd get away from 'em. As I'd get away from 'em, I'd run to the front of the car or jump over the seat or whatever, grab my gun, and start shootin'."

Aileen Wuornos's life story emerged in newspaper stories. She was abandoned by her sixteen-year-old mother three months after she was born; her father, a nineteen-year-old handyman, had left her mother shortly after Aileen's birth. He was later convicted of sodomizing a seven-year-old and sent to prison, where he hanged himself with a bedsheet in his jail cell.

A prostitute since she was fourteen and an admitted drug-user, Wuornos moved to Daytona Beach when she was sixteen. She lived with her lover, Tyria Moore, in a motel on U.S. 1, and frequented the Last Resort. Police identified her as a suspect in the murders and tracked her to the biker bar. She spent the night of January 8, 1991, on a mustard-colored vinyl seat inside the bar—it's still there—and was arrested the next morning.

Nick Broomfield, in his first-rate documentary, *Aileen Wuornos: The Selling of a Serial Killer*, explores both Wuornos's life and attempts by friends, police officers, and others to cash in on her story as she waited on Death Row.

Wuornos remains in prison, and hers is one of hundreds of personalized bricks on a Last Resort wall devoted to the bar's patrons. When Wuornos was in the bar, according to one regular, she always played one song—"Digging up Bones," by Randy Travis. She left her bra here once; it's behind the bar.

But this little stretch of U.S. 1 was famous before Aileen Wuornos ever showed up.

"Al Capone's mother lived right across the street," Bulling says. "Supposedly Ma Barker lived in that house," he adds, pointing to another one just down the road.

"Ma Barker's place is going to be a beauty salon," says Ted E. Bear.

Yes, it's her real name. "Or you can call me Princess," she says, smiling sweetly. "You can quote me on this: if you want a job done right, get a woman to do it."

The artist, who has a studio in Jacksonville, sets up shop at the Last Resort during Bike Week. She rides a Harley; her German shepherd, Barney, has appeared on Letterman (he can tap-dance to "New York, New York"). Ted E. even painted signs for Ron Rice when he was selling Hawaiian Tropic poolside.

"I'm not only beautiful, I can paint," she says.

Ted E. is an American Indian; her mother was a medicine woman in the Carolinas. Her parents moved to Daytona in 1965, "when it was nothing but land; now it's nothing but condos."

Ted E. Bear, artist.

Thirteen, she says, is her lucky number. Why? On February 13, 1985, she was in her brand-new Dodge pickup when it was hit head-on by a drunken driver.

"It tore the top of my face off," she says matter-of-factly. "My lungs were crushed. My right leg was broken. My left leg was sticking out of the skin. I heard the highway patrolman say, 'Oh, she's dead.' I rose up from the sheet and said, 'I'm not dead.' He passed out."

She needed 325 stitches, and took two years to rehabilitate.

In 1992, on another Friday the 13th, she was hit by a motorcycle outside a Daytona Beach bar, suffering serious neck injuries.

Messy contestant in the Last Resort Bar's cornstarch wrestling contest.

Cornstarch wrestler after her shower, Last Resort Bar.

business cards—is here, selling commemorative coins and belt buckles.

"I don't wish anybody bad," he says of his undertaking work, "but business could be better."

"Jesse the Human Bomb will be here tonight," Bulling says later. "He blows himself up all over the world. He's local, a good guy."

More than six hundred thousand bikers will attend the three-week-long Bike Week; more than one million are expected in the year 2000.

"If you're not in a hurry," says Bulling, "U.S. 1 is a nice road."

———

U.S. 1 is Dixie Freeway in New Smyrna Beach. Dr. Andrew Turnbull established the first colony here in 1767 and named it after his wife's birthplace, Smyrna, in Turkey. Trailer parks line the road from New Smyrna south, but they're unlike any trailer parks you've seen, set on beautifully landscaped, palm-tree–shaded lots not far from the ocean. Giant carved heads gaze at U.S. 1 from Art World Gallery in Edgewater, while Whirligig World is on the highway's southbound side in Mims.

Oak Hill was named the state's outstanding rural community in 1994. Manny's Alligator Center ("Florida's finest gift shop") is on the highway. Titusville is named for Col. H. T. Titus, an opponent of abolitionist John Brown in Kansas. Henry Flagler tried to buy choice land here for a resort in the late 1800s, but the price was too high, so he built it in Palm Beach instead.

Titusville ended up doing OK for itself; it is now Space City U.S.A., home of NASA Kennedy Space Center. The U.S. Astronaut Hall of Fame, located just off U.S. 1 on Route 405, is an unsettling experience.

"We suggest people try this last," staffer Susan Peters says of the G-Force Trainer that is among the

"It's like I'm blessed by the Spirit," she says, smiling. "I went through two traumatic experiences and I'm here."

Around her, the party is in full blast. Ponytailed bikers in black-leather jackets saunter past. One of the cornstarch wrestlers returns after a shower dressed in an outfit—skin-tight purple shorts and matching top—that looks like it came from the biker version of Victoria's Secret. Michael Blickenstaff—"The World's Most Famous Undertaker," according to his

Hall of Fame's simulated rides. "It will scramble your eggs."

Not wanting to scramble my eggs, I tried the Mars Explorer, a rocking, rolling, dune buggy–like ride over the surface of the Angry Red Planet; and the 3D–360, which simulates a jet aircraft dogfight, complete with 360-degree barrel rolls. "Those susceptible to motion sickness or sensitive to spinning motions," according to a sign, "should avoid this attraction."

You can sample space sickness on a motion platform, and take a lunar whiff from the Moon Smell panel.

The Hall of Fame, which houses the world's largest collection of personal astronaut artifacts, opened in 1990, thanks to the efforts of the seven Project Mercury astronauts.

Home to U.S. Space Camp Florida (not to mention the Cosmic Cafe and the excellent Right Stuff gift stop), the complex is filled with memorabilia and minutiae of space flight. The *Mercury* capsule Wally Schirra piloted looks so ancient and flimsy you wonder how it ever got him there and back. On the moon, temperatures reach 200 degrees, so astronauts wore underwear threaded with cold-water-filled tubes. The *Apollo 7* astronauts put on such a good show—they opened their TV broadcasts with "Hello, from the lovely Apollo Room, high atop everything"—that they received a special Emmy.

———

The Three Oaks Motel ("neatest little motel on the Space Coast") is on U.S. 1 in Titusville, along with the beautiful, neon-lit Moonlight Drive-In. Don't miss the aptly named Bent Pole Barber Shop on the southbound side. Manatee Hammock trailer park is on 1 in Bellwood. The Space Coast Motel, with its

Now that's a welcome sign!

deep-blue, star-studded neon sign, is on 1 in Cocoa, named for the nut palm that grows here.

There is a billboard for Harvey's Orchards ("73 years, still No. 1") and a sign marking Hoo-Hoo Park. *Florida Today/USA Today* is located on 1 in Pineda. A giant orange sits in front of the Disabled American Veterans J. L. Golightly Chapter 32 headquarters in Melbourne, named by a native Australian after the town of his birth. A sign at Bill's Used Tire, an open-air garage on the highway's northbound side, reads: "No Checks Ever."

Palm Bay is a scenic Indian River community (U.S. 1 in front of the Days Inn became one of my favorite running routes on the entire highway). Malabar ("Where People Care"), Grant, and Micco (from the Seminole word for "chief") flash by. Welcome signs are often bland, but not the one for Sebastian: "13,500 friendly people & 6 ole grouches."

This is citrus country. Christopher Columbus and the Spanish conquistadors brought the first oranges to Florida. A Frenchman, Count Odette Phillipe, planted the first grapefruit trees in Florida near Tampa in 1823.

Today, Florida produces more grapefruit than the rest of the world combined. At Hale Groves, on U.S. 1 in Wabasso, an observation deck, open to

Weeding out the grapefruits. Hale Groves, Wabasso.

the public, overlooks the packing floor. In the road-side store, you can grab a free glass of juice, and buy loose fruit, fruit baskets, and gift items for shipment back home or overseas.

"Towering Indulgence goes on this half of the shelf," reads a note in a storage room. Towering Indulgence is Hale's super-duper gift basket, filled with navel oranges, Ruby Red grapefruit, choco-

Mary Ann Vondiezelski, Hale Groves, Wabasso.

late walnut fudge, mixed nuts, and Golden Walnut cookies.

Roy Beglau, who seems to be Mr. Everything here—he helps move, pack, and grade fruit; does carpentry; gets diesel "for the gol'durned truck"; and gives tours to school and community groups—shows me around the packing plant.

Steve Hale started the business in 1947, opening a little stand on the highway. His wife, Polly, typed labels while Steve packed and shipped fruits to customers. Today, the company has a dozen groves, the packing house, and four stores in the Vero Beach area.

The fruit comes in from the groves green, "but people don't like the looks of green, so they de-green 'em," Beglau explains. "They use gas and heat; leave them in the de-greening room maybe seventy-two hours."

Graders perched on a raised platform snatch less-than-perfect fruit—"anything that isn't pretty," Beglau says—and toss it into a middle chute. This "number two" fruit, which tastes just as good as "number one" fruit but, in the words of Beglau, is "too ugly to pack," goes into specially marked bins outside the store or is sent to the Hale juice-making plant in Vero Beach.

The grapefruit juice in the store juice machine is the best I've had, anywhere; I wish I could put a keg of it on ice and toss it in the back of the Jeep.

Next to the store is the Hale Garden Grove, a self-guided tour through the world of citrus. The taped narrator is named Jake, whose voice drips with southern charm. "Its juice is so sweet and delicious," Jake says of the temple orange. "One taste, and you'll know why it's the cream of the crop."

———

Looking for the "coldest beer in Florida"? You can find it at Consalo's, on U.S. 1 north in Gifford. Mel

Fort Pierce.

Port St. Lucie.

Fisher's Treasure Museum, named after the man who discovered the Spanish galleon *Nuestra Señora de Atocha* and its 400-million-dollar bounty of sunken treasure off Key West in 1985, is on U.S. 1 northbound in Vero Beach.

Twistee Treat, with its swirled ice cream roof, is on 1 northbound in Port St. Lucie, which is also home to Seasick Sam's Grill. Clyde Killer, Attorney, has his office on U.S. 1. Maybe the greatest McDonald's sign of all is on 1 southbound in Stuart, next to the Howard Johnson's. The pink, yellow, and green neon sign advertises 15¢ hamburgers (a small sign says hamburgers are not actually fifteen cents).

Jupiter (Burt Reynolds Park is on U.S. 1) and Juno Beach are modern-day reminders of the so-called Celestial Railroad that linked these towns with the since-vanished settlements of Neptune, Mars, and Venus. The railroad was abandoned in 1894, when Flagler opened a through line from Jacksonville.

U.S. 1 and A1A join briefly, then U.S. 1 swings into Riviera Beach, where the Trylon Tower once

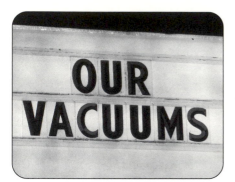

And so . . .

. . . does your
spelling.
Fort Pierce.

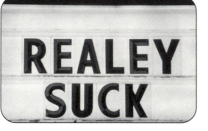

stood. The 230-foot-high three-sided tower, known as "Florida's Tallest Tourist Attraction," was an "exuberant exclamation point on a bustling commercial strip" when it opened in 1960, according to one account.

By the end of the 1960s, though, the Bazaar International shopping center, where the tower stood, was being eclipsed by the nearby Palm Beach Mall. The tower's observation deck was closed to sightseers in the 1970s, and chunks of concrete started to tumble to the ground.

A consultant hired by the state Transportation Department said the tower might be eligible for the National Register of Historic Places, but the state Division of Historical Resources disagreed, calling the Trylon Tower "interesting" but not historic. The tower was demolished in 1998.

———

U.S. 1 through West Palm Beach is a ride on the elegant and wild side, as the highway—by turns Federal Highway, Broadway, Olive Street, and Dixie

Highway—manages to take in not only the world-renowned Norton Museum of Art and the Palm Beach County Courthouse, but also Bell Bottoms Disco, the Hurricane Bar, the Real Life Bar, and several motels that have clearly seen better days.

As the late afternoon shadows lengthen, a half dozen men gather outside Union Baptist Church at 3900 Broadway, across the street from the El Patio Motel. A weather-beaten plywood sign advertises the House of Bread. The men have come for a free meal—and a side order of spiritual guidance and stern advice from the Rev. Isaiah Clark.

"This is a mass feeding program for the nameless, the jobless, and the hungry," explains Clark, standing at the end of a series of long card tables lined up in a narrow church corridor. "What we do is a simple thing—give everybody a hot meal once a day. Don't complicate things, don't add on things."

Clark, friendly, no-nonsense, and partial to black suspenders, opened the House of Bread twelve years ago. Asked how the program started, Clark takes me behind the church.

"See that Dumpster?" he asks. "At night, there were men and women coming through here eating out of that Dumpster. That was their daily meal. We said, 'You don't have to do that; come around front and we'll give you a meal.'"

Three men were present at the House of Bread's first meal; as many as 125 show up for the daily meal today.

"Good evening," he says, addressing thirty men and women sitting at the tables.

"Good evening," they reply in unison.

The regulars include Bill, a grizzled, middle-aged man who wears his bike helmet right through dinner. Bill once had a good job, but suffered a head injury from a fall, according to Clark. That's why he always has the bike helmet on.

Isaiah Clark, founder of the House of Bread, West Palm Beach.

Another familiar face is Kelvin, a young man whose left arm is wrapped in a towel due to an injury that he'd rather not talk about. Everyone who comes to the House of Bread must sign in.

"I've been coming here for years, man," Kelvin says. "It's a survival house for a lot of people. This place is a blessing."

"All right folks, it's time to say grace," Clark announces. "How many of you believe in prayer? Prayer will change conditions. It will change your attitude. It will change your disposition. You've got to do your part, though. There is no lesson plan in the Bible.

"This land is a weary land, and we need to heal it," he says, his voice up a pitch. "Land of the free and home of the brave and this man here can't

Riviera Beach.

find a job. Something wrong with the system. We send millions and billions overseas and we struggle here. Something wrong with the system. Not of all of us are looking for a job. Some of us are hooked on crack."

"Yeah," several men reply.

"We have to ask God for help to stop," Clark says.

Clark, fifty-seven, moved his congregation here eleven years ago from Fourteenth and Douglass in West Palm Beach. He's a full-time pastor, but he once combined ministerial duties with his other job—a project manager for the state Department of Transportation.

"This whole strip, U.S. 1, they're trying to revitalize," Kelvin explains. "It went down with drugs and prostitution. The early eighties was the worst time. Businesses started disappearing. They're coming in now. They even got a Walgreen's on U.S. 1."

The food is donated by church and community groups and cooked by volunteers; Pat Gallagher and Carole Douglass are in the kitchen tonight. Dinner is chicken, corn, a roll, a slice of chocolate cake, served on a Styrofoam plate, and a cup of Coke. The only men who get seconds are those who help set up and clean up.

"The reverend fought to keep us here," Kelvin explains. "They wanted to push him out. But he stood up."

"They still want to shut us down—not the city, but the neighborhood," Clark maintains. "Why? Because we're helping somebody. They say this brings 'undesirables' into the neighborhood."

Later, the tables are folded up, and the men disperse, heading to local motels and shelters. I ask Clark how long the House of Bread will stay open.

"Perpetually," he replies. "Jesus said, 'The poor you shall always have with you.'"

Nicky's Donut, West Palm Beach.

The World's Best Coffee can be found in a classic 1950s doughnut shop on Dixie Highway in West Palm. That's what the big sign says, anyway, outside Nicky's Donut. "Happy Hour—Coffee & Donut" is painted on the window. Under that is a handwritten message: "Yes, You Can Smoke Here."

Inside, a daytime soap flickers on the TV. A Joker Poker machine is bolted to a table. Rows of doughnuts—chocolate-frosted, jelly, butter crunch, Greek raisin, Old-Fashioned Cruller, South Dixie Cruller—are arranged invitingly on shelves. Attached to the wall, instead of the usual plaques and family snapshots, are two pairs of deer antlers.

"Attention Customer," reads a notice. "Check your receipt. You can receive a free doughnut and coffee if it ends with a 20, 60, or 90."

"I am in this country since 1968," says owner Nick Ainis. "Believe it or not, I have sixty-eight cents in my pocket."

He worked at Mister Donut and Dunkin' Donuts shops in several states and Canada. "In Toronto, everybody talking about Florida, everybody going to Florida," says Nick.

So he and his wife, Dina, go to Florida, but only for vacation.

"I called the main office of Mister Donut," he recalls. "I ask, 'Do you have any stores available?' They say, 'West Palm Beach.' I didn't want to come here. I like north—cold weather." He smiles. "My wife says, 'We're not leaving here.'"

Nicky and Dina Ainis outside their West Palm Beach store.

At the time, the Mister Donut on Dixie Highway had been closed. Nicky reopened it in October 1975. He replaced the "Mister" on the marquee with "Nicky's," which accounts for the catchy, if inaccurate, "Nicky's Donut."

But this is more than a story about doughnuts, the World's Best Coffee, or a Greek immigrant's dream to make it in the promised land. In 1991, Nicky asked Dina what she wanted for Christmas. How about hosting a Christmas dinner for the needy? she asked. Nick told her he'd been thinking of the same thing for weeks.

Every year since, the couple has hosted a Christmas dinner—in their parking lot. Scores of volunteers, working under a big tent, cook and serve fifty turkeys, four hundred pounds of ham, forty crates of salad, mountains of vegetables, hundreds of loaves of bread, and sixty pies. Christmas carols play on a loudspeaker, Santa makes an appearance, and there are toys for the children. More than two thousand people are fed every year.

The *Palm Beach Post* called the doughnut man "St. Nick of South Dixie."

"I always want to give something back to this country," Nicky says. "This country has been good to me. Americans," he adds passionately, "are sons of bitches. They don't appreciate their country. I am an American, I can say this. They waste so much. Do you know how much food they throw out at restaurants? If you take the people in this country and send them to South America, India, they come back, all of a sudden, they say, 'This is beautiful country.'"

The doughnut shop is open seven days a week from 5 a.m. to midnight. Whatever is left on the shelves, Nicky gives away.

In 1997, the Christmas dinner almost didn't happen. Nicky was working at the dough mixer when his arm got tangled in the machine. He pulled his arm out, but it was mangled.

"I was out of work six months," he recalls. "Who is going to make the doughnuts? Only I can make the doughnuts."

A friend from Toronto flew down and worked in the doughnut shop until Nicky returned. Then a stranger walked in one day and asked if Nicky needed help with the Christmas dinner. "You can buy twenty turkeys," Nicky said. "That's all?" the stranger replied. "You can get me two hundred yams," said Nicky, not believing his luck. The man—Lawrence Mons, who lives in West Palm—ended up taking Nicky to Costco and buying him twenty-five thousand dollars' worth of food.

"He was my angel," Nicky says.

The doughnut man says the neighborhood is not as safe as it used to be. The shop has been broken into several times, but Nicky shrugs it off.

"They don't find money: I never leave money here," he says. "What are they going to steal, doughnuts?"

Lake Worth.

The Deer Apartments and Little Owl Bar are on U.S. 1 in Lake Worth. Lantana, named for a spiky shrub, is home to the most widely read newspaper in America. Located, somehow appropriately, on the other side of the railroad tracks, is the *National Enquirer*.

Startling Exclusive! Inside the *National Enquirer*!

Or maybe it should say: SPACE ALIEN DRESSED AS U.S. CONGRESSMAN INFILTRATES SUPER-MARKET TABLOID'S TOP-SECRET HEADQUARTERS or, more appropriately, TWO-HEADED REPORTER ON BIZARRE MAINE-TO-FLORIDA ODYSSEY.

It wasn't easy getting inside the *National Enquirer*. Weeks of faxes and phone calls from the road—at one point, I believe, I broke down in tears—finally won over senior editor Charlie Montgomery.

Montgomery was once managing editor of a New Jersey weekly newspaper. He wasn't there long. One day, he wanted to send a reporter to interview a prisoner at the county jail. The editor nixed the assignment. The next day, a rival paper had its own interview on the front page. Charlie rolled the paper up, threw it at his boss, and said,

"Read the motherfucker and get yourself a new number two."

Generoso Pope loved that kind of spunk in his editors and reporters. In 1952, the twenty-five-year-old Pope, whose father owned the Italian-language daily *Il Progresso*, paid $75,000 for a 17,000-circulation weekly called the *New York Enquirer*.

Pope, who once worked for the CIA as a psychological warfare expert, turned the *Enquirer* into a tabloid chock full of crime, sin, sex, and scandal. The *New York Enquirer* became the *National Enquirer*, and in 1971, Pope moved the paper from Fort Lee, New Jersey, to Lantana, a sleepy beach town five miles south of Palm Beach.

"Tabloid Valley" now includes the *Enquirer* and its sister paper, the *Weekly World News*, headquartered

Lantana.

Charlie Montgomery inside the *National Enquirer* newsroom.

in the same building in Lantana, and the rival *Globe*, *Sun*, and *National Examiner* in Boca Raton.

Pope invented supermarket checkout racks to get his paper within easy reach of his largely female, middle-American audience. The paper spared no time, effort, and, especially, expense, to chase down a story.

When Princess Grace died, a team of reporters was flown to Monaco on the *Concorde*. They quickly located the gardener who pulled her from her wrecked car and paid him $12,000 for his story. Two reporters guarded his door and answered the phone so no one else would get the story.

Assigned to get a jailhouse interview with baseball legend Pete Rose, reporter Doug Mays and his wife, Sammie, both musicians, called the Marion, Illinois, correctional facility and offered to give a free concert. Great, the warden said, come on up.

Getting to Rose alone before the concert was the challenge. Money changed hands, and the Mayses were escorted to Rose's cell. While the guards were distracted by the blond-haired Sammie, Doug Mays pulled out a camera and whispered, "Psst, Pete. The *Enquirer*."

"I wondered who'd be the first to figure out how to get to me," Rose said. "I was betting it'd be the *National Enquirer*."

On the way home, as the Mayses stopped in a cafe to call the paper with the scoop, their car was stolen. Fortunately it got stuck in traffic several blocks away. Doug wrestled the perpetrator to the ground and rescued his precious roll of film. All in a day's work for a *National Enquirer* reporter.

The paper handed out miniature cameras to mourners at Elvis's funeral to snap an exclusive front-page photo that became the best-selling *Enquirer* cover of all time. It tracked down, purchased, and published the famous snapshot of Donna Rice sitting on Gary Hart's lap aboard the boat *Monkey Business*, a photo that ruined Hart's political career.

The tabloid has been called everything from "trash" to "resolutely supermarket, peddling death, disaster, divorce, and diet tips to bloated white trash

Lantana.

waiting in the checkout lane, snouts enviously pressed up against the window pane that forever separates them from the Dream."

And yet no other paper was quoted more often by mainstream press during the O.J. case than the *National Enquirer*.

"The *New York Times* called us the Bible on the O. J. Simpson case," notes Iain Calder, who was editor-in-chief and president of the *National Enquirer* from 1975 to 1995.

The Scottish-born Calder, who was known as "The Icepick" around the *Enquirer* newsroom, was part of the wave of Fleet Street journalists who flocked to Tabloid Valley in the 1960s and 1970s.

In the early 1960s, the *Enquirer* "was a horrible paper," recalls Calder, who came on board in 1964. "Gene Pope made this incredible change, overnight."

TV was making inroads on newspaper readership and profits. Pope saw that covers featuring the Beverly Hillbillies sold more than those featuring flying saucers, and beefed up the paper's celebrity coverage.

By 1971, the paper's circulation was one million (it is now 2.7 million). Pope (who died in 1988) and Calder launched *Star Magazine*, *Country Weekly*, *Soap Opera Magazine*, and the *Enquirer*'s twisted sister, the *Weekly World News*, full of all the news you

really can't print elsewhere. *WWN*'s offices are in a back corner of the *Enquirer* newsroom. The walls are decorated with classic *WWN* headlines: SURGEONS CUT MY HEAD OFF. BAT BOY CAPTURED. I HAD BIGFOOT'S BABY.

"We cover Hollywood," Calder says of the *Enquirer*, "the way the *Washington Post* covers the Pentagon. We have contacts all over."

According to observers, the paper started to tone things down after 1981, when it lost a $1.3-million libel suit (later reduced to $200,000) to Carol Burnett.

The tabloids don't have to make anything up. They could have a field day with the strange but true things that happen in Florida every day. Tom Zucco of the *St. Petersburg Times* found these stories on the AP wire in just a thirty-two-hour period: Whirlpool Death. Taco Bell Murder. Plane Crash. Pastor Convicted. Cocaine Lawyer. Eatery Rats. Sex Abuse. Miami Corruption. Elephant Death. Psychic Scam. Human Head. And that was just a partial list!

The *National Enquirer* is located in a one-story building that is practically hidden by a jungle of trees and bush. On the other side of U.S. 1 are the Gypsy Turtle thrift store and a Volkswagen Beetle perched atop a pole in front of a car repair shop.

Starting salary for reporters is about $70,000 a year. Editors can earn $150,000 or more. The current editor is Steve Coz, a Harvard cum laude English major graduate who joined the *Enquirer* in 1981.

There are twenty reporters on staff, and the paper depends on "a great network of stringers around the world," Montgomery says. "We have two guys in Moscow who regularly feed us."

Stringers get anywhere from $100 to $400 for story "lead fees," plus up to $750 for written stories. The *Enquirer* also receives more than a million letters from readers every year (the paper has its own zip code, 33464). News tips pay anywhere from $75 to $500.

Montgomery sits at his cluttered desk in the middle of the *Enquirer* newsroom. Videos are stacked on a filing cabinet. The former marine pulls out a thick folder titled "Charlie's Murder Book," which contains fifty-four *Enquirer* stories—in less than a year's time—on the JonBenet Ramsey case.

There are no more two-headed alien baby headlines in today's *National Enquirer*; the paper, while it has not stopped hounding celebrities, prides itself on its diet, medical, and lifestyle coverage.

"We understand Middle America," Calder says.

Montgomery once stopped in a store in Delight, Arkansas—Glenn Campbell's hometown. He couldn't find a regular newspaper, but there were copies of the *National Enquirer*. He asked the store owner how many copies he received every week. "Forty-seven," he replied.

The former *Philadelphia Bulletin* reporter and *Philadelphia Daily News* city hall bureau chief misses his hoagies so much he occasionally has them Fed-Ex'ed from White House Subs in Atlantic City and another sub shop. "I had one sent from Philly last week, with some Tastykakes," he says. "Cost me fifty-four bucks."

The newspaperman is itching for a cigarette, so he heads outside, into the near-blinding Florida sunshine. "When I can't have fun, when I can't get excited, that's when it's time to get out of the business," he says. "In the meantime, you just wait for the next phone call." He smiles. "It could be the biggie of all time."

———

Hypoluxo, just south of Lantana, has one of the more intriguing names of the Florida U.S. 1 towns.

The name may be of Indian origin. "Hapo" was Seminole for "mound or pile," while "poloski" means "round or circular."

Hypoluxo could refer, then, to the many shell mounds along the Florida coast, Allen Morris points out in *Florida Place Names* (Pineapple Press, 1995). Early settlers agreed upon "hypo" instead of "hipo" for the first syllables; they did not want people to call the settlement Hippoluxo.

According to its official welcome sign, Hypoluxo is the "Home of the Barefoot Mailman." The Barefoot Mailman was the collective name given to mail carriers in the 1880s and 1890s who would pick up mail at Lake Worth, row a skiff twelve miles south to Hypoluxo, then walk sixty miles on the sand to Miami—often in their bare feet.

The journey took the better part of three days. There was no railroad at the time, not even horse or bicycle trails. The Hypoluxo post office, located on U.S. 1, closed in 1954; mail is now handled by Lantana. The Barefoot Mailman Motel is on 1 northbound. *The Barefoot Mailman* is Theodore Pratt's 1943 "romantic adventure" novel about the mailmen and their exploits, not all of them having to do with stamps.

"Steve sat stunned," begins chapter eight. "The touch of her lips, giving him his first kiss, was fresh and tenuous. It darted in before it was to be seen, was gone almost before it could be known it had been there. What it left behind jolted and quickened him."

Mailmen should have it so good.

Boynton Beach—many Finnish farmers settled here and in Lantana—is home to several roadside attractions on U.S. 1. The "World's Smallest Recliner" is in the window of a store at the corner of Federal Highway and S.E. Twenty-third Street. Sun Wah Restaurant, with its corroded but splendid sign, is

Boynton Beach.

here, along with the Homing Inn and Anne Marie Motel.

Exclusive Boca Raton means "mouth of the rat," an apparent mistranslation from an Indian phrase that referred to the area's rocky shore. The International Museum of Cartoon Art, on U.S. 1, is America's only museum devoted to the collection, preservation, exhibition, and study of cartoons.

The museum, founded by Mort Walker, creator of Beetle Bailey, is staffed by friendly guides, most of them senior citizens, who will tell you which way to Little Nemo in Slumberland, Brenda Starr, the Fantastic Four, and Calvin and Hobbes. Don't miss the gift shop.

Richard Outcault is credited with creating the first newspaper comic strip—*Superstar*, featuring a street urchin known as the Yellow Kid. The strip debuted in the *New York World* in 1895. In 1902, Outcault also created Buster Brown.

One strip on display shows Dennis the Menace coming out of the Tunnel of Love with an unhappy-looking little girl.

"What didya expect?" Dennis says. "I'm only five years old."

Pompano Beach, 8 miles south of Boca, was named during dinner. An engineer doing surveying work for the railroad was delighted by the fish served him at a restaurant. When he learned it was pom-

pano, he wrote the word on his map as the village's name.

"Dead Bug Edwards, The Termite Professional," proclaims a billboard on the highway's northbound side.

Fort Lauderdale, the Broward County seat, was once spring break mecca for millions of college students; the city now projects a "family" image. In probably no other city along U.S. 1 is neon more the fashion; just check out the pink and blue lighting at the Roxy Theater, or even the familiar "Hot Doughnuts Now" sign at the Krispy Kreme shop at N.E. Twenty-second Street. In Fort Lauderdale, U.S. 1 runs through the Kinney Tunnel. Blink once and you're through it, but it's a tunnel nonetheless, the only one on the highway. At night, the Coral Ridge Presbyterian Church at 5555 Federal Highway, Fort Lauderdale, is a spectacular sight, its sleek white illuminated tower soaring heavenward.

A good portion of South Florida's huge sex industry is located along U.S. 1. Adult bookstores, video shops, go-go bars, bondage supply stores, massage parlors, and escort service offices jam the strip. The sex industry rakes in more than 500 million dollars a year and employs about seventy-five

Two employees, Krispy Kreme shop, Fort Lauderdale.

hundred people, according to the *(Fort Lauderdale) Sun-Sentinel*. Adult Video News reports that Americans will spend more than 8 billion dollars this year on X-rated videos, sexual devices, sex magazines, peep shows, cybersex, and live sex acts.

Fort Lauderdale was for many years South Florida's X-rated playground. Scores of go-go bars and bookstores called the city home. Fort Lauderdale could boast the nation's first topless doughnut shop, topless carwash, topless hot-dog vendor, and topless check-cashing operation.

In the late 1980s, the city started cracking down on the video shops and bookstores, driving them out completely. The businesses just set up shop elsewhere. Today, the strip clubs Pure Platinum and Solid Gold are members in good standing at the Greater Fort Lauderdale Chamber of Commerce. At the Greater Fort Lauderdale/Broward County Convention Center, the 575,000 conventioneers who visit every year can get a free ride to four area nude clubs listed on the center's entertainment courtesy board. 9 1/2 Weeks, the Atlanta-based sex novelty chain, opened its first store outside Georgia on Federal Highway (U.S. 1) in Fort Lauderdale in late 1997. The neon-lit store is strategically located across from the elegant strip club Pure Platinum. Low-rent adult bookstores and clubs still litter the highway through South Florida, but the well-lit, supermarket-like operations are the wave of the X-rated future.

"The age of the sex bookstore, with the small booths in the back so men could masturbate, is gone forever," Michael Brannon, who teaches human sexuality at Nova Southeastern University, told the *Sun-Sentinel*. "Now you're dealing with places that look like a Publix."

The Graves Museum of Archaeology and Natural History is on 1 in Dania. A huge billboard for Dania Jai Alai towers over Dixie Highway in that town,

Dania.

named by the Danish families who migrated here in the late 1800s, but it is a betting attraction of another kind that awaits in Hallandale.

———

In the interest of full and accurate reporting, I forced myself to go to Gulfstream, on Federal Highway in Hallandale, one warm, sunny winter afternoon. There was just one question on my mind: If I lost a whole lot of money, could I get reimbursed by my publisher?

Admission is just three dollars, and includes parking and program as well as entrance fee. I load up on racing forms—a *Gulfstream Park World-Class Racing and Simulcast Past Performance Program*, thicker than a phone book, which comes with two free supplements; and *The Gulfstream Park Handicappe*r. I have absolutely no idea what I'm supposed to do with either.

Gulfstream is open from January to March. The track's customer base—what the *(Fort Lauderdale) Sun-Sentinel* called "the cigarette-puffing oldster

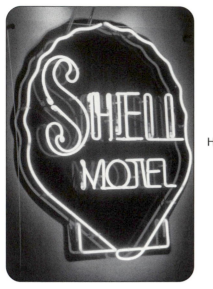

Hollywood.

wearing polyester Sans-a-belt slacks clutching a rolled-up program"—is dying off. So Gulfstream is going after the twenty-five-to-forty-five-year-old crowd, using rock concerts, direct mail, even Howard Stern radio spots to entice a younger clientele.

Gulfstream, which celebrated its sixtieth anniversary in 1999, is also boosting its purses. The Donn Handicap, won by glamour horses Skip Away, Formal Gold, and Cigar in 1998, 1997, and 1996, carried a $500,000 purse in 1999, up from $300,000 the year before. The race was aired on Fox Network the day before the Super Bowl, held less than 10 miles away at Pro Player Stadium in Miami.

At Gulfstream, the first race is ready to go off. I scan the selections by five track experts in *The Gulfstream Park Handicapper*. For some reason, I don't know why, Raffie's Majesty, Bryce Soth's pick, sounds intriguing. Two bucks on Raffie's Majesty.

Raffie's Majesty, at about 5–1, wins. I collect my $8.80 at the window, and decide to go with Mr. Soth in the second race. His pick: Silvercircle. Silvercircle wins, and I pocket $10.

Who does Mr. Soth pick in the third race? I've Been a Gem? Two bucks to win on Gem, two bucks

to place on Brenda's Babe. I've Been a Gem wins, and I collect $15.

This is *easy*. My new best friend Mr. Soth tabs Silver Launch in the fourth, so I go with the Blue Goose Stable entry (like I know the Blue Goose stable from Orange Duck Stable). Silver Launch wins, of course. After four races, I am up $38.20.

How does that saying go? Quit while you're ahead?

Mr. Soth's winning touch deserts him, and I have losers in the next three races. But, picking on my own, I rebound nicely in the eighth race, as my win horse wins and my show horse shows, and I collect $15.60.

In the ninth race, I put $5 to show on number nine, Blazeable, and the woman behind the counter apparently thinks I said five and gives me a ticket showing horse number five. When I protest, she says tickets can't be exchanged. It's not my fault, I say. The ticket lady looks as if she's about to call security or something, and anyway, the race is off.

The horse I wanted, Blazeable, finishes back in the pack. Squat. The horse I didn't want places second. I'm a winner!

The big race of the day is next, the $300,000 Donn Handicap. Greedy, I put down two $5 bets and a $2 bet. Nothing.

Later, I do the math. I wagered $59 in all, and won . . . $59.80!

———

U.S. 1 crosses into Dade County at N.E. 215th Street. It is by turns Biscayne Boulevard, Brickell Avenue, and, once again, Dixie Highway. The Miami city line is at N.E. 87th Street. Dig the naked mermaids in front of the Vagabond Motel at N.E. 74th Street! The imposing white-walled building at 3801 Biscayne Boulevard is the American Police Hall of Fame and Museum, the nation's only memorial and museum to police at all levels. You can't miss the place; look for the police car that looks like it's climbing the side of the building.

Exhibits upstairs describe the exploits of America's most famous criminals—Bonnie and Clyde; Baby Face Nelson; John Dillinger; Al Capone (his hat is here, courtesy of the Ness family); and Machine Gun Kelly, a bootlegger, small-time bank robber, and "good-natured slob" who "never fired a shot at anyone and certainly never killed anyone."

Look, there's another *National Enquirer* exclusive—the tabloid's photo of Lee Harvey Oswald on a morgue slab at Parkland Hospital in Dallas.

On display is a poster dated March 24, 1882, Las Vegas:

> Notice! Thieves, Thugs, Fakirs and Bunko-Steerers
> Among whom are J. J. Harlin, alias "Off Wheeler"
> Wm. Hedges, Billy the Kid
> Billy Mullins, the Cutter
> Little Jack
> Pock-Marked Kid
> and Twenty Others
>
> If Found within the limits of this city
> after ten o'clock p.m. this night,
> you will be invited to attend a grand neck-tie party,
> The expense of which will be borne
> by 100 substantial citizens.

One display is devoted to hidden weapons— knives inside crucifixes, hairbrushes, and lipstick holders. Another is devoted to public hangings. The hangman's noose was not always dependable, or humane. "One possibility was the head being snapped off the body. It wasn't uncommon to find a head at your feet."

Surveillance equipment here includes a Letterbomb Detection and Envelope Compromise Spray, donated by the CIA, "that facilitates discreet agent opening of envelope contents without tearing."

Also on display are tear-gas canisters and a 120,000-volt Zap Stick, cooking spoons and other drug paraphernalia, a 1949 Electro-Matic Radar SpeedMeter, a real guillotine (Dr. Joseph Guillotine was a victim of his own invention), and a full-size replica of a gas chamber.

"Please feel free to sit on the gas chamber seat and have your photograph taken," announces a taped message. "Enjoy yourself."

In a side room, you can test your shooting skills— with a shotgun, assault rifle, or grenade gun—on video machines. "Don't shoot the innocent bystanders," one of the machines says helpfully.

Downstairs are a gift shop and the Hall of Fame, where the names of more than six thousand fallen officers are engraved on Italian marble. Friends and families leave flowers, notes, cards, and baby pictures.

"In memory of Kevin Easter," reads one note. "I miss you very much! You will forever be in my heart. I love you. My soulmate and my love. Julie."

A widow tells her husband about the son he never saw grow up: "Do you know that he looks just like you? Right down to your size 14 shoes! You would be so proud of the man he's become. He's tried to live his life as he knows you'd want him to, but with a little of my dramatics thrown in. I miss you and still love you. Stay by us. Becky."

———

The late, great TV show *Miami Vice* portrayed a tropical paradise awash in guns, drugs, and corruption. Viewers followed the adventures of Sonny Crockett (Don Johnson) and Ricardo Tubbs (Philip Michael Thomas), whose wardrobes ran to Guccis without socks and Versace suits without ties. Guest stars included everyone from rocker Ted Nugent to G. Gordon Liddy. No other show in the history of television used locale, atmosphere, and music so well.

Javier Giovane, Metro Dade police officer.

If *Miami Vice* wasn't the best cop show ever, it was certainly the coolest. Before *Miami Vice*, Florida, according to novelist James Hall (*Bones of Coral*), "virtually did not exist. It was a place your grandmother went to retire, the place you'd visit only if you were really desperate for rubber alligators and garish T-shirts, this strange place that really didn't belong to America."

Metro Dade Officer Javier Giovane certainly doesn't wear Guccis and Versaces on the job, and dinner during his shift is more apt to be a booth at Miami Subs than an oceanfront table at a South Beach restaurant.

With the cooperation of the Metro Dade Police Department, I spent an afternoon and evening riding with Giovane, most of it up and down Dixie Highway—U.S. 1—in Cutler Ridge, Perrine, Goulds, and Naranja, south of downtown Miami.

"First thing, we don't call it Route 1," says Detective Pat Brickman, who will ride in the back seat tonight as our escort. "Down here, it's Dixie Highway, Federal Highway, or U.S. 1."

"Or just the Highway," says the twenty-four-year-old Giovane, settling into the driver's seat of Car 15345, a Caprice Classic.

Metro Dade's jurisdiction runs from S.W. 136th Street south to Homestead. Giovane, born and raised in Queens, New York, heads north on 1. He wears a semi-automatic handgun; there's a Remington shotgun in the trunk.

"White Volvo four-door," a dispatcher's voice crackles over the radio almost immediately. Possible stolen car.

Giovane pulls over and waits for backup. Another car arrives, and the two officers drive to a nearby development. Two Metro Dade cars are already there.

"He advised us the car belonged to his nephew," one of the officers says on the radio. "He advised us he and his ex-wife were going through an altercation. . . . Maybe the ex-wife called it in."

The main radio in the car is connected to headquarters. Giovane wears a shoulder mike that is hooked to a radio on his hip; the smaller radio, set on a different frequency, allows him to talk to fellow officers.

He turns down a street in Goulds, past rundown homes and garbage-strewn lots. "This house right here," he says, "has always been known for a certain narcotic, in this case, marijuana."

"They used to store the drugs in trees," Brickman says.

Giovane turns back on Dixie Highway and pulls up alongside a known prostitute, a leggy redhead in a black fishnet blouse, cutoff jeans, and black boots. "Where are you coming from, where are you going?" he asks. Satisfied with the answer, he drives away.

"She's one of the newer ones up here," he says. "The vast majority of them have AIDS. They say it's a victimless crime. That's what bothers me. Ninety percent of [the men] are married, with kids. They take this home to their wives."

He circles a neighborhood off S.W. 220th Street, in Goulds. "This is another of our infamous drug areas," he explains. "It is notorious for shooters."

Heroin?

"Firearms. Heroin is supposedly making a comeback, but it isn't making much of an impact here."

He hooks up with Officer Jason Gambill. "Great drug house," says Gambill, pointing to a long, low gray dwelling. "It's like Fort Knox. Lights rigged up, alarms, everything."

"For the most part, the Highway," Giovane says, back on 1, "is almost like a river. You have people who drive it, shop at the markets on it, eat at the restaurants. In the old days, with the Native Americans, everyone tried to make camp by the river. Same way with the Highway today. It's a river."

The police officer follows a white Honda Civic for a few blocks, then hits his flashers. "Are those white folks?" Brickman asks from the back seat. "You see white kids around here, pretty good chance they're buying drugs."

> "Miami was good that way . . . from running red lights to holding up a 7-Eleven, hey, the cops didn't have time for that dinky stuff, man. They're too busy bulldozing the bodies off Biscayne Boulevard."
>
> James W. Hall, *Gone Wild*, Delacourte, 1995

Giovane walks up to the driver's side door. A young man in the back seat fingers a circular tuft of hair on his otherwise bald head. The driver, a girl in her late twenties, tells Giovane she's on probation for grand theft auto. But she checks out clean, and Giovane lets her drive away.

He gets on the radio and asks Gambill if they want to do a "jump-out" in an apartment complex along U.S. 1.

"A jump-out?"

"We just come in rapidly and jump out," he replies. "They run away, ditch the narcotics. Sometimes it works, sometimes it doesn't."

They drive their cars, lights flashing, into the complex. Giovane runs one way, Gambill another. A minute later, they are standing outside one apartment.

"Man, I just woke up," the tenant says.

"Someone ran out of this house," Giovane says.

"I don't know, man, I just woke up," the man insists.

"Don't lie to me, I saw someone run out."

"We ain't done nothing wrong, we innocent people," the man says.

Back on the highway, Giovane drives past a Toys 'R' Us and Home Depot. A half dozen men are gathered behind a deserted warehouse, but the police officer doesn't give them a second look. "Radio-control-plane fliers," he says.

It's dark by now. Giovane drives through a development of modest but well-kept homes. He pulls up behind a new, apparently abandoned pickup truck. A man is standing by the side of the road a good fifty feet away.

What follows is worthy of an *Outer Limits* episode. The man tells Giovane he's the owner of the truck and that he was over there because he heard "noises." Then he says he was there "for other reasons," which he doesn't specify.

"I don't have any weapons," he says suddenly.

He pulls out the registration from the glove compartment, and tells Giovane the truck is his sister-in-law's. Says he's checking out the noises for her.

"Why were you standing over there?" Giovane asks.

"I wasn't doing anything wrong," the man replies.

"I didn't say you were doing anything wrong," the police officer says. "What were you doing over there?"

"I know it may look weird to you . . . ," the man begins.

"What were you doing there?"

"I wasn't doing anything wrong."

"Look," Giovane says, trying to reason with the man, "if you were me and you came over here and saw me where you were, what would you think?"

"I don't know, man," he says. "I wasn't doing anything wrong."

Giovane is getting nowhere, but there's not much else he can do. He drives away.

"I love this district," he will say later. "Wouldn't trade it for anything. A lot of things going on."

A call comes in over the radio. A woman says she took a ruined blouse back to her dry cleaner, who, insulted, brandished a staple gun in her face. Giovane drives to the woman's house. She doesn't want to press charges against the dry cleaner. "I don't know what she's capable of," the woman says, trembling. "I don't know if I'm going to come home, find my tires slashed or a car bomb. I don't know."

Ten minutes later, Giovane gets another call, and joins Gambill and two other officers at a well-to-do condo development. They all know this guy—Angel, who works on Harleys in his garage. His neighbor has complained—again—that Angel is beating his dog. The two have a long-running neighbors' dispute.

"I'm the dog beater," proclaims Angel, a big smile on his face. "I go from house to house beating up all the dogs."

There is no furniture in his living room; Angel says his wife just left him. One of the officers suggests Angel find out what his neighbor drinks and sit down with him to "bond."

"I don't drink," Angel says.

A half hour later, Giovane pulls into a cheap roadside motel on U.S. 1. Two middle-aged men are standing in front of a Ford Explorer with two poorly dressed young women.

"Look what we got here," say another officer on the scene. "Double dating."

"We were just walking," one of the two prostitutes says in a screechy voice. "They asked us what we were doing tonight."

One of the men is retired army. He says he just stopped for a smoke.

"Little professional courtesy," Giovane tells him. "Get out of here."

The men get in the Explorer and drive away.

At 10:15, Giovane stops at a Miami Subs on Dixie Highway and gets a steak sandwich on a pita. Brickman has a grilled chicken sandwich.

A half hour later, we're back on the highway. "LOVE" is emblazoned in neon atop a pawnshop. Another call comes in. Giovane listens, and immediately hits his siren. "Burglary. Ex-boyfriend with a restraining order," he says quickly.

He guns the Caprice down U.S. 1, then turns down an unlit country road in Naranja. The speedometer hits 60, then 70, then 80. Siren blaring and lights flashing, he races into an apartment complex, drives around back, and is out of the car before it comes to a stop. We run after him, turn a corner, and find Giovane and two other officers wrestling the suspect to the ground.

"Me and Tasha been sleeping together for two months," the twenty-three-year-old suspect, Arthur, says later, handcuffed in the back seat of the police car. "We just had a fight the other night. I got a key to the apartment. The key's in my pocket."

It turns out that he is to appear in court the next morning for violating an earlier restraining order forbidding him from getting near his ex-girlfriend. She was the one who called in the report tonight as Arthur tried to break into her apartment.

He will be charged with violation of an injunction, burglary, aggravated assault, and stalking (one neighbor saw Arthur hanging outside his ex-girlfriend's apartment for several hours before she came home).

"Wait a minute," Arthur says from the back seat. "You're charging me with aggravated assault?"

"What do you want to be charged with?" Brickman asks.

Arthur thinks a moment. "With being me," he replies.

The woman, thirty, is attractive and well-dressed. She shows the officers the bedroom window where her ex-boyfriend tried to break in. The paperbacks on her bookshelf include *Hot Blood: Crimes of Passion*.

"She says I broke in?" Arthur says in the police car. "The window was already broke in. Jesus Christmas, I might as well be a dope dealer, I'm being treated like one."

Giovane returns to his patrol car; his work here is done. It's midnight; his shift is over.

"People expect shootings and carjackings," he says back at the station. "That happens, but this job

Biscayne Boulevard, Miami.

Miami.

is more about life experiences and people. This job shows you a lot of things."

———

U.S. 1 dashes through the commercial heart of Miami, showing you everything A1A, winding through fashionable Sunny Isles, Bal Harbour, and Miami Beach, doesn't. "Miami's show street" is how the WPA guide described Biscayne Boulevard in the 1930s, and it still holds true today.

Pawnshops, fast-food restaurants, doughnut shops, bodegas, laundromats, churches, schools, go-go bars, newsstands, convenience stores, police stations, and 1940s-era motels line the route. Miami Spy, part of a chain of eavesdropping/surveillance equipment stores, is at U.S. 1 and N.E. 26th Street.

The Spanish baroque–influenced Freedom Tower, at 600 Biscayne Boulevard, was built in 1925 for the *Miami Daily News*; in the 1960s, it was used to process more than a half million Cubans who had fled Castro's regime. On the other side of U.S. 1 is the American Airlines Arena, home of the NBA's Miami Heat. The fifty-five-story First Union Financial Center, at 200 South Biscayne Boulevard, is Florida's tallest building.

Freedom Tower, Miami.

U.S. 1 crosses the Miami River and becomes Brickell Avenue, a canyon of skyscrapers, including the largest concentration of international banking offices in the country. I-95 ends in Miami, off-ramping onto U.S. 1 at 32nd Road in Coconut Grove.

The Grove, South Florida's oldest settlement, was swallowed up by Miami in 1925, but still protests the annexation by periodic and unsuccessful secession movements.

When it was founded in the 1920s, Coral Gables was promoted as "The City Beautiful," where the Old World met the New. In the early 1930s, Kendall was a citrus-growing settlement with just 300 residents;

South Miami Heights.

Bert Wexelbaum, owner of Lee's Bakery, Goulds.

its population is now about 90,000. A billboard on U.S. 1 here, courtesy of Miami Cardiac and Vascular, says: "You're on one of the few arteries we can't unclog."

At S.W. 232nd Street and U.S. 1, a whitewashed little shop stands out in a tawdry stretch of go-go bars, pawnshops, and weed-choked vacant lots. "It's Here!" screams a hand-painted message above the awning. "A Slice of Sunshine" is stenciled on the window.

Inside, Bert Wexelbaum, wearing a red baseball cap that looks like it had been run over repeatedly by trucks on 1, stands behind a wooden display case filled with pies. Not just any pies, though.

"This is the best pie in Miami," the eighty-one-year-old owner of Lee's Bakery says. "Somebody took one to Germany yesterday. Down in the Keys they get fourteen dollars for a pie this size and it's lousy. I got the best pie in the world."

He has no phone, does no advertising, and his shop is the kind of place the local chamber of commerce representative would run away from, screaming. A refrigerator that looks like it was fished from a landfill stands in one corner; a battered, rusted-out couch sits in back. "Appalachian Spring" plays on an old radio.

"You know who stopped here once?" Bert says. "Jimmy Hoffa. Short guy, blue eyes. Very polite. Bought two pies. 'Radar' from *M*A*S*H* came in one day, bought all my pies to use in a pie-throwing scene. When President Nixon lived on Key Biscayne, he would send a noncommissioned officer over to buy pies. He didn't have to pay for them, but always did."

Bert's from Brooklyn; you can still hear it in his voice. On vacation one year in Miami with his wife, Bert found himself on the beach thinking, "Man, this is the life."

He was a surgical supply salesman in New York City, but when he moved to Miami he noticed bakery trucks were doing well, so he bought a bakery

Lee's Bakery, Goulds.

truck and parked it on Key Biscayne. "I sold danish, pastries, doughnuts, bread, anything I could get ahold of," he recalls. "Then I got the idea of selling Key lime pies."

He parked his truck on U.S. 1 south of here, in Naranja. "People were lined up for three blocks trying to buy my pies," he says. "The building inspector came by one day. He said, 'What are you doing?' I said, 'What do you mean what am I doing? I'm selling Key lime pies.'"

In 1949, he bought the little building in Goulds, a former real estate office. It's called Lee's after his son, Lee, whose photo is on the pinkish wall. Bert remembers the endless procession of army trucks rumbling down U.S. 1 on their way to Homestead during the Cuban missile crisis. "Never seen so many trucks in my life," he says.

Until a year ago, Bert made the pies himself, but it became too exhausting, so a baker in southwest Miami now makes them.

"I supervise everything," he says. "Make sure it's browned right."

The pieman won't reveal his recipe, but says this much: "We have a good crust. The filling is tangy. We don't use condensed milk; it overshadows the lime. [Competitors] don't cook it right; they swish it around. I get all the customers in the Keys; they come up here."

Once Bert sells his pies, he closes up shop, no matter if it's noon or 5 p.m., and goes home to watch *Geraldo* or *Wall Street Week*.

How long will the pieman stay in business?

"I have arthritis, aches and pains, I got things for which there are no names," he says, smiling. "But as long as I can get up in the morning, I'll be here."

———

Princeton, just south of Goulds, was originally named Modello. But a group of Princeton grads opened a lumber mill in 1905 and put up a huge Princeton sign. Although it was repeatedly removed, the sign always reappeared, and the name eventually stuck.

Naranja.

At S.W. 286th Street in Homestead is one of the stranger sights, and stories, on U.S. 1. From the highway, Coral Castle looks like just another tacky South Florida tourist attraction, a prehistoric rock version of a children's playground.

The king and builder of this castle was Edward Leedskalnin, born in Latvia in 1887. A frail and often sickly young man, he was engaged at age twenty-six to a sixteen-year-old girl named Agnes.

"Cupid's arrow found its mark," a voice purporting to be Ed's says on the Coral Castle audio tour tape. "My Agnes was ten years younger, but I was smitten by her charm. I failed to see the danger. The night before our wedding she left me, claiming I was too old and poor."

The voice on the tape is soft, insistent, and hypnotic, like Bela Lugosi doing "Dracula."

Crushed by Agnes's rejection, Leedskalnin emigrated to the United States, working his way across the country as a mason, logger, and ranchhand, eventually settling in Florida City. In 1923, he bought an acre of land for twelve dollars, and started

Coral Castle exterior, Homestead.

Admission marker, Coral Castle, Homestead.

Homestead.

to build a rock garden, making furniture and fixtures "from the stones under my feet."

"My neighbors' curiosity got the best of me, and soon I was giving tours of my Eden for ten cents. Life was good and I was happy until civilization started moving in around me."

In 1936, he bought a ten-acre parcel of land on U.S. 1 in Homestead. Using simple tools—crude winches, iron wedges fashioned from truck springs, a ladder built from pieces of an old car—Leedskalnin excavated, carved, and moved tons of coral rock.

In his new surroundings, he completed his life's work: a nine-ton gate, balanced on ball bearings, that moved at the touch of a finger; a 60,000-pound stone along the north wall; eleven half-ton chairs; a forty-seven-foot-high, thirty-ton obelisk, and other pieces.

"People would look at me, all five foot and 100 pounds, and almost laugh. I hated it when asked how I moved and carved such pieces. Everyone knows if you understand the principles of weight and balance as were used in Egypt to build the pyramids, you can move the world."

A stargazer, he carved Mars, Saturn, and a crescent moon out of massive rock. "I used to sit in that moon and wave at cars on Route 1," he recalls on the tape. "A few years ago a rock star named Billy Idol did the same thing."

Leedskalnin carved beds, a cement-lined tub, and a heart-shaped, two-and-a-half-ton Feast of Love table listed in *Ripley's Believe It or Not* as the World's Largest Valentine.

He built a Repentance Corner for "when my Sweet Sixteen sasses me back," although by that time Agnes had long since left him.

"Let me say here that when I refer to Sweet Sixteen it is not the age I talk about; rather I mean a brand-new girl, one not soiled."

The King of Coral Castle needed a throne, so Leedskalnin built his Throne Room, with its massive chairs. The only chair that was uncomfortable, he would point out, was the one designed for his future mother-in-law; he wanted to keep her visits short.

He lived in the two-story, 240-ton main tower. Sixteen steps ("perhaps Sweet Sixteen is on my mind too much") led upstairs. He lived there by himself. His "real love" was experimenting with electromagnetic force. He kept his life savings—thirty-five hundred dollars—in an old tripod he used as a radio stand.

In December 1951, he put up a sign out front that read "Going to the Hospital" and checked into Jackson Memorial.

"Three days later I passed on to another life, but I can still look down and see my beloved rock garden, which passed on to my nephew Harry in Detroit. He didn't want it, so a man in Chicago bought it to operate as a tourist attraction. He sold it in 1980 to his cousin, who owns it to this day."

Doris Wishman, director of several dozen sexploitation shockers (*Bad Girls Go to Hell*, *Let Me Die a Woman*, etc.), filmed her 1963 cult hit *Nude on the Moon* at Coral Castle. In 1984, Coral Castle was placed on the National Register of Historic Places.

"There's plenty of competition," says Frommer's Florida guide, "but Coral Castle is probably the zaniest attraction in Florida." The grounds behind the castle are tree-shaded; there are benches where you can relax and ponder the intricacies of Ed's universe.

"As a tourist attraction, I like to think Coral Castle is an attraction for the mind. It will cause you to think and dream. Did I really do this with my physical strength alone? With only a fourth-grade education was I really capable of understanding the universe?

"When you go into the gift shop don't forget to buy the four-color book which tells the story of Coral Castle. . . . It has been my extreme pleasure to have you here today. Please tell a friend of your remarkable discovery. So long . . ."

———

Homestead and Florida City, packed with hotels, restaurants, and gas stations, are jumping-off points to the Everglades and the Keys. Hurricane Andrew left Homestead a shambles in 1992; today, the rebuilt city hosts NASCAR Grand National and Craftsman Truck Series races and CART FedEx events at the Homestead Motorsports Complex. The Fiftieth Annual Homestead Championship Rodeo was also held there in 1999. A sign along the road says this is also the home of the Everglades Mounted Posse Drill Team.

Florida City, the southernmost mainland town in the United States, was originally called Detroit, thanks to a group of settlers from Michigan. But the local post office said the name was confusing, so residents changed it to Florida City.

It may come as a surprise to learn U.S. 1 runs through the Everglades. "There are no other Everglades in the world," Marjory Stoneman Douglas began *The Everglades: River of Grass*, her 1947 classic. "They are, they have always been, one of the unique regions of the earth, remote, never wholly known."

Douglas helped lead the campaign to have the Everglades' core preserved as Everglades National Park. Douglas, a former assistant editor at the *Miami Herald*, railed against poor land management and overdevelopment that both polluted and drained the Everglades.

When the 1.5-million-acre park was dedicated by President Harry Truman on December 6, 1947, there were fewer than two million people living in the entire state. Now there are six million in South Florida alone.

One million people will visit the Everglades this year, but more people will visit Ford's Theater in Washington, where Lincoln was assassinated. Nearly

Marathon.

as many foreigners (21 percent) visit the park as Florida residents (29 percent).

"It is the last honest place in Florida," Cyril Zaneski and Geoffrey Tomb wrote in a *Miami Herald* series marking the park's fiftieth anniversary. "Elsewhere, you find subdivisions named for trees developers chopped down long ago and beach towns named for golden sand the waves have swept away. Here, places are called The Nightmare, Snake Bight, Graveyard Creek, Lostmans River, and Hell's Bay. It's simple: In Everglades National Park, man is not in charge."

But the park is imperiled on many fronts. Fertilizer-laced water washes in from Lake Okeechobee; drums of flammable and toxic chemicals are dumped here. The population of South Florida is

expected to triple by the year 2050. The Everglades, a sponge that soaks up rain for underground aquifers, will be sorely tested.

"It seems miraculous that the Everglades haven't been completely parched, poached, or poisoned to stagnation by the six million people who've moved in around them," says novelist and *Miami Herald* columnist Carl Hiaasen.

Ranger-led programs and hikes are held year-round at the park's visitor centers.

Giving a talk about birds behind the Royal Palm Visitor Center, ranger Yvette Daniels says, "Sometimes you see him in the shallows, in the water; he be everywhere." Someone asks her about alligators, and, as if on cue, one surfaces in the pond behind her. South Florida is the only place where both alligators and crocodiles can be found in the wild; the Everglades are home to about four hundred American crocodiles.

"There are two seasons here: buggy and more buggy," ranger Tanya Stiers tells a group on the Anhinga Trail. "You have the fortune of being here in the buggy season. Congratulations."

I get a painful introduction to the number-one bug—the mosquito—on a solo hike along Long Pine Key Nature Trail. The mosquitoes are voracious—and it's noon.

On the road to the Pa-hay-okee Overlook, a sign announces: "Rock Reef Pass. Elevation 3 feet." Pahay-okee looks out over a sea of sawgrass, bending slightly in the softest of breezes. A plaque quotes Loren Eiseley: "If there is magic on the planet, it is contained in water. . ."

Marjory Stoneman Douglas died May 14, 1998. She was 108. Although nearly blind for the last two decades and in failing health, she continued to lecture and lobby on behalf of Florida's wild places. Her ashes were scattered, per her wishes, in the Everglades.

The Last Chance Saloon, on 1 southbound below Florida City, is aptly named; just beyond it, the highway plunges into the swamp, mangrove, and

The Everglades.

"No Passing" signs that mark the true beginning of the Florida Keys.

———

The Florida Keys, which are the only West Indian islands you can drive to, were created more than one hundred thousand years ago from oceanic limestone and ancient coral reefs. American Indians lived in the Keys for thousands of years before the first Europeans arrived.

Just south of Florida City.

Florida Keys.

According to Fodor's Florida guide, the Overseas Highway (U.S. 1) can be, depending on the time of day and your outlook, "a 110-mile traffic jam lined with garish billboards, hamburger stands, shopping centers, motels, and trailer courts," or "a mystical pathway skimming the sea."

For me, the Keys will always be more mystical pathway than commercial strip. Billboards, strip malls, hamburger joints, seafood markets, humble motels, exclusive resorts, even a WalMart and Home Depot clog the highway, but development has not run amok.

Then again, I'm from New Jersey, so any place that doesn't have a multiplex theater and strip mall every quarter mile seems like paradise.

In the Keys, U.S. 1, with the possible exception of the Maine coast, is at its most beautiful. Maine may be more wild and rugged, but in the Keys you don't have to worry about ice. A common Maine road sign you'll never encounter in Florida: Moose Crossing.

———

Key Largo is the first stop on the Overseas Highway. Key Largo Station was originally a stop on the Florida East Coast Railway, which connected Key West with the mainland. At Key West, passenger cars were shunted onto ferryboats bound for Cuba. You could step into a Pullman car in New York City and step out of it in Havana. But the great hurricane of 1935 wiped out 40 miles of track, and service was discontinued.

Key Largo was originally called Rock Harbor, but the name was changed to cash in on the Humphrey Bogart–Lauren Bacall movie *Key Largo*. Bogart's presence lingers in Key Largo. The *African Queen*, the boat used in the Bogart–Katharine Hepburn movie, is docked along U.S. 1.

Mel Fisher Treasure Castle, Key Largo.

The Shell Man, at Mile Marker 106 bayside, calls itself "The United States' most unique store." Next door is the Florida Keys Visitors' Center. There are plenty of hotels in Key Largo, but none like Jules' Undersea Lodge (MM 103.4 oceanside), the world's only underwater hotel. Rooms, accessible by scuba diving only, are thirty feet underwater and encircled by windows, putting guests right in the middle of the marine environment. A tamer adventure lies ahead. It's time to go snorkeling.

The nation's first undersea park is located along U.S. 1. It's hard to imagine the same highway that spirals through downtown Boston, runs through the Bronx, and vaults over Jersey City as the Pulaski Skyway also provides access to one of the best places in the world to sample marine life.

John Pennekamp Coral Reef State Park (MM 102.5 OS) and adjacent Key Largo Marine Sanctuary provide 178 square miles of ocean wonderland. Snorkeling, scuba diving, and sailing trips, plus glass-bottom boat tours, are available. Check the board inside the office for wave and visibility conditions.

"There's a marine head in the back," says Rick Warriner, captain of the *Tons o' Fun* boat taking twenty of us on a snorkeling trip. "It's nothing like

The *African Queen* heads out to sea. Key Largo.

the toilet you have at home. We'll explain how it works." He smiles. "If you don't learn how to use it, we'll have a lot of people with their knees together on the way home."

The boat is heading to the Grecian Rocks. One famous diving spot in Pennekamp is the Christ of the Deep statue, its arms outstretched in twenty feet of water.

Conditions look ideal—bright, sunny skies, and only a one–to–two–inch chop, according to the board, but by the time we reach our dive spot the waves are much higher. If it's one to two inches, it's in whale not people inches. It's not so much snorkeling as bouncing around in some underwater thrill ride at Disney World. I bob around for a while, and at one point find myself in the middle of a school of multicolored fish.

Shark, barracuda, even stingrays are common sights, according to first mate Jim Segroves.

"Last week, a twelve-foot shark came up alongside the boat," he says. "All the snorkels went in the water."

Across from Pennekamp is the Maritime Museum of the Florida Keys (MM 102 BS), which displays silver and gold coins spanning four hundred years of New World history, and a reconstructed shipwreck site.

The *African Queen*, tied up next to the Holiday Inn Key Largo (MM 99.7 OS), is somehow smaller than one expected. In John Huston's *The African Queen*, Bogart played gin-swilling Charlie Allnut, while Hepburn was Rosie Sayer, a slain missionary's spinster sister. They elude pro-German forces, are captured, blow up a pursuing gunboat, escape on the *Queen* and wash ashore to live happily ever after.

There were two *African Queen*s. One was blown up in the movie. The other bounced from owner to owner, finally ending up in Ocala, Florida. That's when Jim Hendricks, a native of Palisades Park, New Jersey, and a former marine, heard about her.

A big fan of *The African Queen*, he bought the thirty-foot boat in 1981 for sixty-five hundred dollars. But he couldn't operate the British-built 1912 steamer because of something called the Jones Act, a 1921 law that says only boats with American-built hulls can ply U.S. coastal waters.

In 1989, then-president George Bush signed a bill exempting the *African Queen* ("the greatest thing he did as president," Hendricks says).

The *African Queen*'s skipper now takes passengers on cruises around the Key Largo waterfront, chugging 1,000 feet into the placid Atlantic Ocean before turning back.

"I don't know anywhere else in America where it's easier to get into the ocean than here," he says, piloting the boat one hot, sunny afternoon.

Hendricks, who wears a raffish red scarf and a polo shirt with "African Queen Key Largo" stitched above the pocket, uses specially packaged African Queen Stoking Fuel to fire the diesel engine. With three ear-shattering whistles, the boat slides from the dock, and Hendricks becomes tour guide, captain—and raconteur.

"See that?" he says, pointing to a sprawling waterfront home. "It was a drug smuggler's place. It was originally listed at 1.4 million dollars, then 900,000 dollars. I called the other day; it's down to 575,000 dollars. That's a great buy. These houses go for 1.5 million dollars."

Hendricks and Hepburn have corresponded informally over the years. "Is it really the *African Queen*?" she wrote in her first letter. "I thought it was blown up in Africa."

She refers to the boat as "Dear Old *Queen*." Hendricks once asked the actress if she would cross the

Islamorada Chamber of Commerce.

English Channel with him on the *African Queen*; Hepburn politely declined.

He sent her roses on her birthday in 1992. "That certainly is a great big splotchy bright bouquet of red roses," she replied. "Really gorgeous. And they make me feel really important. I just must be somebody. Thank you. Thank you."

———

At the Florida Keys Wild Bird Rehabilitation Center (MM 93.6 BS) in Tavernier, sick and injured birds are nursed. The center was founded by woodcarver and teacher Laura Quinn. The *Reporter*, the Keys' weekly newspaper, is located on U.S. 1 in Tavernier.

Islamorada, "The Sport Fishing Capital of the World," actually takes in four keys—Plantation, Windley, Upper Matecumbe, and Lower Matecumbe. Viewed from the air, Upper Matecumbe often appears lilac-colored; thus, Islamorada, Spanish for "purple island." Marker 88, one of the Keys' top restaurants, is located, naturally, at MM 88, bayside.

To many, U.S. 1 may look like one nonstop commercial strip from Key Largo to Key West, but many of the stores, restaurants, cafes, and motels are colorfully named (Pay Fair Market, Josie's Junk Alley, Finnegan's Awake bar/restaurant, etc.) and creatively if not zanily decorated. A whale mural enlivens the

Islamorada.

facade of the Kmart on U.S. 1 in Marathon, which is also home to a WalMart, Home Depot, and Deadhead George's Mexican Grill. About the last place you'd look for the Museum of Natural History of the Florida Keys (MM 50 gulfside) would be across the street from Kmart, but that's where it is.

Crane Point Hammock is home not only to the natural history museum, but a Children's Museum and the Adderly Village Black Historical Site. Crane Point is named after Francis and Mary Crane, who

moved here from Needham, Massachusetts. A shopping center, resort hotel, and residential development were envisioned here, but the Florida Keys Land and Sea Trust, a nonprofit organization, stepped in and purchased the property in 1988.

The natural history museum is a good place to learn about the Keys' geology, wildlife, and history (pirates were such a nuisance that in 1822 the U.S. navy established a West Indies Anti-Piracy Squadron in Key West). Also headquartered on 1 in Marathon is the Turtle Hospital, which cares for sick and injured sea turtles. The hospital is run by Richie Moretti, a retired auto mechanic, and his team of vets and volunteers. The building houses an operating room, recovery tanks, nursery, and imaging equipment; there is even a Turtle Hospital ambulance.

Museum of Natural History of the Florida Keys, Marathon.

In memory of Charlie. Lower Matecumbe Key.

At MM 59 GS in Grassy Key, a thirty-foot-high statue of a dolphin seems poised to leap over U.S. 1. There are three dolphin research centers in the Keys, and several more marine zoos, but only the Dolphin Research Center, on U.S. 1, can say it is the home of Flipper.

Remember the theme song?

They call him Flipper, Flipper,
Faster than lightning.
No one you see
Is smarter than he.
And we know Flipper
Lives in a world full of wonder,
Lying there under,
Under the sea.

Flipper actually was a dolphin named Mitzi, and she belonged to Milton Santini, a commercial fisherman who lived in the Keys. One day, Santini jumped on the back of a dolphin as it swam in the boat's wake and went for a ride, a trick he repeated many times. Santini began catching and selling dolphins to zoos, aquariums, even the U.S. navy.

In 1962, after breaking his back in an accident, Santini began training dolphins, opening Santini's Porpoise Training School on U.S. 1 in Grassy Key on November 22, 1963—the day John F. Kennedy was assassinated.

One day, a movie crew scouting for a dolphin to play the title role in a movie called *Flipper* saw Santini playing with Mitzi, his pet dolphin. Mitzi became "Flipper" in the 1963 movie starring Chuck Connors; Santini served as consultant for both the movie and the TV show that followed. Mitzi died unexpectedly at the age of twenty-two in 1971. A monument to the original Flipper is on the grounds of the Dolphin Research Center.

In 1971, Santini sold his school to an entertainment conglomerate, which reopened it as Flip-

Feeding time, Dolphin Research Center, Grassy Key.

per's Sea School. Signs outside the building in the seventies proclaimed: "This is it. Best show in the Keys, except for the sunsets. Flipper's Sea School."

Six years later, it was sold to whale conservation activist Jean Paul Fortom-Gouin, who closed the facility to the public and used it to concentrate on dolphin research. In 1983, he gave the facility to Mandy and Jayne Rodriguez, his general manager and head trainer, respectively. A year later the couple opened the Dolphin Research Center.

Twenty Atlantic bottlenose dolphins and three California sea lions live in saltwater lagoons with low mesh fences. Tours are held at 10, 11, 12:30, 2, and 3:30. Busloads of schoolchildren are often found here, screaming with delight at the antics of Buck, Luther, Santini, and the other dolphins.

A big kiss. Dolphin Research Center, Grassy Key.

The center's Web site (www.dolphins.org) describes the center's work and programs and gives personal data about each dolphin.

"Dolphins have about one hundred sharp teeth, but they don't use them for chewing," says trainer Danielle Kadas, leading a tour. "Food goes right down the hatch."

Each dolphin goes through twenty-five to thirty pounds of fish a day, mostly herring and capelin, a smelt relative. The diet is supplemented with vitamins, which are slipped inside the food fish.

Several programs allow you to get up close and personal with the dolphins. Dolphin Encounter is a two-and-a-half-hour program that includes a twenty-minute structured swim with the dolphins. In DolphinInsight, participants, working from the floating dock, communicate with the dolphins by hand and verbal signals. Another program brings together physically and mentally handicapped children and the dolphins.

"Our mission is strictly for the dolphins," explains administrative assistant Laura Catlow. "We're not here to make money. We're not here for entertainment."

Researchers from around the world come here to study Rainbow and pals. "One researcher from England has asked to study humor in dolphins," Catlow says. "Is there such a thing?"

———

When it is not running past the Keys' seemingly nonstop parade of signs, billboards, markers, and colorfully decorated shops, U.S. 1 vaults over the water on a series of bridges.

The most spectacular is the Seven-Mile Bridge connecting Key Vaca (Marathon) and Little Duck Key. Top down in a convertible on the Seven-Mile Bridge is, to me, the ultimate Keys experience. You can walk, jog, or fish along the 4-mile-long segment of the old bridge, called "the longest fishing pier in the world."

Pigeon Key, at MM 47, was used as a CIA staging area during the Bay of Pigs invasion. Now the five-acre island is a favorite spot for painters. At the end of Seven-Mile Bridge, at MM 37, is Bahia Honda State Park, a relaxing oasis just steps from the highway.

The hurricane-severed end of the bridge in Pigeon Key was used in the Arnold Schwarzenegger movie *True Lies*. The hurricane on September 2, 1935, spelled the end of the Florida East Coast Railway, dubbed Flagler's Folly. "From coach windows or the favored observation car, travelers on it could watch dolphins leaping from deep channels or sharks pacing the train as it moved slowly across the great bridge," wrote the late Pat Parks in her excellent book *The Railroad That Died at Sea* (Langley Press, 1996). More than four hundred people died, half of them highway workers (the Hurricane Monument is at MM 81.6 OS in Islamorada).

The Overseas Highway fared better than the overseas railroad. When the road to Key West was completed in 1928, it was hailed by *American Motorist* magazine as "the world's most wonderful automobile drive," even if motorists were forced to use two car ferries to bridge the 40-mile gap between Lower Matecumbe Key and No Name Key, and the entire Miami–Key West journey took eight hours.

Incorporating portions of the old railbed and bridges, the Overseas Highway was completed in 1938 at the cost of 8.5 million dollars. More improvements were made over the next six years. On May 16, 1944, then-governor Spessard Holland cut a ribbon at a dedication ceremony in Florida City, signaling the opening of the last link in U.S. 1 from Fort Kent to Key West.

———

Three kinds of souvenirs are available along U.S. 1 in the Keys: junk, worthless junk, and the custom-made license plates available from the Prince of Plates, parked at MM 30.5 in front of Coconuts Lounge on Big Pine Key.

"I've been doing this for fifteen years, and I'm not going to tell you more than that," says the bare-chested Lenny Elfers, a k a the Prince of Plates, standing inside his twelve-foot step van. Over the next two hours, though, he tells all.

"All kinds of people have tried to imitate me," he says. "They think they can make a million dollars doing this. If I was making a million dollars, I wouldn't be doing this, I'd be on a fifty-foot Hatteras."

Born on Kelly's Island in Ohio, he was a contractor and commercial fisherman for thirty-plus years. "Never worked for anybody; can't go for that," he explains. "They pay you enough to get back to work on Monday. Ask anybody who works for anybody."

Fifteen years ago, he spotted a guy making crude license plates at a car show. Larry knew he could do it better, so he built a special license-plate machine. Took him a year.

He spent the next three years traveling to shows selling his custom-made plates. At one show, he did well. He makes me promise not to reveal how much. "Then these shows started demanding higher fees. They wanted five hundred dollars [rent] a day and 20 percent of the business. I said—you can write this—'Fuck that.'"

The Prince of Plates, Big Pine Key.

He gave up the cross-country wandering, finding a home—and a perfect business location—under a palm tree in the Keys. His nephew owns the Coconuts Lounge.

"People say they can buy this up in Miami for ten dollars," says Lenny, sporting an earring in one ear and flip-up sunglasses. "I say, well, why aren't you up in Miami buying them fucking there? Another guy said, 'Twenty-two dollars, that's too much.' I said, 'What are you, a price consultant?'"

Sample plates cover the inside and outside of his truck. LYF SUX. RU RICH 2. On a Quebec plate: 2 COLD. On a Nebraska plate: BUFLO CHPS. One plate's cryptic message: EM TAE.

"It's backwards," Lenny explains. "Cute, huh? It looks real cute when you pull up in back of a cop car."

"Our credit manager is Helen Waite," says a sign above his table. "If you want credit, go to Helen Waite."

His worst customers?

"I can tell you exactly where they're from—New Jersey," he says, grinning wickedly. "New Jerseyans are the only people who stand up here and tell you you're doing this wrong."

His nickname is Snake, so the bartenders at Coconuts gave him a freeze-dried snake, which sits on his dashboard. He pulls out his legendary rattlesnake Panama hat, which he made himself. The snake's preserved head is on the hat, the rest of it is in his truck somewhere.

"When someone asks, 'Is that a snake sticking out of your head?' I say, 'No, it's a fuckin' rat.'"

Two British guys pull up in a rent-a-car. "They tell me America is full of entrepreneurs; now we know,"

Clyde Perkey's bizarre bat tower, Sugarloaf Key.

port and then follow the road 0.3 of a mile until it forks. Bear right and you'll see a weather-beaten forty-five-foot-high tower.

Holy Mosquito, Batman, it's the bat tower! Developer Clyde Perkey was determined to rid the Keys of mosquitoes, so he built a tower and stocked it with bat aphrodisiac to lure the mosquito-loving animals. The bats showed up, but didn't stay long. Mosquitoes everywhere celebrated. The bat tower still stands, a testament to Perkey's bizarre vision.

———

At MM 8, U.S. 1 splits the U.S. Naval Air Station Key West on Boca Chica Key. Painted on the side of the Coral Isle Bar on Stock Island are these not-so-encouraging words: Free Beer *tomorrow*. The highway enters Key West as Roosevelt Boulevard, skirting the waterfront. A fiberglass shark is perched atop a car in the marina. "Welcome to Paradise," says a sign in front of the Ramada Inn.

Roosevelt Boulevard becomes Truman Avenue. The street is a riot of color: a yellow "Eat Me" sign atop a pink car owned by Breakfast Anytime Delivers (BAD), a bright green Volkswagen mini-bus advertising Island Bicycles. At 1205-B Truman Avenue is the whitewashed storefront of the National AIDS Brigade.

marvels Roger Hamilton, of Meriden. Hamilton, in the "automotive electronics" business, says this is his ninety-seventh trip to the United States. He's visited nearly every month for the past ten years.

"You can stand up on the bumper and watch," Lenny tells the two.

"You're assuming we can stand up," Hamilton says.

"Drinking?"

"Not yet, but we'll get to it soon enough."

Also on Big Pine Key is radio station U.S. 1 (104.7 FM). Mangrove Mama's, a cool Keys bar/restaurant, is at MM 20, across the road from the KOA campground.

Possibly the strangest site in all the Keys can be found at MM 17. Turn at the sign for Sugarloaf Air-

Words to go thirsty by. Stock Island.

Key West.

Key West.

"We're right on the street, we're in the real world," says Paul Smyth, director of NAB's Key West drop-in center.

The National AIDS Brigade was founded in 1983 by Jon Stuen-Parker, then a medical student at Yale. Stuen-Parker began the nation's first IV-drug-user education outreach program. In 1986, NAB launched the nation's first needle exchange programs; in 1995 it undertook what it says is the first AIDS prevention outreach in the history of Cambodia.

"If you prick your arm," says a poster inside NAB's Key West office, "arm your prick." Brochures fill a rack. One is titled "Reach for the Bleach. Clean Works Before and After Use."

The Scottish-born Smyth ("I had some experience with substance abuse in my country") had been working at NAB's drop-in center in Boston when he was offered a job in Key West. He drove down from Boston in July 1995, opening up the office in a former cobbler's shop.

Only in Key West.

The National AIDS Brigade's Key West office.

Smyth has since handed out thousands of condoms to students from Key West High School. "Our basic philosophy is abstinence, but nationwide, abstinence is not where it's at with high school students," he says.

HIV testing and counseling is done here twice a week. "It's all walk-ins, no appointments," Smyth explains. In March, the Brigade hosts an AIDS Walk through Key West. The group has also started a condom distribution program in Cuba.

"A two-piece road, a fit companion to a one-piece bathing suit, both covering very little anatomy. . . . We shall soon as see a road to the mainland from Key West as we shall see angels flitting down from heaven to Key West on sunbeams."

Early skepticism about Overseas Highway, 1920s

Donations "go straight into the rent," says Smyth, who eats at a local soup kitchen. Asked how long he will stay here, he says, "For as long as it's needed.

"I don't want to sound pompous," he adds, "but it comes down to human suffering. I'm not a crusader. You go out and help people, and don't expect anything back."

From Smyth's office, U.S. 1—Truman Avenue—makes a right turn onto Whitehead Street. At 907 Whitehead is the Ernest Hemingway Home and Museum. Hemingway wrote many of his greatest works—*Death in the Afternoon*, *To Have and Have Not*, *For Whom the Bell Tolls*, *Green Hills of Africa*, among others—on U.S. 1.

He owned the Spanish colonial–style house from 1931 until his death in 1961. His study, situated in a pool house loft, was connected to the main house by a precarious catwalk to discourage visitors.

There is a little cat cemetery for the celebrity-named felines who called 907 Whitehead home. Kim Novak, 1975–1997. Spencer Tracy, 1974–1997. Frank Sinatra, 1979–1996. Charlie Chan, 1985–1995.

Cat gravestones,
Hemingway Home and Museum, Key West.

"This is my friend Archie MacLeish," says pony-tailed tour guide John Brooks, pointing to a cat sleeping in the master bedroom. "I'm trying to get him in the *Guinness Book of World Records* for longest nap."

First editions of *The Old Man and the Sea*, *A Moveable Feast*, and *For Whom the Bell Tolls* line a display case. There are photos of Hemingway's four wives, photos of Hemingway on safari. Clippings describe his exploits as a Red Cross ambulance driver. According to one story, a mortar round caused him to be wounded in "237 places."

"The wounds from the mortar didn't hurt a bit, and the machine gun bullet just felt like a smack on the leg by an icy snowball," he wrote.

Hemingway's pool, built in the late 1930s at a cost of twenty thousand dollars, was the first pool in Key West. The price prompted the writer to take a penny from his pocket and press it into the wet cement of the patio and announce jokingly, "Here, take the last penny I've got!" The penny is still there.

From Hemingway's house, U.S. 1 continues down Whitehead Street to Fleming Street. Just before the corner, in front of the Monroe County Courthouse, a sign proclaims:

> End of the Rainbow.
> And End of the Route U.S. 1.
> Key West, Florida.
> Unlimited Opportunities.
> Tropical Vacationland.

It may be the end of the rainbow, but it is not quite the end of the highway. There are a few more homes and shops—Girl Friday of the Florida Keys; Sophia, Tarot Card Reader and Psychic—and then a sign with the word END above the number 1.

———

U.S. 1 is not the longest highway in the United States, nor the most scenic, nor the most romantic, maybe not even the most historic. It is simply the best damn highway in America, and, at the corner of Fleming and Whitehead in Key West, it finally comes to an end.

This is where it ends. Key West.

WHERE TO EAT ON U.S. 1

MAINE

Jade Palace, Caribou

Irving Big Stop, Houlton

Coffee Express, Maine Coast Mall, Ellsworth

Riverside Cafe, Ellsworth

Belfast Bay Brewing Co., Belfast

Hideaway Diner, Northport

Lighthouse Espresso, Rockland

Rockland Cafe, Rockland

Thomaston Cafe and Bakery, Thomaston

Moody's Diner, Waldoboro

Miss Wiscasset Diner, Wiscasset

Red's Eats, Wiscasset

Brunswick Diner, Brunswick

Thai Place, Brunswick

Congdon's Doughnuts, Wells

Maine Diner, Wells

NEW HAMPSHIRE

Dinnerhorn Seafood Oyster Bar, Portsmouth

Molly Malone's, Portsmouth

Southwestern Grill, Portsmouth

Uncle Tai's Restaurant, Portsmouth

Galley Hatch, Hampton

MASSACHUSETTS

Agawam Diner, Rowley

Bel Air Diner, Peabody

Sunrise Pizza and Sub Shop, Peabody

International House of Pancakes, Norwood

CONNECTICUT

New England Country Store and Bakery, Branford

White's Family Diner, Bridgeport

Fairfield Diner and Vegetarian Enclave, Fairfield

Super Duper Weenie Wagon, Fairfield

Silver Star Diner, Norwalk

NEW JERSEY

White Mana, Jersey City

Queen Elizabeth Diner, Elizabeth

Luna Bell, Woodbridge

Frank's Italian Hotdogs, Edison

On the Border, New Brunswick

T.J.'s Cafe, North Brunswick

PENNSYLVANIA

City Line Diner, Philadelphia

Llanerch Diner, Llanerch

MARYLAND

Daniel's, Elk Ridge

The Little Tavern, Laurel

Tastee Diner, Laurel

Gringada, Beltsville

VIRGINIA

Aunt Sarah's Pancake House, Glen Allen

Little Pig Barbecue, Petersburg

Waffle House, Petersburg

NORTH CAROLINA

Tip-Top Restaurant, Business U.S. 1, Henderson

International House of Pancakes, Capitol
    Boulevard, Raleigh

Food Lion Deli-Bakery, Tramway

Mac's, Southern Pines

Huddle House, Southern Pines

SOUTH CAROLINA

Hard Times Cafe, Cassatt

GEORGIA

Amigo's, Augusta

Krispy Kreme, Augusta

Huddle House, Louisville

El Potro Mexican Restaurant, Waycross

Huddle House, Waycross

Huddle House, Folkston

FLORIDA

Waffle House, Jacksonville

Waffle House, St. Augustine

Sonny's Real Pit Bar-B-Que, St. Augustine

Charlie T's Truck Stop, south of St. Augustine

Armadillo Grill, Holly Hill

Dixie Donuts, Holly Hill

International House of Pancakes, Daytona

Songkram, South Daytona

Sam's Italian Seafood Restaurant, New Smyrna
    Beach

Moonlight Drive-In, Titusville

Nicky's Donut, West Palm Beach

The Original Pancake House, Deerfield Beach

Anna's, Fort Lauderdale

The Caves, Fort Lauderdale

Tina's Spaghetti House, Fort Lauderdale

Jack's Hollywood Diner, Hollywood

Jimmy's East Side Diner, Miami

Thai Silk, Miami

Pollo Tropical chain, Miami area

Shivers, Homestead

International House of Pancakes, Cutler Ridge and
    Homestead

Mutineer Restaurant, Florida City

Islamorada Fish Company, Islamorada

Marker 88, Islamorda

Mangrove Mama's, Sugarloaf Key

ACKNOWLEDGMENTS

I met so many wonderful people in the two years I spent on the road that to single out a handful would slight many more, so I will just thank all those folks on these pages who made this book, and the journey down U.S. 1, such a memorable experience. WIth few exceptions, I never scheduled interviews, just dropping in on people in the middle of the day or night. Not one person told me to go away or come back another time. Thank you for that, and for your stories.

Up at the north end of the highway, thanks go to the Topsfield Fair front office, which let me pore through their great collection of old-time photos and records. To Larry Cultrera, for the kind use of his vintage postcards. To Arthur Krim, for taking me on that nighttime ride down U.S. 1 in Saugus, Massachusetts. And Bob Paino, of Route 1 Miniature Golf, for graciously lending me his family album.

Special thanks are due Richard Weingroff of the Federal Highway Administration, who made my day, and saved me countless hours of work, by preparing a mammoth file stuffed with newspaper clippings and documents related to U.S. 1.

To Bob Foster of the Hoboken Historical Museum, for persuading me to visit the Coral Castle.

To Stew Leonard Jr. for the tour of his store, and the use of company archival pictures.

To my colleagues at the *(Newark, N.J.) Star-Ledger* who offered encouragement and support, especially Sue Livio, Ana Alaya, and Editor Jim Willse.

To Tara Maguire, who heard this book long before anyone read it.

To the friendly, expert nurses and staff at the Maine Medical Center in Portland, for treating the worst case of poison ivy I've ever had—contracted, I might add, neither in Maine nor on U.S. 1.

Once again, thanks to Kathie and everyone at Freese Camera in New Brunswick, N.J.

To my mom, Connie Genovese, who was always on the lookout for stories about U.S. 1.

A special thank-you goes to radio stations up and down the coast for providing the soundtrack to a long, strange, and fascinating trip: WERU (89.9

FM), Blue Hill, Maine; WWMJ (95.7 FM), Ellsworth, Maine; WMDI (107.7 FM), Bar Harbor, Maine; WKIT (100.3 FM), Brewer, Maine; WBYA (101.7 FM), Searsport, Maine; WTOS (105.1 FM), Skowhegan, Maine; WCLZ (98.9 FM), Brunswick, Maine; WPKM (106.3 FM), Scarborough, Maine; WFNX (101.7 FM), Lynne, Mass.; WGBH (89.7 FM), Boston, Mass.; WZLX (100.7 FM), Boston, Mass.; WWRX (103.7 FM), Westerly, R.I.; WCNI (91.1 FM), New London, Conn.; WNHU (88.7 FM), West Haven, Conn.; WHCN (105.9 FM), Hartford, Conn. (especially for playing "Alice's Restaurant" on Thanksgiving Day); WKHL (96.7 FM), Stamford, Conn.; WXPN (88.5 FM), Philadelphia, Pa.; WARW (94.7 FM), Bethesda, Md.; WHFS (99.1 FM), Annapolis, Md.; WAMU (88.5 FM), Washington, D.C.; WCVE (88.9 FM), Richmond, Va.; WAFX (106.9 FM), Suffolk, Va.; WUNC (91.5 FM), Chapel Hill, N.C.; WRDU (106.1 FM), WIlson, N.C.; WKQB (106.9 FM), Southern Pines, N.C.; WRJA (88.1 FM), Sumter, S.C.; WHOG (95.7 FM), Ormond Beach, Fla.; WBGG (105.9 FM), Fort Lauderdale, Fla.; WZTA (94.9 FM), Miami Beach, Fla.; WWUS (104.7 FM), Big Pine Key, Fla.

Finally, I'm not sure where I'd be without the wonderful people at Rutgers University Press. This is my third book for the press, and each experience has been special. I am proud to call them collaborators and friends. To Marlie Wasserman, who came up with the idea for this book (I blame her for all those warm, sunny days I endured in Florida). To Helen Hsu, supervising editor and fellow Krispy Kreme lover. To Marilyn Campbell, for her wisdom and advice during *Roadside New Jersey* and *Jersey Diners* and her editing of and guidance with this book. To Tricia Politi, senior production coordinator, who also played a key role in all three books. To Ellen C. Dawson, who designed and typeset the book. To Amy Rashap, marketing and sales director; and the wonderful women in the warehouse—Janet Tamburrino, Barbara Gillard, and Carmen Rodriguez. And to Lisa Gillard Hanson, best publicist in the galaxy, postcard pen-pal and all-around nice person, despite being a Rangers fan.

To all those I met in two years on the road, thank you for your hospitality, your kindness, and your candor. I hope I have done your stories, and this highway, justice.

ABOUT THE AUTHOR

PETER GENOVESE is a reporter for the *(Newark) Star-Ledger*, for which he also does the weekly "Eat with Pete" column. A series he did in 1994 on the Rwandan refugee crisis was nominated for the Pulitzer Prize. Genovese is the author of *Roadside New Jersey* and *Jersey Diners*, also published by Rutgers University Press, and has appeared on CNN, the History Channel, the Food Network, and elsewhere. He lives in Manasquan, New Jersey.

Welcome to Frenchville,
a Small Town with a Big Heart

Welcome to Presque Isle.
The Spirit is Here

Welcome to Princeton,
Sportsmen's Paradise

Welcome to Perry, Halfway between
the North Pole and Equator

Welcome to Cherryfield,
Blueberry Capital of the World

Welcome to Ellsworth,
Crossroads of Downeast Maine

Welcome to Belfast,
a Waterfront Community

Welcome to Waldoboro,
Home of the 5-Masted Schooner

Welcome to Kennebunk,
the Only Village in the World So Named

Welcome to Stamford,
the City That Works

Welcome to Kittery,
Oldest Town in Maine

Welcome to Philadelphia.
Enjoy Our Past. Experience Our Future!

Welcome to Sanford,
Brick Center of the U.S.

Welcome to Richmond County,
Small Town Charm in the Fast Lane

Welcome to Cheraw,
South Carolina's First Tree City U.S.A.

Welcome to Elgin,
Home of the Catfish Stomp

Welcome to Lyons,
Home of the Southeast Georgia Soapbox Derby

Welcome to Alma,
Georgia's Blueberry Capital

Welcome to Hilliard,
Florida's 1 Gateway

Welcome to Mims,
the Friendly Town

Welcome to Melbourne,
the Harbor City

Welcome to Grant,
Home of the Seafood Festival

Welcome to Malabar,
Where People Care